LAGONDA

The author's 1930 3-Litre Tourer (top) and 1934 4½-Litre Pillarless Saloon.

LAGONDA

An Illustrated History 1900–1950

GEOFFREY SEATON

The Crowood Press

First published in 1988 by
The Crowood Press
Ramsbury, Marlborough,
Wiltshire SN8 2HE

British Library Cataloguing in Publication Data

Seaton, Geoffrey
    Lagonda: an illustrated history, 1900–1950
    1. Lagonda automobile – History
    1. Title
    629.2'222   TL215.L3/

    ISBN 1 85223 107 6

Typeset by PCS Typesetting
Printed in Great Britain by Butler & Tanner Ltd, Frome and London

This book is dedicated to all for whom the marque Lagonda is a way of life, rather than simply a desirable means of transport.

CONTENTS

ACKNOWLEDGEMENTS

One of the most gratifying aspects of writing this book has been the kind response to my request for Lagonda photographs and literature, a response so great that, in order to keep the work within practical proportions, some of it could not be used.

My sincere thanks then, not only to those whose names appear with their respective photographs, but to all who have offered assistance, be it material or verbal. But, in addition, special mention must be made of those without whose advice or expertise this book could never have satisfactorily materialised. In no preferential order, I am more than grateful to the following:

Phil Ridout for providing so many photographs from his collection, in addition to copying countless others to such a high standard, and for his technical help with the 2 Litre models and 2 Litre Register history; Captain Ivan Forshaw for the loan of a lifetime's collection of Lagonda brochures, photographs and press cuttings and also for sparing so much of his valuable time answering endless technical questions during my many visits to Aston Service, Dorset; the editors of *Motor* and *Autocar* for the use of their material; likewise those of *The Hereford Times* and *Belfast Newsletter;* the staff of the Quadrant Picture Library, Chas K. Bowers & Sons, BP Oil, Brooklands Society, Esler Crawford Photography, Paul Oatway Studios, the Farnham Museum, V.S.C.C., the Brooklands Museum and also, for photographs, Cyril Posthumus and Geoffrey Goddard; Mrs V. E. Davies for the loan of her late husband's photo albums and scrap-books, not forgetting the amusing reminiscences of her days at Staines; Arnold Davey and Anthony May for photographs and valued advice and, of course, their remarkable book *The Marque Lagonda* (David & Charles), which has been a constant source of reference; Mrs Jean Taylor, daughter of Bert Hammond, for the loan of her father's collection of photographs and documents; for help in many ways, including much needed encouragement, Alec Downie, Roger Cooke, Dennis Flather, Richard Hare, John Oliver, Michael Jones, Peter Whenman, Dick Sage, Mrs V. E. May and Mrs F. Roberts; Mrs Esme Humphreys, daughter of Major W. H. Oates, for an insight into her father's rallying and racing days, and also for the loan of her superb collection of photographs; J. W. T. Crocker, President of the Lagonda Club, for his professional help and advice; the Rapier Register for access to their photograph albums and technical archives, and, for technical advice on the Rapier models, Mrs Ann Pilgrim, Peter Cripps, Colin Banks and Alan Lamburn; Denis Jenkinson (Jenks) for his valued advice, and his kindness in writing a foreword to this book; Jeff Ody, Chairman of the Lagonda Club, for starting me on this mammoth but enjoyable task, not forgetting his encouragement along the way; last, but certainly not least, my wife Joan, for typing the entire draft.

Geoffrey Seaton, 1988

FOREWORD

It is always very satisfying to become involved with a book written and compiled by a member, or members, of a one-make car club, because their fund of knowledge on the subject is certain to be unsurpassed. No matter how keen you are on motor cars, or how much of a motoring enthusiast you are, it is impossible to accumulate a vast store of knowledge on more than a handful of makes, whereas those who specialise in one particular make can channel all their energies and research into the one subject and thereby do a thorough job. This applies in particular to Lagonda enthusiasts, and none more than Geoff Seaton who has written and compiled this illustrated history of Lagonda cars.

Geoff's dedication to the make Lagonda is not purely academic, as all Lagonda Club members will know. His beautifully maintained 3-Litre Tourer is the envy of a great many people, while his recent restoration of an M45 Saloon is something that I applaud wholeheartedly, and is an object lesson to the club. In various parts of this book Geoff decries the current habit of destroying original Lagonda saloon cars in order to create facsimilies of period tourers. In this he has my full support, and after reading this book even the least historically minded reader will realise that saloon-bodied Lagondas were a major factor in creating the great name of Lagonda and the Staines factory. While we all like a sports/racer or a sporting tourer, some of the saloon bodies built by Lagonda themselves illustrate the true meaning of the word elegant, and more to the point, they were both elegant and fast.

Specialising in Lagonda cars and Lagonda history is not an easy task, for the firm not only covered fifty years of manufacture at the Staines factory, but embraced a varied and interesting range of diverse types and models, all of which are dealt with in the following pages.

Throughout the years of Lagonda, competition and racing was always at the forefront of the firm's activities, ranging from simple Brooklands Handicap races to the 24-hour race at Le Mans. It was the Le Mans victory in 1935 by John Hindmarsh and Luis Fontes that really fired my enthusiasm for the cars from Staines, for since the Bentley withdrawal from the annual 24-hour classic in 1930 (which was before my interest in motor racing developed) there had been no one from Great Britain to continue waving the Union Jack. The Fox & Nicholl 4½-litre cars had put up a good fight in the 1934 Tourist Trophy race in Ulster, which had focused attention on the sporting potential of the M45 model, and the Le Mans victory the following year set the seal on the M45 Lagondas being of outstanding quality. Being a young schoolboy at the time, only interested in sports cars and racing, the management tribulations of the Lagonda company passed over my head. Lagonda was something special to me in those formative years, enhanced by the arrival of the Le Mans winning car in the hands of Douglas Hull in S.E. London, where I was living in 1939. The Hull family were near neighbours and that tall radiator, those big headlamps, the regulation minimal mudguards, the small fin on the tail and the bright red colour was a transport of delight for a young lad to see.

In 1939, the entry of the two special V12 Lagondas for the Le Mans race diverted my attention from my first love, which was Grand Prix racing. The story of these 12 cylinder cars is well told and illustrated in the following pages, but to those of us following the sport in 1939, albeit only by magazine and newspaper in my case, the Le Mans result was a foretaste of what to expect in 1940. This anticipation was heightened by the races on the Brooklands Outer Circuit in August 1939 and the test-run of the streamlined V12 Saloon at Brooklands, all of which Geoff Seaton has dealt with in the closing chapters of this book. In September 1939 when war was declared on

Germany it seemed impossible that all the Lagonda plans would not go ahead; but alas it was not so, and 1940 passed into the 'might-have-been'.

By this time I had got myself on the inside of motor racing in the form of a very junior mechanic to a private-owner racing an Alta, but it did permit me to stand alongside some of the great racing cars of the time. I well remember the thrill of seeing the two V12 Le Mans Lagondas in the Brooklands Paddock, and seeing 'Charles the Brack' win his race at 118.45 m.p.h., with a lap at 127.7 m.p.h., a speed that must have given him 140 m.p.h. down the Railway Straight. I was very impressed by the smooth and quiet running of those remarkable V12 engines. Add to all this excitement the sight of Lagonda LG45 Rapides, with that fascinating tail, like the Fox & Nicholl TT cars, and the flexible chrome outside exhaust pipes, like a 38/250 or 540K Mercedes-Benz, and its road-test speed of well over 100 m.p.h., and it is not surprising that Lagonda cars inspired me. I never had the chance to ride in an LG45 Rapide when they were in production, but a 90 m.p.h. run in an M45 Rapide Tourer with a racing driver of the time, convinced me of the power and performance of the big Lagondas.

In recent years, through the generosity of Lagonda Club members, I have been able to drive numerous Lagondas, and of special satisfaction has been the opportunity to drive all three of the Fox & Nicholl 1934 Tourist Trophy cars, including the 1935 Le Mans winner BPK 202.

All in all, this book is something special for me, as I know it will be for all Lagonda Club members, whether they own a humble 11.9, a magnificent V12 or a buzzy little Rapier. The cars that emanated from the Staines factory have drawn together enthusiasts for every model, all combined in the Lagonda Club which is one of the foremost of the one-make car clubs. That super-enthusiast Geoff Seaton has done a fine job in compiling this illustrated history of the Lagonda range of cars. The support he has had from numerous club members is indicative of the strong fellowship within the Lagonda Club, and I am very pleased, indeed very honoured, to be allowed to pen this foreword to a book that will stand alongside the Arnold Davey & Anthony May *magnum opus, Lagonda – A History of the Marque*. With these two books the Lagonda Club can justifiably feel proud of making worthwhile contributions to the documention of the history of one of Great Britain's truly great names in the motor industry.

Denis Jenkinson
Crondall, Hampshire
January 1988

PREFACE

Good photographs can be invaluable to both the restorer and prospective purchaser of a car, whatever the make. With this in mind, the Lagonda photographs for this book have been carefully selected, and most show the cars when new. Where it has not been possible to reproduce original photographs, the cars shown are those that have been lovingly preserved, or faithfully restored.

Though the extensive range of Lagonda cars produced at Staines is in year order as far as possible, to do this accurately proved an impossibility. This is due to the long production overlap of some models, and the extensive range of cars being manufactured alongside each other. Furthermore, it is not unusual to find that earlier examples of models were supplied long after the known introduction of their later counterparts.

'Wilbur Adams Gunn. A good engineer, a dapper man, more English than the English, active in local affairs, and a good man to work for.'

G. H. (Bert) Hammond, 1964

Wilbur Adams Gunn, 1859–1920.

INTRODUCTION

Lagonda. A proud and respected name in motor engineering since the turn of the century, and a legend in the ranks of the finest of automobiles since the mid-1920s. The All-British Lagonda, however, owed its origins to an American, one Wilbur Adams Gunn.

Born the second child of The Revd John W. Gunn, Wilbur spent most of the early years of his life in the village of Lagonda, situated on Buck Creek, Springfield, Ohio. The origin of the name Lagonda was seemingly derived from Ough Ohonda, the Shawnee Indian name for Buck Creek. This was later changed to La Ohonda, eventually to be corrupted into Lagonda, from which the village took its name. It is reasonable to assume that Wilbur named the company after his home town.

The young Wilbur Gunn was apprenticed to the Singer Sewing Machine Company and eventually became an inspector with that company. Wilbur also had musical interests and, without doubt, talent, as he sang at concerts at the Opera House in Springfield. It is uncertain what brought him to Britain, but it is a possibility that it was an attempt to further his ambitions of becoming an opera singer; it is believed that he sang at the Lyric Theatre. But whatever his intentions were, soon after his arrival he set himself up as a consulting engineer and, in the late 1890s, bought a large house in Staines, fitting out the greenhouse as a workshop. Here he built a steam yacht, which he named *Giralda*, reputed to be the fastest boat on the Thames, and used on several occasions as the umpire's boat for the Oxford and Cambridge Boat Race.

About this time Alfred H. Cranmer joined Gunn in his greenhouse workshop. Alfie Cranmer had just completed his apprenticeship with the Staines Lino Works, and was keen to make a career in engineering. Cranmer remained with the company for over 30 years, for most of the time holding the position of Technical Director.

In 1899 Wilbur Gunn set up a business called the Lagonda Engineering Company, specialising in the manufacture of steam marine engines. These were followed by motor cycles, the first being introduced in 1900. However, in 1904, the company was re-formed into a limited liability company called the Lagonda Motor Co. Ltd.

During 1904, a young G. H. (Bert) Hammond joined the Lagonda Motor Co. Ltd. Bert had commenced his working life at the tender age of 13, with Knights, a local cycle maker. Like Alfie Cranmer, Bert was to play an important role in the company in the years to follow.

In the factory now growing up around Wilbur Gunn's home, he went on to introduce tricars, followed by a varied range of four-wheeled vehicles. Sadly, Wilbur Gunn died in 1920. Fortunately, the company continued, and from the mid-1920s to the present day, Lagonda has been associated with the finest of motor cars the world over.

Chapter One

Lagonda

THE EARLY YEARS

Two views of the first motor cycle, dated 1900. Gunn made the engine for these early machines, the frame being supplied by Knights of Staines. But by 1903 the entire motor cycle was made in the Lagonda works, a 3½hp (78 × 82mm, 392cc) and a 4½hp (86 × 96mm, 558cc) being offered. Both machines were priced at 50 guineas. The engine had a cast-iron piston and automatic inlet valve. A Longuemare carburettor was fitted. The frame was 22in of diamond pattern, with rigid forks and 26in wheels.

Lagonda motor cycles were very successful in competition and won many awards. A Lagonda also represented Great Britain in the International Cup races. Unfortunately none of these motor cycles is known to exist now. (Photos: Lagonda Club)

THE LAGONDA TRICAR

The single-cylinder Tricar. Two of these machines were made to special order in 1903 and were originally 3½hp belt drive. They were found to be underpowered, and also suffered from belt slip. One was converted to 5hp and chain drive. The photograph shows this vehicle after conversion. A two-speed gearbox was used. The single-cylinder models were further increased in capacity to 6hp towards the end of the production period. The price was 90 guineas. The Tricar was not formally announced to the press until April 1904. These machines were said to be extremely reliable.

The two-cylinder Tricar was announced late in 1904, the first production model being sold in January 1905 at a price of 100 guineas. The engine was a 45° V twin of 1221cc (90 × 96mm), driving through a three-speed gearbox with chain final drive. Handlebar steering was retained, but the saddle was now replaced by a seat. The passenger seat was also improved. A Lagonda Tricar won a gold medal in the London–Edinburgh in 1905, and many other successes followed. (Photos: Lagonda Club)

Mr S. Southall on his 1904 Lagonda Tricar. This is the oldest known survivor and thought to be a prototype model. The machine has run in the London–Brighton on many occasions since 1937, and is the only Lagonda Tricar eligible for this event. It has a 1220cc V twin air-cooled engine with automatic inlet valves, and a three-speed gearbox.

Mr Southall acquired the Tricar for 7/6d (37½p) when a student in 1935 and says it cruises comfortably at 25–30 m.p.h., but on the 1937 London–Brighton run, when he was younger and rasher, achieved some 45 m.p.h. – a brave man indeed. (Photo: *Hereford Times*)

In an attempt to remove the Tricar's bath chair appearance and present something of a car image, a steering wheel replaced the handlebars for 1906. The vehicle was again improved for 1907, when water cooling was adopted. (Photo: Lagonda Club)

The V Twin Commercial Tricar of 1906. (Photo: Lagonda Club)

Wilbur Gunn's first four-wheeled car was a 10hp Twin, many of the Tricar parts being used. It was water-cooled and had coil ignition. The foot-brake operated on the intermediate shaft, while the handbrake lever operated internal expanding brakes on the rear wheels. The wheels were non-detachable, but a Stepney spare was carried. Few of these cars are thought to have been made.

The 10hp car was replaced by the 14/16hp model in 1909. The chassis was similar to that of the 10hp car, but the three-speed gearbox now had a right-hand change lever, instead of the centre change of the earlier cars, and the brake lever was also on the right-hand side. Both levers were outside the body. For the first time in the company's history, Gunn fitted an engine that was not of his own design or manufacture, the power unit being a four-cylinder side valve Coventry Simplex. The cylinders were cast in pairs, water-cooled with pump assistance. This was, at least to my eyes, a most attractive motor car. But, again, few were made, as it was superseded in the same year by a 16/18hp car. Again, a Coventry Simplex engine was used, but larger this time, which suggests that the 14/16hp car was underpowered. The 16/18hp was still side valve, with four cylinders cast in pairs, but was now 2140cc (86 × 92mm). A Polyrhoe carburettor was fitted. The chassis specification was similar to the earlier car, but wire wheels of detachable type now became an option; and, in addition to the two to three-seater, a full four-seat Tourer was on offer. Like all Lagondas, these cars were beautifully engineered.

The elegant 14/16hp, two to three-seater of 1909. (Photo: Lagonda Club)

G. H. (Bert) Hammond joined the Lagonda Motor Co. Ltd in 1904 as a shop boy. Bert remained with the company for over 31 years. In the early days he seemed to be a jack-of-all-trades, but his talents were soon recognised and he became Wilbur Gunn's personal mechanic and test driver. He successfully raced some of the early cars and finished his career with the company as Chief Tester. Many of the pictures, and a lot of the facts relating to the early period of the company's history, have come from the Bert Hammond albums and notes, now held by his daughter. Bert died on 26 August 1966, aged 78.

In the 1909 Brooklands Summer Handicap, Bert Hammond drove a lightweight 18hp two-seater, winning the race. It is understood that the body was constructed of aluminium panels over light angle steel frames.

Bert Hammond in the 18.2hp lightweight two-seater, after winning the 1909 Brooklands Summer Handicap. This car had several outings during the season but this was its only victory, though it was fourth in the Relay Race, second in the Senior Handicap and fourth again in the O'Gorman Trophy Race. (Photo: Lagonda Club)

The lightweight two-seater in action. The venue is again Brooklands but the event and driver are unknown; it may well be Wilbur Gunn having a go, as he sometimes liked to. Wilbur often used this car as his personal transport, but no doubt wings were fitted for these occasions. (Photo: National Motor Museum)

(Below)   The Lagonda in Russia: the 16/18 Lagonda at the start of the 1910 Russian Trials, outside the Tsar's palace, Tsarsko Selo, near St Petersburg. (Photo: Mrs E. Humphreys)

During 1910, Gunn had negotiated with the Russians to supply cars for the wealthy. A British agency was appointed in St Petersburg and Bert Hammond spent some time with them, supervising and training the staff.

For the 1910 St Petersburg Reliability Trial, Gunn entered a 16/18hp four-cylinder Tourer. This was a very advanced machine for the period, boasting a freewheel, magneto ignition, CAV dynamo lighting system, and so on. The body was finished in white, coated with gold size, then dusted with aluminium powder while the size was still wet to provide a sort of metallic finish. Lagonda was painted along the sides in nine-inch letters. This car was the first Torpedo model. The trial took place over a circular route of some 2,000 miles, starting at St Petersburg and finishing in Moscow. The crew were Wilbur Gunn, Bert Hammond, co-driver and mechanic,

a Mr Thornton as interpreter, and a Russian observer, who was apparently in full army uniform, complete with spurs.

On completion of the 16-day trial the cars were put on show for a week in Moscow, the crews not being allowed near them. At the end of the week, when the results of the trial had been worked out, many competitors had a similar number of points, so to find a clear winner, a special award was offered to any car that returned to St Petersburg in one day, under observation. This was a run of some 400 miles. Wilbur Gunn was the only one to take up the challenge, and completed the journey in 12 hours, including stops, over terrible roads, averaging 40–50 m.p.h., and winning the gold medal. The observer was so impressed that he ordered a Lagonda on the spot and a considerable number of sales followed.

The 16/18hp four-cylinder Lagonda, seen in Russia prior to the start of the 1910 St Petersburg Reliability Trial. Note the complete absence of weather equipment. (Photo: Lagonda Club)

The Lagonda

"THE CAR FOR THE EXPERIENCED MOTORIST."

British Manufacture throughout.

A Car which has been produced for many years, and has gained a high reputation, but has never been advertised before.

NOT A "CHEAP" CAR.

20 h.p. TORPEDO Model - Price £525

(Including Hood, Screen, Spare Wheel and Tyre, &c.)

LAGONDA RELIABILITY in the RUSSIAN RELIABILITY TRIAL.

In July, 1910, a Four-cylinder LAGONDA secured a GOLD MEDAL in the Russian Reliability Trial (then 3,000 versts, a much longer distance than this year), gaining maximum marks, and being the only car to complete the trial on one set of tyres, and without damage to the springs. No shock absorbers were used.

Two Models only :—20 h.p. 4-cylinder (58 b.h.p.) and 30 h.p. 6-cylinder (80 b.h.p.)

WHAT OWNERS SAY:—

"32,000 miles, and still runs like a new car." (Ref. No. 8.)

20 H.P. MODEL—
"My first LAGONDA was excellent in every way, but this one is a revelation, and "I have yet to meet the car under 40 h.p. that I cannot pass on hill or level."
(Ref. No. 30).

30 H.P. MODEL—
"5,600 miles and haven't had the toolbox open yet." (Ref. No. 42.)

During Olympia Show the Cars may be seen and tried at **Addison Bridge Place.** Please make appointment with—

THE BURLINGTON MOTOR COMPANY, LTD., 176, PICCADILLY, W.

Telegrams—" BURLMOCO, LONDON." Telephone—Mayfair 4666.

CALL BEFORE YOU GO INTO OLYMPIA.

We have a few District and Colonial Agencies open.

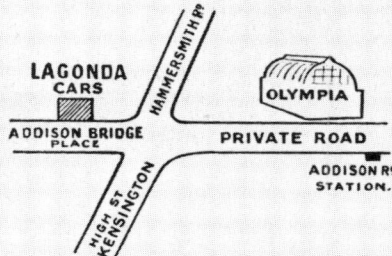

LAGONDA CARS — ADDISON BRIDGE PLACE — HAMMERSMITH R? — OLYMPIA — PRIVATE ROAD — ADDISON R? STATION. — HIGH ST KENSINGTON

Towards the end of 1910, a 20hp car was marketed. It was fitted with a Lagonda engine of 3054cc (90 × 120mm), four cylinders, side valve, with non-detachable heads. The chassis was a more robust version of the 16/18hp car, and in 1911 a 30hp Six was introduced (4590cc), again an all Lagonda power unit and again side valve, with non-detachable heads. These cars were well engineered and extremely reliable. Practically all the cars were exported to Russia, only a few being made available to the home market. None are known to exist today.

The 20hp Side Entrance Torpedo pictured at a motor exhibition, probably in Russia. (Photo: Lagonda Club)

The illustrations below are taken from the Lagonda catalogue of 1912 and relate to the four-cylinder 20hp models of that year. (Catalogue Photos: Mrs E. Humphreys)

The Lagonda Chassis with 4-Cylinder Engines

The Lagonda 4-Cylinder Engines
Near Side View   Off Side View

THE LAGONDA LIMOUSINE

A delightfully appointed closed in car—forming a perfect all weather carriage.

Complete with lamps, spare wheel and tyre, all tools and spares.

20 h.p., 4 Cylinder	£600 0 0
30 h.p., 6 Cylinder	£750 0 0

A 20hp Landaulette of ungainly appearance.

(Below) A 30hp Six with similar coachwork, yet looking quite elegant, possibly due to the increased chassis length. (Photos: Lagonda Club)

The 20hp four-cylinder two to three-seater Cabriolet of 1912.

(Below) The rather more elegant six-cylinder 30hp model, again of 1912. Unfortunately the negatives of these historic photographs have suffered with the passage of time. (Photos: Lagonda Club)

Chapter Two

Lagonda

ECONOMICS – OR JUST PLAIN SENSE?

THE 11.1hp

Wilfred Valentine Denison, Managing Director of Tollemache & Griffin Ltd, and a director of the Lagonda Company, accompanies William

Henry Oates in an 11.1hp Coupé demonstrator, Autumn 1913. (Photo: Mrs E. Humphreys)

A complete change of policy was adopted by the Lagonda Company in 1913, with the introduction of the little 11.1hp car. These cars were now aimed at the lower end of the market, whereas previous Lagondas had been mostly for the wealthy enthusiast. The design of the car was basically the work of Wilbur Gunn and was revolutionary for the period. Alf Cranmer was responsible for the detail design and development.

This was the first car to be made of unit construction and, in this respect, was very many years ahead of general thinking in vehicle design. Most manufacturers eventually followed the lead, but not for years after Gunn's brainchild.

The 11.1 was very simple and almost the entire car was made in the Lagonda works at Staines. The chassis body unit was constructed from angle steel longerons and frames, with sheet tinned-steel panels flush-riveted to them – in effect, almost the stressed skin principle used on aircraft. The cast aluminium sump, clutch housing and gearbox units all bolted together formed the main stress member. Should the engine need to be removed, the cylinder block and top half of the crankcase was separated from the lower half of the crankcase-sump unit, still retaining its oil if this was required.

A four-cylinder overhead inlet, side exhaust valve engine was used, the integral head/cylinder block and upper half of the crankcase being of cast iron. The bore and stroke was 67 × 77.8mm, giving 1097.18cc. An SU carburettor was chosen, but this was soon to be changed to a Zenith.

The wheelbase was 7ft 9in with a track of 3ft 10in. Initially only one body style was available, this being the two-seater Coupé, but towards the end of 1913 a four-seater Tourer was introduced on a longer chassis of 8ft 9in. The cars were complete with oil, side and tail lamps, acetylene headlamps, horn, spare wheel and tools, the two-seater being priced at £150. This was reduced slightly as production got under way. During the early period of the 1914–18 war, vans were produced using the Coupé chassis, but with harder road springs.

The oldest recorded 11.1hp Lagonda. Officially Veteran Car Club-dated 1913, this smart and original little Coupé has spent much of its life in Ireland, but now resides a mere few miles from its birthplace, Staines.

From all angles, the design of the 11.1 was practical, yet in its own way attractive. The tubed radiator was of Lagonda manufacture. This car is fitted with acetylene headlights and oil side lamps typical of the early models. (Photos: Steve Lawrence)

(Left) Typical of the period, one of the beautifully cast wheel hub nave plates. (Photo: Steve Lawrence)

Two illustrations from an 11.1hp car
instruction book. (Photos: Lagonda Club)

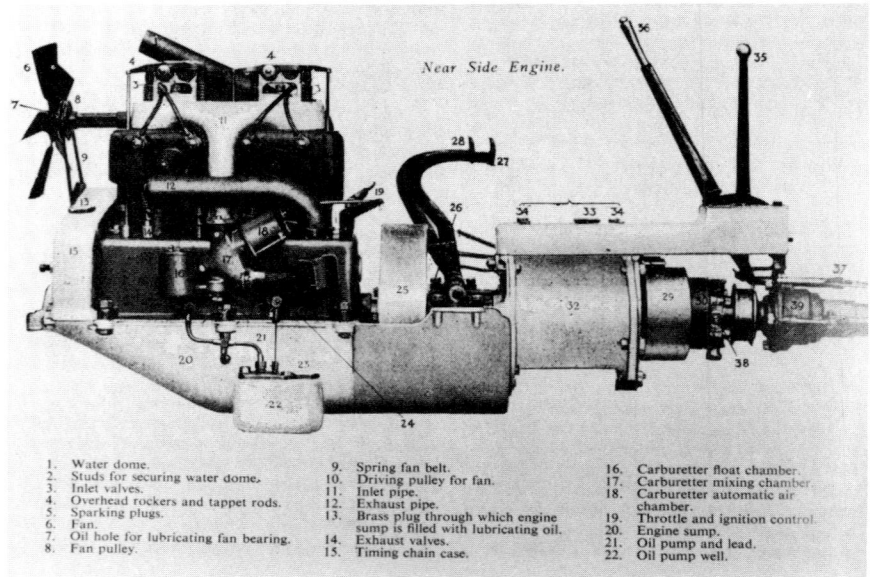

Near Side Engine.

1. Water dome.
2. Studs for securing water dome.
3. Inlet valves.
4. Overhead rockers and tappet rods.
5. Sparking plugs.
6. Fan.
7. Oil hole for lubricating fan bearing.
8. Fan pulley.
9. Spring fan belt.
10. Driving pulley for fan.
11. Inlet pipe.
12. Exhaust pipe.
13. Brass plug through which engine sump is filled with lubricating oil.
14. Exhaust valves.
15. Timing chain case.
16. Carburetter float chamber.
17. Carburetter mixing chamber.
18. Carburetter automatic air chamber.
19. Throttle and ignition control.
20. Engine sump.
21. Oil pump and lead.
22. Oil pump well.

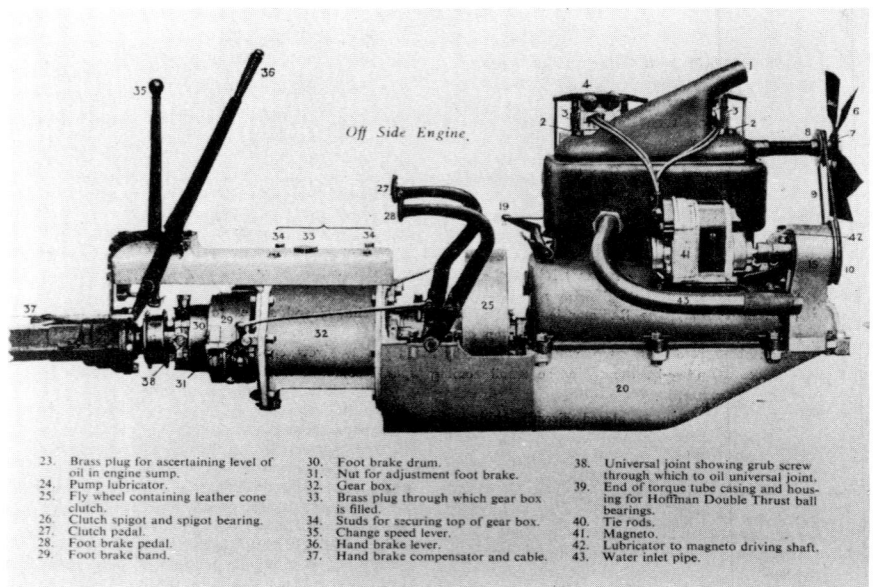

Off Side Engine.

23. Brass plug for ascertaining level of oil in engine sump.
24. Pump lubricator.
25. Fly wheel containing leather cone clutch.
26. Clutch spigot and spigot bearing.
27. Clutch pedal.
28. Foot brake pedal.
29. Foot brake band.
30. Foot brake drum.
31. Nut for adjustment foot brake.
32. Gear box.
33. Brass plug through which gear box is filled.
34. Studs for securing top of gear box.
35. Change speed lever.
36. Hand brake lever.
37. Hand brake compensator and cable.
38. Universal joint showing grub screw through which to oil universal joint.
39. End of torque tube casing and housing for Hoffman Double Thrust ball bearings.
40. Tie rods.
41. Magneto.
42. Lubricator to magneto driving shaft.
43. Water inlet pipe.

A period photograph of the four-seater Tourer. This is a 1913–14 model, equipped with oil and acetylene lamps, though electric lighting was soon to become available, if, in fact, it was not so already. (Photo: Lagonda Club)

RECENT SUCCESSES.

London to Gloucester and back	BRONZE MEDAL.
The Colmore Cup Trial	GOLD MEDAL.
Oxford to York and back (24 hrs. Sealed Tool Bag)	GOLD MEDAL.
General Efficiency Trial	CERTIFICATE.
Birmingham M.C.C. one day trial	SILVER MEDAL.

LAGONDA CARS

RELIABILITY

FOR COMFORT AND

£150   £150

TOLLEMACHE & GRIFFIN, LTD.,
195, HAMMERSMITH ROAD, LONDON, W.

Telephones: 575 & 502, Hammersmith.

Telegrams: "Lagondy, Hammer, London."

Careful study of the 11.1 hp Coupé illustrated in the Tollemache & Griffin advertisement, dated April 1914, clearly shows the car to be fitted with electric lighting, contrary to general belief that this was a post-war luxury.

MAJOR WILLIAM HENRY OATES OBE

Shortly after the introduction of Wilbur Gunn's 11.1hp light car, one William Henry Oates was engaged by Lagonda to fill a managerial vacancy created by the new Lagonda sales outlet and the service department of Tollemache & Griffin Ltd, at 195 Hammersmith Road, London. Bill Oates soon became a frequent competitor with Lagonda cars, in both road and track events. As early as 1914, he had achieved a class win at Brooklands, in the MCC's high-speed tests and, somewhat encouraged, soon started work on a Special Sports model, but it is believed the war prevented its completion.

Like many, Oates spent the 1914–18 war years in the army. A born leader, he soon rose to the rank of Major, and was also awarded the OBE. He returned to 195 Hammersmith Road after the war, and within a short space of time was waving the Lagonda flag, winning count-less awards in trials, and later in speed events, at Brook-lands. He also became a Steward at the Brooklands Motor Course and, in this capacity, attended almost every meeting until the track closed for racing in 1939.

After the collapse of Lagonda Motors in 1935, Major Oates, together with Tim Ashcroft and Nevil Brockel-bank, bought from the successors, LG Motors (Staines) Ltd, the lease of 195 Hammersmith Road, together with all remaining stocks of Lagonda Rapier components, to form the new company of Rapier Cars Ltd. Unfortunately this turned out to be a misadventure for all concerned.

Major Oates' next calling was the Ministry of Supply, and here he carried out yeoman service throughout the Second World War. This remarkable man was never one to retire, so, with the war over, he was soon back in business with an engineering shop and filling station; this he ran until his death on 4 April 1974, aged 89. Sadly, his wife followed him a week later.

A lifelong radio ham, Major Oates was better known to many simply as '5YJ'. Wireless led to television, and during the 1930s he devoted an immense amount of time to experiments into the Baird system. Such was his enthusiasm that part of the flat above the Hammersmith Road showroom was converted into a television studio and from here, with the assistance of his daughter Esme, he made several fairly successful television transmissions to Alexandra Palace.

Major Bill Oates in his capacity of Steward at the Brooklands Motor Course. (Photo: Mrs E. Humphreys)

Bill Oates with his navigator Wilfred Denison on their way to winning a gold medal in the Colmore Cup Trial of 1914. The car is an 11.1hp Lagonda Coupé, with its windscreen removed for the event, in which he took many awards prior to the outbreak of war. (Photos: Mrs E. Humphreys)

THE FIRST WORLD WAR 1914–1918

Van and car production continued on a smaller scale after the outbreak of war until 1916, but gradually the factory had been converting its efforts to the demands of war, the whole factory devoting its production mainly to munitions from 1916 onwards. Hundreds of women were employed and Bert Hammond was night superintendent for the duration of the war. Wilbur Gunn worked excessive hours during this period, often being in the works both day and night.

The change from car production to war work necessitated the laying down of special and costly machinery and the employment of a very large number of both skilled and unskilled workers. Owing to the necessities of the time, the firm practically revolutionised its production activities, Lagonda becoming a large and important works. Most of the company's energies were directed to the manufacture of shell fuses, but other highly technical military products were also made for both the army and the navy.

Lagonda manufactured all its own tools, and both the tool room and machine shops were amongst the largest and most advanced in the country at the time. Many automatic machines were introduced, allowing large numbers of unskilled and semi-skilled staff to be employed, the factory working most of the period on a 24-hour basis.

General view of the works taken from the main entrance. The overhead power shafts and exposed drive belts are a nostalgic sight. But just as well shop stewards had little power in those days – or did they? Not a soul to be seen in this picture.

These girls are carrying out the second operation on fuse bodies. Note the 11.1hp car wheels on the barrow. These barrows continued in service at Lagonda during the entire period the company were at Staines; in fact, some were known to continue in service after Petters had taken over the old works, and may even be in service today. (Photos: Bert Hammond Collection)

Tapping and finishing operations on shell fuse adaptors. Note the small boy, centre foreground; it is doubtful whether he was much over twelve years of age. Immediately behind him, the section charge-hand maintains a close watch on his staff — hard days indeed.

With the ever-increasing demand for a higher rate of production, Lagonda took the opportunity to virtually re-equip their machine shops, and they were soon to become some of the largest and most advanced in the country. This is a section of the tool room machine shop, where the turning, milling and grinding operations were carried out for the tool room itself. (Photos: Bert Hammond Collection)

After the armistice most of the girls returned to more feminine duties, their places to be taken by men returning from the war, who soon got car production under way. By the middle of 1919 both the 11.1hp Tourer and Coupé were back on the market. There were a few modifications, the most significant of these being electric lighting as standard equipment, a worm and sector steering box and nickel-plated radiator shell. At the time of reintroduction, they were priced at 275 guineas for the Coupé and 285 guineas for the Tourer. These prices were to increase rapidly as inflation took hold.

During the war years Wilbur Gunn seldom seemed to be out of the factory and it is thought that these long hours, plus the worries of getting the cars back into production after the armistice, were the prime reasons for his rather premature death in 1920. He was buried at Englefield Green Cemetery, where his grave is maintained by the Lagonda Club.

Following Wilbur Gunn's death, Colin Parbury filled the post of Managing Director; the other directors during this period were Henry Tollemache and Wilfred Denison and the Company Secretary was Alberta Beeby.

A post 1914–18 war 11.1hp Tourer. Electric lighting was now standard equipment, and the radiators were nickel-plated. Trade plates appear to be fitted, so it is likely the car was on test prior to final finishing. (Photo: Bert Hammond Collection)

(Below) A section of the service department, about 1919–20. The engineless car in the foreground is one of the rare 20hp Cabriolet models; almost all of these cars were exported to Russia. Lined up behind it, looking somewhat dwarfed, is a selection of 11.1hp two and four-seaters in various stages of overhaul. (Photo: Lagonda Club)

THE 11.9 LAGONDA

An 11.9hp car was introduced in 1920, the engine being similar to the 11.1, but increased to 1420cc (69 × 95mm), with the block now separate from the crank-case. Aluminium pistons replaced the cast-iron ones of the 11.1. The short chassis was abandoned and both Coupé and Tourer were on the 8ft 9in chassis. The rear of the Coupé was lengthened to form a dicky seat, giving the car a far more balanced appearance than the bobtailed 11.1 Coupé. The car illustrated is the model 'L', priced at £495. (Photo: Lagonda Club)

The Model K Coupé. The K type was the cheapest of the 11.9 cars and easily identifiable by the wing-mounted headlamps. This car was first registered in 1923.

The engine of the same car. (Photos: Alan Audsley)

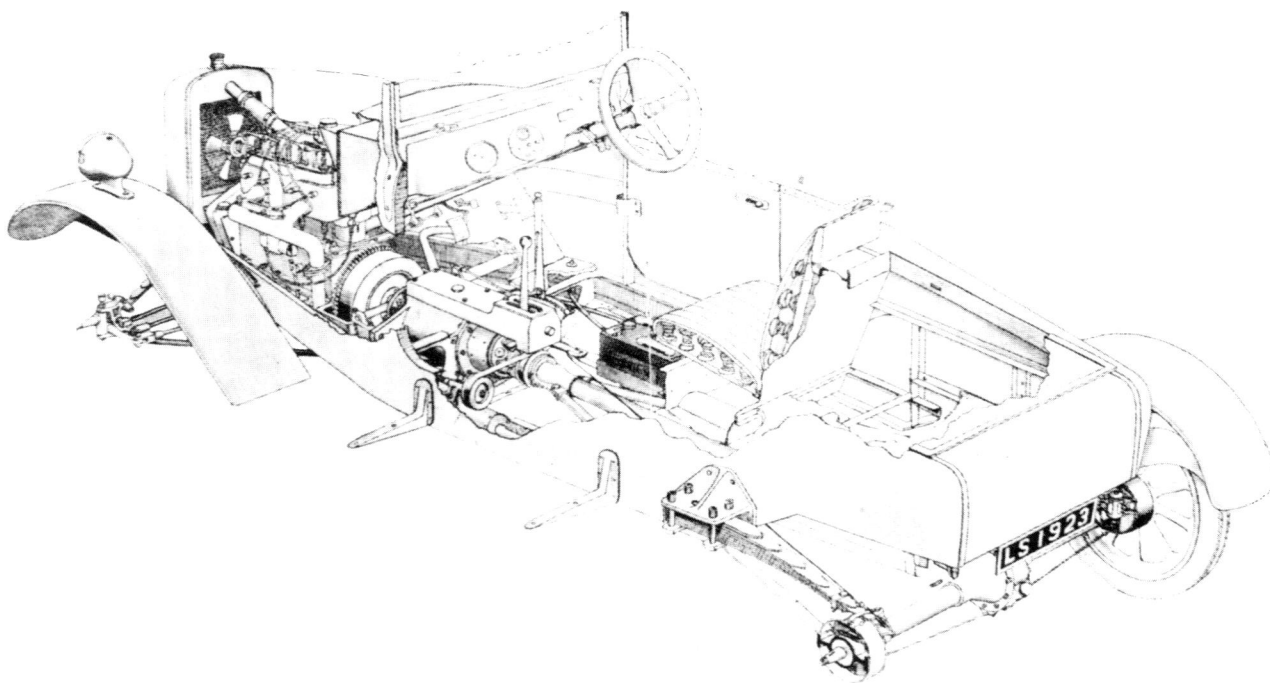

(*Above*)   This superb cutaway illustration of an 11.9hp Coupé was drawn for the Lagonda Club by Alan Audsley.

A well-restored 11.9hp Model K Coupé. (Photo: Lagonda Club)

Major Bill Oates' 11.9hp Lagonda at the finish of an MCC trial in 1922.
(Photo: Mrs E. Humphreys)

THE 11.9 LAGONDA RACERS

Though factory-sponsored, the 11.9hp single-seat racer was built at the Lagonda sales and service department in Hammersmith. Bert Hammond was made available for testing. However all competitive events were privately entered in Major Oates' name.

Both chassis and body of the car were single-seat width, but built on the same principles as the production model, although clad in aluminium. A spiral bevel back axle was used but the track remained the same as the production car. The engine was bored out from 69mm to 70.5mm, giving a capacity of 1483cc; it is also possible that the compression ratio was increased. A Claudel Hobson carburettor replaced the Zenith instrument used on the production model.

The car was run in many events during the 1921 season,

winning the Brooklands JCC Junior Short Handicap, and taking second and third places in other races.

Modifications were made to the nose fairing for the Autumn Brooklands BARC 75 m.p.h. Short Handicap. It won this event, and on 5 October took five light car class records as follows:

1.   The flying start mile, at 86.91 m.p.h.
2.   10 laps in 20 minutes 9.30 seconds: 82.36 m.p.h.
3.   One hour at 71.17 m.p.h. with a 2½ minute stop for a wheel change.
4.   50 miles in 36 minutes, 18.82 seconds: 82.61 m.p.h.
5.   100 miles, 1 hour 14 minutes 49.55 seconds: 80.19 m.p.h.

Bert Hammond in Major W. H. Oates' single-seater racing car. The damaged appearance of the body is due to a faulty negative. (Photo: Bert Hammond Collection)

Major Oates' daughter Esme (now Mrs Humphreys) congratulates her father with a kiss for winning the Brooklands BARC 75 m.p.h. Short Handicap. An equally happy Mrs Oates waves her programme, while mechanic Ernie shows some surprise at the proceedings. (Photo: Mrs E. Humphreys)

For the 1922 racing season the single-seater car was fitted with wire wheels, and Major Oates was back at Brooklands, taking many second and third places, and in August won the 75 m.p.h. Short Handicap, putting in a best lap of 85.87 m.p.h. In July, he had also claimed three first class awards, and took fastest time of the day at the Kop Hill climb. All in all, an impressive achievement for a car of under 1500cc in 1921–2.

Major W. H. Oates poses with the 11.9 single-seater in its 1922 form.
(Photo: Mrs E. Humphreys)

During 1921, the Lagonda works at Staines had been building two two-seater racing 11.9hp cars for the JCC 200-mile race at Brooklands, to be held on the 22 October. One of these cars is pictured on slave artillery wheels, wire wheels being used for the race.

A normal production chassis was used, but undertrayed, and the axles were damped by André-Hartford shock absorbers. The engine measured 69 × 100mm (1496cc). The tail housed a large petrol tank with a capacity to complete the race without a refuelling stop. (Photo: Bert Hammond Collection)

Bert Hammond (car number 43) at speed on the Members' Banking at Brooklands during the 1921 JCC 200-mile race, his riding mechanic Clem Logan crouching low to reduce wind resistance. Hammond finished 11th at an average speed of 76.9 m.p.h. His superior, and team-mate, Major Oates could only manage 13th place, resulting in Bert being severely reprimanded for beating an officer and a gentleman, and not allowed to race again, though in later years he was nominated as reserve driver on some occasions.

Bert Hammond with hand on wheel, and Clem Logan, looking very pleased with themselves after the JCC 200-mile race. Clem Logan was employed in the Lagonda engine test department.

A despondent-looking Bert, by this time no doubt having had a few hard words from his superior Bill Oates. Only one of the two-seater cars was entered for the 1922 200, perhaps because Bert Hammond was still in disgrace. However, Major Oates put in some very fast laps with his car before a forced retirement due to engine trouble. (Photos: Bert Hammond Collection)

Major Oates and his intrepid riding mechanic Ernie, on the line with the 11.9 before the start of the 1922 JCC Brooklands 200-mile race.

This fine action shot shows Oates trying hard to fend off the very fast GN, prior to the Lagonda's engine blowing up on the 17th lap. Both the two-seater racers languished back at Staines for some years, before eventually being broken up. (Photos: Mrs E. Humphreys)

THE LAGONDA FACTORY: EARLY 1920s

The factory as it was in about 1921.

(Below)   The general machine shop. The machine shop foreman is the smartly dressed gent second from left. Almost every part of the Lagonda car was made on the premises, even down to the manufacture of nuts and bolts. (Photos: Lagonda Club)

The components inspection and standards department.

(Below)   A section of the carpenters' shop. Every piece of timber was hand-shaped and finished to a remarkable degree of accuracy. (Photos: Lagonda Club)

(*Above*)   The upholstery department.

Just one corner of the vast stores.
(Photos: Lagonda Club)

The following delightful series of photographs was taken about 1921 and shows the 11.9hp cars in various stages of production. Automation was a long way off in those days, every car being virtually hand-built.

The 11.9 fitting shop. To the right of the picture a worm drive rear axle is being assembled and, in the foreground, steering gear and engine assembly is taking place.

The test shop. The department head, Bert Hammond, is the man in the dark suit on the right of the picture. (Photos: Lagonda Club)

Angle steel frames and longerons being assembled. The body panels were attached to these with countersunk copper rivets, then soldered and cleaned off flush. Note the bottom half of the engine *in situ* in the lower section of frame (bottom right-hand corner of the picture). This was the main stress member, in this instance being used as a jig during frame assembly.

Completed chassis/body units in the paint shop. The cars were hand-painted and, after the final colour coat, varnished.

Coupé and Tourers in the trim shop. Most 11.9s were upholstered in Rexine.

The final assembly shop. Axles can be seen being fitted to the chassis/body units. The completed cars were then returned to the test shop for Bert Hammond's tuning and road tests.

Chapter Three

BIRTH OF A BREED

THE 12/24 LAGONDA

The 12/24 was introduced in June 1923 and, although it was a direct follow-on from the 11.9, extensive modifications were made to both engine and chassis. The most important of these modifications were drip-feed lubrication for the valve gear, a cast aluminium rocker cover, Roto-plunge oil pump, and the magneto (either a Fellows or Watford) was mounted across the front of the engine, taking its drive from the dynamo shaft via a skew gear, the former being chain driven. The integral head and cylinder block castings were also altered, enlarging the water passages, and the push rods now operated within the cylinder block casting. In addition, there was a completely new rear axle of the spiral bevel type and a fully compensated cable-operated braking system, with separate shoes for foot and handbrake. These worked within 10in drums. A 12-shoe braking system was to become a feature of Lagonda on subsequent models for many years. The gearbox and propeller shaft also received attention, as did the front axle. The radiator took on a new shape, its design eventually developing into the classic radiators of the late 1920s and 1930s. Pressed steel wheels with 4.95 × 28in tyres were fitted as standard. Lagonda catalogue number 26 illustrated four body styles, all featuring pneumatic upholstery.

S Type, four-door Saloon: £370
R Type, four-door all-weather Saloon: £365
MC Type, two-door Coupé: £330
LC Type, two-door Tourer: £295

As was usual, the new car was entered in the classic trials, and in 1924 ten gold medals and three silver were taken, followed in 1925 by five gold and five silver. The works entries were driven by Oates, White and King.

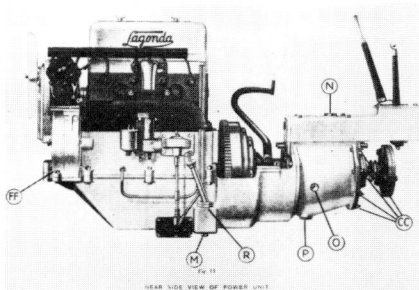

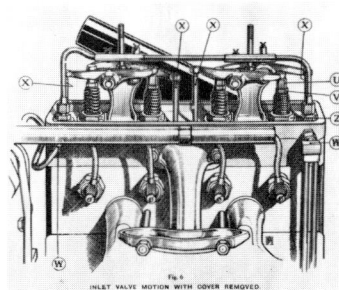

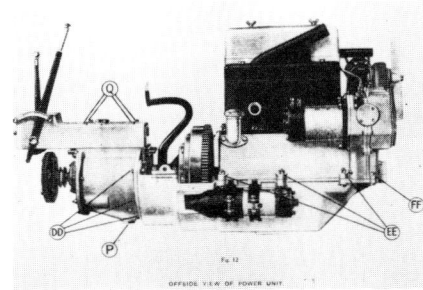

The 12/24 engine and gearbox assembly. This unit was both designed and manufactured by Lagonda. Four cylinders, monobloc of 69 × 95mm bore and stroke (1420.9cc). 11.9hp. A Zenith carburettor was fitted, the clutch was dry single-plate type, and the gearbox three-speed centre change. (Catalogue illustrations: Ivan Forshaw)

(Above)   The prototype 12/24 Tourer photographed at the works in 1923. (Photo: Lagonda Club)

The 12/24 Model S four-door Saloon. Blue was the standard colour, with fawn Bedford cord interior. These cars were very well appointed for the period and were the forerunners of a line of cars that were to bring Lagonda back into the sporting and luxury class.

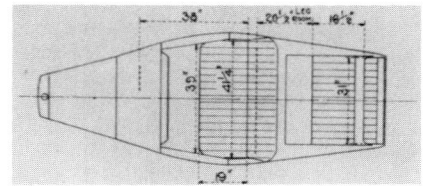

The 12/24 Coupé Model MC. The car described as ideal for the lady driver, and well suited to the needs of the professional man, had a hood of finest quality leather that could be raised or lowered without leaving the driver's seat, glass wind-up windows, and two additional seats in the dicky. The standard colour scheme was blue with fawn Bedford cord upholstery. (Catalogue illustrations: Ivan Forshaw)

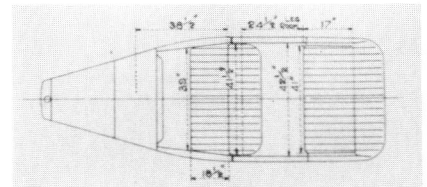

Though the 12/24 Model R had a soft top, Lagonda marketed it as the all-weather saloon, possibly because it had frameless glass windows with winding regulators. It was claimed that the hood could be raised or lowered by one person. The standard colour was fawn with matching upholstery. (Catalogue illustrations: Ivan Forshaw)

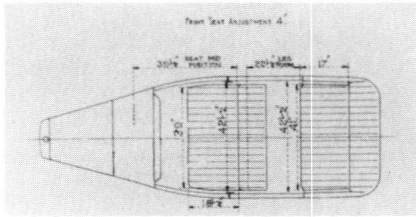

MODEL "LC"

The cheapest car in the 12/24 range, the Model LC Tourer. A feature of the car was the neat stowage for the side curtains, each one being stowed in its respective door. The standard colour for upholstery and paintwork was fawn. Front seats on all models were movable, the backs of which could also be adjusted for angle. (Catalogue illustrations: Ivan Forshaw)

An aerial view of the Lagonda Works at Staines in 1925.

(Below) Motoring as it used to be, and surely as it was intended. This delightful winter scene completely captures the joys of Lagonda motoring in the early 1920s. (Photo: Ian Jack)

In 1952, Lagonda Club member Hamish Moffat drove a similar 12/24 from London to Cape Town. The route, which crossed the Sahara Desert, totalled some 12,500 miles, this epic drive completed in six weeks' driving time.

The car, now back in Britain, is still in service.

The later examples of the 12/24 were of conventional design. The unit construction was dropped and a return was made to a normal chassis to form the basis of the car.

(Above)   Major Oates at it again: there can have been very few trials
he missed during the 1920s. He is seen here with a 12/24, on an MCC
trial in 1923. (Photo: Mrs E. Humphreys)

One of the late models during restoration. The car, now completed,
is fitted with its correct pressed steel wheels, and not with wires as
shown here. (Photo: R. Norman)

THE 14/60 2 LITRE OH LAGONDA

In August 1925 the 14/60 2 Litre was announced to the press, though the 12/24 remained in production at a slightly reduced price. The later models of the 12/24 had become more conventional in design and, in fact, now had a separate chassis, the body being bolted to it. The 14/60 was similarly constructed, but of exceptional quality, and of classic design throughout. Lagonda had completely changed its image with the introduction of the 11.1hp cars back in 1913; now, with the mass market being more than catered for by Austin, Morris and many others, the company decided to seek its clientele elsewhere, or were possibly forced into that position. It was a fact, however, that the old 12/24 had become far better appointed since its introduction in 1923, and these later examples were now often the choice of the nobility. The 14/60 was definitely aimed at this top end of the market.

W. R. Buckingham had been responsible for many of the modifications in body design and equipment of these later 12/24s, and it was he, with two new men, A. E. Masters in charge of chassis design and Arthur Davidson responsible for the engine, who were to form the new design team for the 14/60.

The 14/60 2 Litre was of advanced design throughout and beautifully engineered. With its twin-cam engine, right-hand change, four-speed gearbox, powerful Rubery type 12-shoe braking system with right-hand fly-off handbrake, plus the superb Marles steering box, all the ingredients were there for a truly thoroughbred sporting machine. As it turned out, the 14/60 was not a great performer, though the Lagonda catalogues of the period referred to it as a fast car. In practice little over 65 m.p.h. was possible from the open version, with the high 50s being about the figure for the saloons. But the foundations were there for all to see and, with the market crying out for an advanced sports tourer, the company were not long in seeing the possibilities for such a car, and were soon to put into production the famous 2 Litre Speed Model, the car which changed Lagonda's image for all time, and put the name amongst the most élite of manufacturers.

Designed by Arthur Thatcher, the noble radiator of the 14/60 2 Litre Lagonda.

OH Type Gearbox

Gear Ratios	Top	Third	Second	First
Semi-Sports	4.6	7.46	11.65	18.64
Tourer and Saloon	5.44	8.7	13.6	21.76

In the case of the Semi-Sports, a higher gear ratio was available at an extra cost of £5. Tyre size was 4.75 × 21in on wire or artillery wheels to choice.

An early 14/60 2 Litre chassis. Clearly visible are the right-hand change, four-speed gearbox, semi-elliptical springs and spiral bevel back axle. The chassis has a centralised lubrication system, wheelbase 10ft, track 4ft 6in. Chassis price was £495.

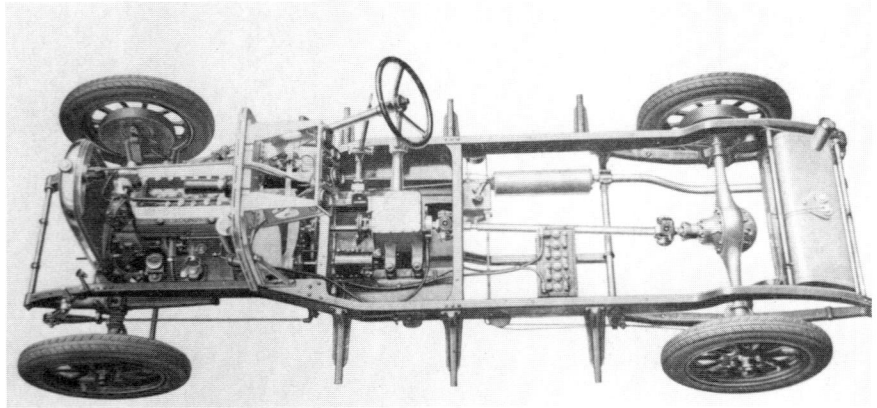

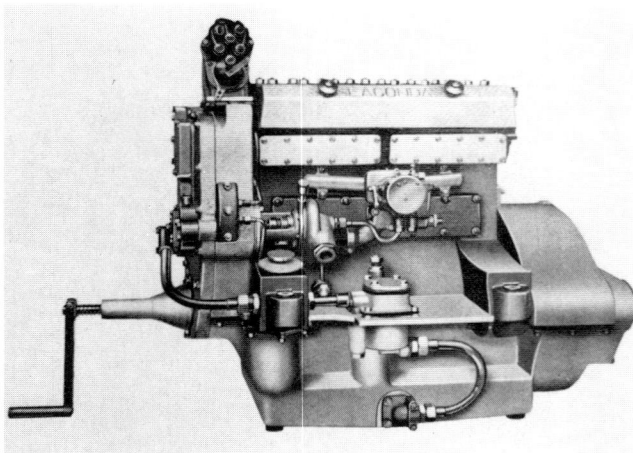

Nearside and offside views of the 14/60 engine, the latter with valve cover removed: four cylinders, monobloc casting, bore 72mm, stroke 120mm, 1954.32cc; detachable head with overhead valves. The two camshafts were mounted in extensions to the cylinder block above the lower face of the head, the valves being operated by rockers adjusted by eccentric fulcrums. The cylinder head was removable without disturbing either valve or ignition timing. The design, though good for ease of maintenance, led to poor porting arrangements. The fully machined and counterbalanced crankshaft ran in five main bearings. A Zenith 30HZ carburettor was fitted, fed by Autovac from a 12-gallon petrol tank. A magneto ignition system was driven by skew gear from the offside camshaft.

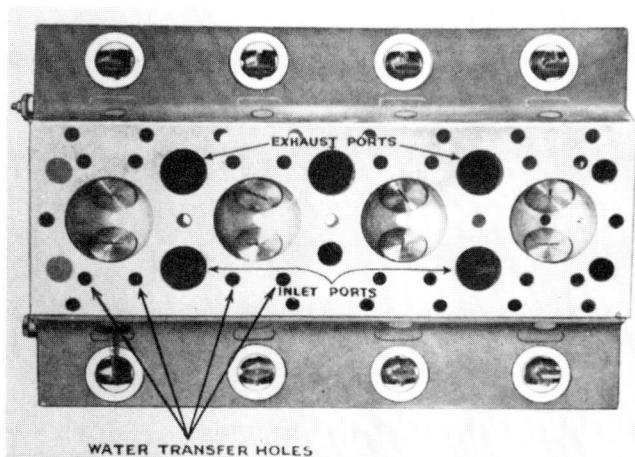

The underside of the cylinder head showing the hemispherical combustion chambers and porting arrangements. (Photos: Ivan Forshaw)

Interior view of the Saloon. Bucket or bench-type front seats were optional, a bench seat being used in this configuration. A partition and two occasional seats were also available at extra cost. Upholstery was leather or Bedford cord, according to choice. (Catalogue illustrations: Ivan Forshaw)

The 14/60 2 Litre Saloon. The 14/60 was the first Lagonda to be finished by the 'new' cellulose paint scheme, the cars being treated with Cerric lacquer. A wide range of colours was available, but the wings, wheels and chassis were normally black, other colours being supplied at extra cost. All fittings were nickel-plated, while handles and so on were of German silver. Body style S.

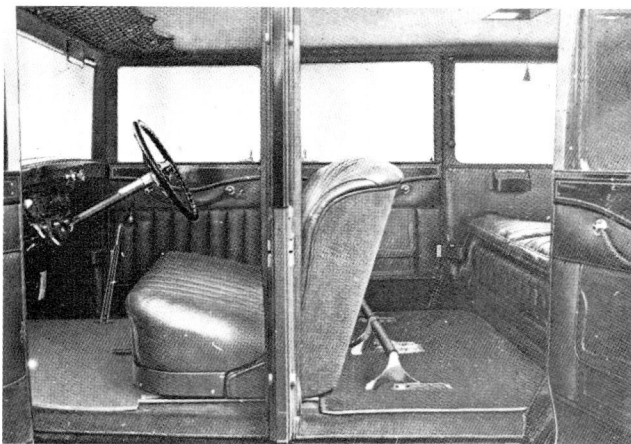

The 14/60 Semi-Sports 2 Litre Tourer. An imposing and beautifully made motor car. As on the Saloon, a Cerric finish was used, a wide range of colours being available. Wings, wheels, etc. were normally black. Body style SS.

The polished aluminium fascia board. The V windscreen and tool locker are all visible in this picture. The upholstery is leather. A three-panel rear windscreen could also be fitted to cars that had a bench front seat, bench or bucket seats being optional. The car was priced at £650. A five-seater Tourer was also available at the same price. This was body style T. Illustrations and prices are from catalogue 29. (Catalogue illustrations: Ivan Forshaw)

All 14/60 models were available on wire or artillery wheels. Tyre size was 4.75 × 21in in both cases. The Saloon was priced at £785. A Weymann fabric Saloon was also available priced at £770. (Catalogue illustrations: Ivan Forshaw)

(Opposite and above) Both these magnificent 14/60 2 Litre Semi-Sports Tourers continue to give reliable and enjoyable motoring to their owners and, who knows, perhaps some pleasure and happy memories to many they pass on the wayside. (Photos: above, Lagonda Club; opposite, G. Robbins)

THE 16/65 SIX-CYLINDER Z TYPE LAGONDA

The 16/65 made its début at the Olympia Motor Show of 1926. The chassis, with the exception of the front cross member and a few minor details, was virtually the same as the 14/60 but, in order to cater for a larger engine, was longer by 9in, giving a wheelbase of 10ft 9in. Alternatives of artillery or wire wheels were available, these fitted with 5.25 × 21in tyres in both cases.

Like the 14/60, Arthur Davidson was responsible for engine design. It was again a monobloc casting of iron, with a detachable cylinder head of similar material, but other than this the new engine had little in common with Davidson's earlier design. The six-cylinder engine had push rod operated overhead valves, and a peculiarity was the complete absence of valve overlap — low-speed torque and smoothness obviously being uppermost in the designer's mind. The camshaft itself ran in a tunnel on the nearside of the engine, the cam followers being in the form of rocking levers, the latter again an unusual feature, but completely silent and trouble free. The fully machined and balanced crankshaft ran in seven main bearings, and the generator was directly driven from its nose. Steel connecting rods and aluminium pistons, with fully floating gudgeon pins, were fitted. The bore and stroke was 65 × 120mm (2389cc), this was soon increased to 69 × 120mm (2692cc). Like the 14/60, an OH-type gearbox was fitted, but the back axle was a new Z type, this soon to become known as the 'heavy' axle. The gear ratios were 21.2, 13.25, 8.48, top and final drive 5.3:1. Other ratios were available. Catalogue number 29 quoted the chassis price as £570.

Lagonda body types were:

Saloon: Type S
Semi-Sports: Type SS
Five-seat Tourer: Type T
Weymann Saloon: Type WS

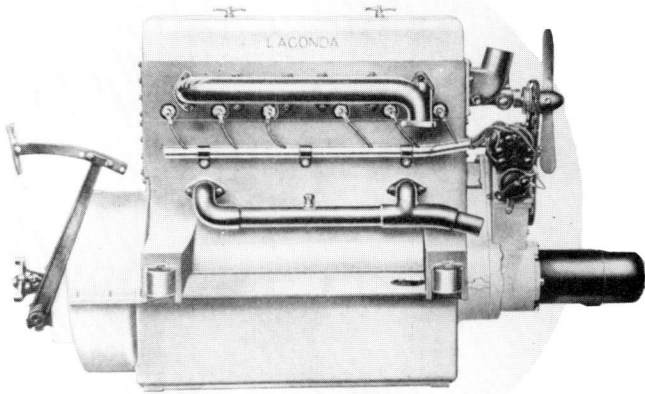

Nearside and offside views of the 16/65 engine. The carburettor is a Zenith. Both illustrations show the later 2692cc engine. The valve cover is removed in upper picture. (Catalogue photos: Ivan Forshaw)

The 16/65 Tourer shown here in open and closed form. The side curtains were neatly stowed in a holdall behind the rear seat when not in use. Bucket or bench front seats were optional. A three-piece rear windscreen was a standard fitting on this model when a bench seat was fitted. The car was priced at £740.

The Semi-Sports Tourer, rear screen erected, and fitted with twin side-mounted spare wheels. What an elegant motor car it is. Body finish and specification were virtually the same as the 14/60.

The 16/65 five-seater Tourer. An almost identical body was also available on the 14/60; body style T on both chassis.

This five-seater Saloon on the 16/65 chassis is outwardly very similar to the 14/60 Saloon, though the increased bonnet length gives this model a more balanced appearance. Lagonda referred to it as an elegant motor carriage, and in its day it certainly was. The price was £860, partition extra.

The interior of the Saloon was lavishly appointed. Silk blinds were fitted to the rear windows, loose cushions on the rear seats, and there was a lady's and gentleman's companion, etc. Bucket or bench front seats were to customers' choice, with a partition and two occasional seats also being available in cars supplied with the latter. Upholstery was Bedford cord or finest leather, as desired. (Catalogue illustrations: Ivan Forshaw)

The 16/65 Weymann Saloon. These four-seater fabric bodies were built by Lagonda under Weymann patents. The extreme lightness of this body and total lack of drumming made the body style very popular. Note the fabric covering the bonnet also. The car was priced at £845. (Catalogue illustration: Ivan Forshaw)

THE 16/65 h.p. Six-Cylinder Lagonda upholds the craftsman's art in every detail.

Vibrationless at all speeds—because of its sturdy crankshaft carried in seven main bearings and true engine balance.

Wonderful flexibility—from walking pace it will accelerate rapidly to its maximum speed.

Perfect suspension that levels the roughest road and makes driving a delight.

16/65 h.p. 6-cylinder Chassis .. **£570**
16/65 h.p. 6-cylinder Saloon .. **£860**
14/60 h.p. Two-Litre Models
　　from (Chassis) **£450**
Dunlop Tyres fitted as standard.

Catalogue M28 on request.

LAGONDA LTD. - STAINES - MIDDLESEX.
Telephone: Staines 122-123.　　　　*Telegrams: "Lagonda, Staines."*
Sole London and District Distributors:—EUSTACE WATKINS, LTD. Retail Showrooms: 91, New Bond Street, and 50, Berkeley Street, W.1. Wholesale Showrooms: 91, New Bond Street, London, W.1.

Chapter Four

A NEW ERA OF MOTORING

THE OH 2 LITRE SPEED MODEL

The High Chassis 2 Litre Speed Model Lagonda is today one of the most respected and sought after cars of the vintage period. These beautifully made, taut motor cars were remarkably quick for the period, 80 m.p.h. in top, and 70 in third being guaranteed by the manufacturer. The open car was also endowed with a lightweight but practical body of attractive design, which is as eye-catching today as it was when the model was introduced in July 1927.

The Speed Model evolved as a result of the public's insistent demand for a car with the reliability of the 14/60, but unfettered by the weight and wind resistance of the earlier car. With increased engine efficiency, higher and closer gear ratios, and impeccable handling, the smoothness of this model brought a new era of motoring to the sportsman and enthusiast who required a car of modest engine size. It was also the first of the long line of thoroughbred sporting and luxury machines for which the Lagonda company has now been so long renowned.

The car was a direct development of the 14/60, and the very early examples of the Speed Model had few mechanical changes other than a higher compression ratio, a close ratio OH gearbox and the OH rear axle with a ratio of 4.2:1 (10 × 42) for the open car. The solid crankshaft of the 14/60 was retained, but the inlet camshaft was changed, the new camshaft having exactly the same profiles as the exhaust camshaft, increasing the valve overlap from 3 degrees to 9 degrees. The radiator badge also remained as on the 14/60. At least one of these very early Speed Models survives.

However, for the 1928 model, considerable changes were made. Though the compression ratio remained the same as on the 14/60 at 6.2:1, important changes were made to the crankshaft and lubrication system. The crankshaft now had hollow crankpins with aluminium end caps, but as before ran in five white metal bearings. The oil suction filter was moved to within the sump, the Roto-plunge oil pump now delivering the oil to a main gallery in the crankcase. Cross drillings from the gallery through the crankcase webs led to each main bearing, from where, via drillings in the crank webs, oil was fed to the big end bearings. The camshafts ran in three bearings and were partially submerged in oil, and the camshaft tunnel cover plates were changed from aluminium to steel, though many of the cars existing today have aluminium plates fitted, possibly for cosmetic reasons. BHB pistons were used with fully floating gudgeon pins and bronze end caps. A Zenith triple diffuser carburettor was fitted and fed by Autovac from a rear-mounted 14-gallon petrol tank. The clutch and flywheel assembly was also lightened, and a simpler 12-shoe braking system was compensated on the rear wheels only, thus making a far safer system, as the danger of losing the foot-brake, should a rear cable break, was now eliminated. A badge of new design adorned the attractive radiator, though the latter was unchanged. Wire wheels were fitted as standard, with a tyre size of 4.75 × 21 in. Many fine examples of this model exist today.

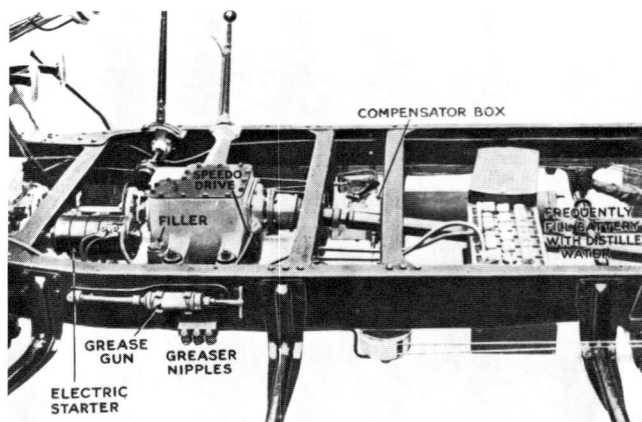

Centre section of Speed Model chassis. The battery position varied with body style.

Nearside of the 2 Litre Speed Model engine. The single Zenith triple diffuser carburettor, steel camshaft tunnel side plates, and large diameter pipe to the crankshaft oil feed gallery are all visible. The four-cylinder engine measured 72 × 120mm, bore and stroke (1954.32cc).

(Above and right) The high chassis Speed Tourer is equally attractive with the hood either raised or lowered. Side curtains are neatly stowed behind the rear seat squab when not in use. The saucy wings were a feature of the model, irrespective of body type. Though smart, it was not much fun for those travelling behind on wet days. This is Model Type SM, priced at £675. (Catalogue photos: Ivan Forshaw)

(Above)   The Speed Model Weymann Saloon. These lightweight bodies were said to be rattle-free. The fabric finish covered the bonnet. The Saloon body type is SMW. The price of the car was £750. The prototype Tourer had a door on the offside, but production models were normally fitted with the more familiar body, with two doors only on the nearside, and though the bonnet side panels were fabric covered, the top was painted. A wide range of colour schemes was available, and the interior was leather throughout.

(Top right and above)   Two superb examples of the Speed Model Close Coupled Saloon. The model is surely one of the most attractive closed cars of the late 1920s. In the interior of the car (right), with the nearside seat folded, note the three-inch flat pleating of the leather seats and side panels. This style was typical of all Lagonda upholstery until 1931, when it was changed to two-inch pleating. It is a pity that many otherwise excellent restorations are spoilt in this department by the use of heavily stuffed pleating which is quite out of keeping with the period. Body type CCS.

The Barker headlamp dipping mechanism fitted to many high chassis 2 Litre cars. Shown here is the lever at the right-hand side of the seat, through a system of rods and levers dipping both lamps to the ground when pushed to the forward position.

(Far right) Detail of the lever and pivot assembly. (Photos: Ivan Forshaw and Phil Ridout)

A new era of motoring for the sportsman and enthusiast. A contemporary picture of the attractive high chassis 2 Litre Speed Model Lagonda of 1928. (Photo: Geoffrey Goddard)

(Above)   This superb H/C Speed Model was the Lagonda company's entry for the 1929 Southport Rally. The car took first prize in Class II. (Photo: National Motor Museum)

The 1928 Land's End Trial, Sammy Davis storms Beggar's Roost. (Photo: Quadrant/Autocar)

Driven by J. Hathaway, this unusual H/C 2 Litre took a silver medal in the 1931 Land's End Trial. Note the door on the driving side, windscreen mounting, and bench front seat. The blisters on the side lamps are parking lights, presumably fitted with very low wattage bulbs. On the right of the picture can be seen Lord de Clifford who became a very notable competitor with Lagonda cars during the late 1920s and 1930s, driving 2, 3 and 4½ Litre models, and also the delightful little Rapier. This photograph was taken at the Brooklands MCC one-hour, high-speed trial on 28 September 1930. (Photo: Bert Hammond Collection)

The first of several Lagonda Fêtes was held at Brooklands in July 1926. The track was hired for the day, and any Lagonda owner could have a go. Demonstration races also took place, the professionals all driving Lagondas in two and three-lap events. Other goodies were a parade round the track, and an annual *Concours d'Elégance*. None of the events were serious affairs; it was all just a jolly good day out.

BROOKLANDS LAGONDA FÊTE APRIL 27th

INVITATION

The Directors of Lagonda Ltd. invite all readers of "The Autocar" and their friends to the 3rd Annual Lagonda Fête on Saturday, April 27th, at 11.30 a.m.

Races and competitions with prizes for every event. Tickets of admission, inclusive of tea, can be obtained FREE from Lagonda Ltd., Staines, Middlesex, or through any Lagonda agent. Please mention "The Autocar."

The new Lagonda 2-litre "Special" (6-cyl.) and the new Close-Coupled Saloon models will be available for inspection and trial.

Lagonda Ltd., Staines, Middlesex.

The Ladies' Run of 1928 is about to start. Posing for the camera are Mrs Oates in the 2 Litre, with daughter Esme at the wheel of the Tricar. In a similar event during 1926, it is rumoured that one Mrs Church stood so hard on her 12/24's accelerator pedal that it vanished through the floor, turning an old Brooklands joke into a reality. (Photo: Mrs E. Humphreys)

Edward Sawers with his 1929 Speed Model at Vintage Prescott in 1949. He clocked 74.27 seconds on his first run of the day. A lifelong enthusiast on two and four wheels, he started his motoring in 1905 with a 1903 Mercedes and owned many Norton and Douglas motor cycles. In 1921 he had some success at Brooklands with a flat twin Douglas-engined car, taking two second places at the Whitsun meeting; he could also boast that he attended both the first and last Brooklands Race Meetings, and most in between. Edward died on 4 July 1976 aged 87. The 2 Litre is now in the Ridout stable. (Photo: Richard Hare)

Photographed with two of the 1928 works team cars are some of the personalities responsible for design and development. They are, left to right, Eddie Bolton (Works Manager), W. R. Buckingham (Body Design), A. E. Masters (Chassis Design), 'Alf' Cranmer (Technical Director), Bertie Kensington Moir (Racing Manager) and Bert Hammond (Chief Tester and Reserve Driver).

The four cars of the 1928 racing team outside the factory before leaving for Le Mans. (Photographs: Bert Hammond Collection)

THE 1928 2 LITRE RACING TEAM

In 1928, Francis Samuelson (later Sir Francis Samuelson) had some success in the Monte Carlo Rally with the company's 2 Litre Speed Model PH 3928. Arriving at Monte Carlo without penalty, he went on to win the 2-litre class in the Mont des Mules hill climb, and finished a creditable 22nd overall in the event. All at Staines were highly delighted with Samuelson and the 2 Litre and, fired with enthusiasm, four special 2-litre cars were developed for the 1928 Le Mans 24-hour race.

The 1928 Le Mans team were, in effect, high-chassis cars modified to accept what has become known as the low-chassis engine, which was under development for production the following year (1929). The L/C cylinder block incorporated improved exhaust porting (three separate ports instead of a gallery partly in the block), and required a new exhaust manifold which used the space previously occupied by the generator, the latter now mounted directly to the front of the timing chest, and driven from the crankshaft nose. The generator incorporated a dog for the starting handle, this now being removable. Other modifications for the racing cars were special camshafts, increased compression ratio, and twin Zenith carburettors. The new position of the generator necessitated a change to the front chassis cross member. This was now heavily dished in its centre, with the radiator slightly relieved at the bottom and the generator protruding between the two. The radiator was also slightly lowered, as was the bulkhead. Additional shock absorbers and an oil tank to replenish the sump, with its control in the cockpit, were also fitted for the race, and the fuel tank capacity was increased to 25 gallons.

The four cars were registered PH 8595, PK 1058, PK 1059 and PK 1060. A team of three cars was to run at Le Mans, with the fourth car as reserve. The drivers were Baron d'Erlanger and Douglas Hawkes in car number 16, Francis Samuelson and Frank King in car number 15, and Clive Gallop and E. J. Hayes in car number 18. Bert Hammond was reserve driver. The cars were entered in the name of Brigadier-General F. E. Metcalfe, who at that time was Managing Director of Lagonda Ltd.

During practice the cars ran well, lapping at 68 m.p.h., with a best lap of 68.5. However, in the actual race, Samuelson skidded into the sand at Mulsanne on lap twelve and rolled back into the path of Baron d'Erlanger, who promptly shunted the car back into the sand and through a wooden fence. Samuelson lost over two hours excavating the car, only to find that the gearbox was damaged and he had to retire on reaching the pits. But the Baron's car, though severely damaged with a bent and cracked chassis, the radiator pushed back, damaged brakes and steering, and lamps pointing to the sky, was drivable. Meanwhile, the Gallop and Hayes car was leading its class and in eighth place overall, but eventually had to retire due to loss of water caused by a crack in one of the radiator mountings. D'Erlanger and Hawkes battled on in the very bent number 16 and, despite another long stop to do something about the lamps, worked through the field to eleventh position overall by 4 a.m., holding this place to the end of the race. The car had covered 1,353 miles in the 24 hours at an average speed of 56.39 m.p.h.: quite an achievement for a badly damaged car of only 2 litres. The race was won by a 4½-litre Bentley driven by Barnato and Rubin.

Back at Staines, the racing department prepared the cars for the TT, to be run on the Ards circuit on 18 August. The chosen drivers were Baron d'Erlanger, Eddie Hall and Major E. J. Hayes. The cars put up a good show in the first half of the race, but were again dogged by bad luck, and all retired with mechanical problems of one sort or another. None of these cars survive today, but enough evidence exists to suggest that they became the 1929 racing team, though in very much modified form.

The Le Mans cars were tractable enough for road use and were driven from Staines, stopping at Samuelson's home in Sussex prior to crossing on the Newhaven boat and the drive to Le Mans.

The cars resting at Samuelson's before commencing the journey to Le Mans. Presumably the fourth car is still in the barn. The team were accompanied by General Metcalfe, his Saloon just visible in the picture. (Photo: Samuelson/Sage)

Somewhere in France: Sir Francis Samuelson, with Frank King in the passenger seat, prior to the 1928 Le Mans. (Photo: Ivan Forshaw)

This magnificent photograph shows the three Le Mans cars alongside the Lagonda pits before the race. W. R. Buckingham (hatless) chats at the rear of number 16, Frank King can be seen immediately to the right of the gent strolling in the foreground, and Samuelson is the taller of the two men in caps behind number 15. (Photo: Samuelson/Sage)

Samuelson in serious trouble at Mulsanne after skidding into the sand. Note the bracing rods for the headlamps; they were fitted after leaving Staines and were possibly found to be necessary in practice. The ballast is also clearly visible, being bolted to the top of the dumb irons. Lead ballast was also carried at the rear. The cars had to be at full touring weight to comply with the race rules. The Bentleys were similarly penalised.

Samuelson attempts to push his car out from the other side of the fence. Much against the Le Mans rules, a spade was smuggled to him, possibly by the man in the picture above. Some two hours were spent in excavating the car, but all to no avail, as the gearbox was damaged and the car was retired on reaching the pits.

The d'Erlanger/Hawkes car, badly mangled, but going well shortly before the end of the race. Despite being severely damaged, the car averaged 56.39 m.p.h. and covered 1,353 miles during the 24 hours, even though one hour was lost after the crash.

(Photos: Quadrant/*Autocar*)

LAGONDA
AT LE MANS

Bad luck redeemed by heroic endeavour and mechanical endurance—that is the brief history of LAGONDA'S first effort at Le Mans.

In the second hour of the race the first LAGONDA driven by Capt. F. H. Samuelson was involved in a thrilling crash with the second LAGONDA driven in turn by the Baron d'Erlanger and W. D. Hawkes.

In spite of personal injuries to the driver, and the fact that the car had sustained a twisted axle, a broken frame and disabled brakes the race was continued.

The engine bonnet was never raised from start to finish, and despite its enormous handicap, it actually maintained an average speed of 56 m.p.h. over the whole 24 hours, i.e. in spite of one hour lost after the crash.

LAGONDA thus qualified for the Rudge-Whitworth Cup race next year—a tribute to the skill and endurance of the drivers and above all to the stamina and power of their all-British LAGONDA.

The above performance was put up by an absolutely standard model such as can be supplied by any Lagonda agent. Specification gladly supplied on request.

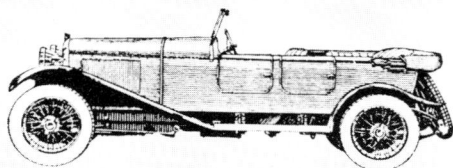

Cerric Finish and Dunlop Tyres are Standard on the All-British Lagonda.

THE 1928 RAC ULSTER TOURIST TROPHY

The Lagonda team of drivers and mechanics pose with their cars outside the service post in Chichester Street, Belfast, prior to the start of the 1928 Ards TT. The drivers are: third from left, Baron d'Erlanger, fifth from left, Major E. J. Hayes and sixth from left, Eddie Hall. Hall retired due to loss of oil, having covered some 205 miles, when in fourth place. Hayes was also forced to retire a few laps later. Meanwhile d'Erlanger, in seventh place, had several stops to change broken rocker arms, but retired during the fifth hour of the race. The eventual winner was Kaye Don, on a blown Lea Francis. (Photo: *Belfast Newsletter*)

(*Above and right*) This very authentic replica 1928 Le Mans 2 Litre is the result of countless hours of dedicated hard work. The owner, Dick Sage, scoured the country for information, original photographs, etc., in order that the car should be correct to the last detail. The petrol tank is believed to have survived from one of the original cars, and it was this find that prompted the owner into such a costly and time-consuming project. The car, still awaiting its hood, is shown at the Lagonda Club's 1985 AGM. (Photos: Phil Ridout and Geoff Seaton)

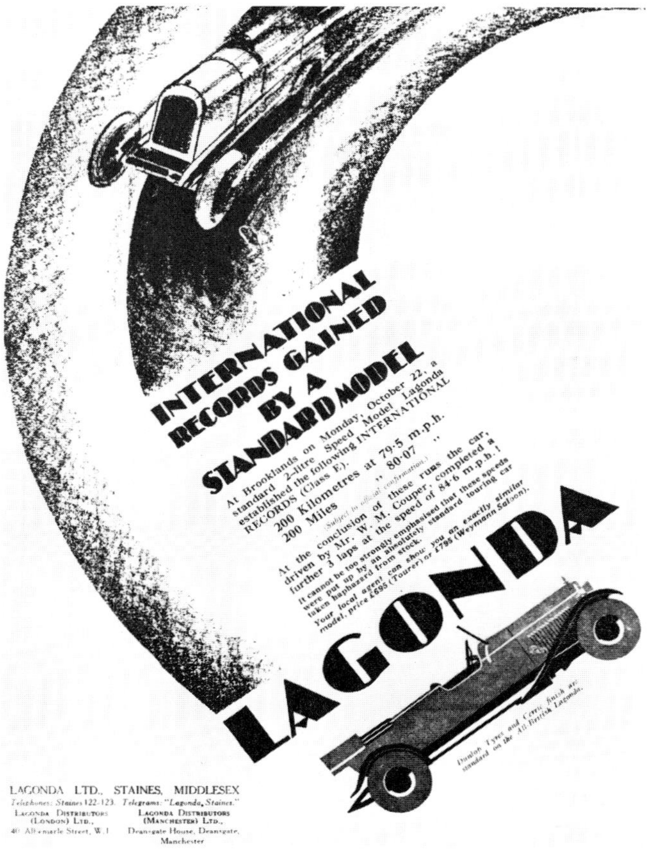

INTERNATIONAL
RECORDS GAINED
BY A
STANDARD MODEL

At Brooklands on Monday, October 22, a
standard 2-litre Speed Model Lagonda
established the following INTERNATIONAL
RECORDS (Class E):-
200 Kilometres at 79·5 m.p.h.
200 Miles " 80·07 "

Subject to official confirmation.

At the conclusion of these runs the car,
driven by Mr. W. M. Couper, completed a
further 3 laps at the speed of 84·6 m.p.h. I
It cannot be too strongly emphasised that
these speeds were achieved from stock, you an exactly similar
taken is a standard that these speeds
Your local agent
model, price £695 (Tourer) or £795 (Weymann Saloon).

LAGONDA

LAGONDA LTD., STAINES, MIDDLESEX
Telephones: Staines 122-123. Telegrams: "Lagonda, Staines."
LAGONDA DISTRIBUTORS   LAGONDA DISTRIBUTORS
(LONDON) LTD.,   (MANCHESTER) LTD.,
40 Albemarle Street, W.1   Deansgate House, Deansgate,
                            Manchester

This Lagonda advertisement appeared in all the leading motoring journals after W. M. (Mike) Couper's successful attack on the International Class E records (200 kilometres and 200 miles) at Brooklands on 22 October 1928. The car, said to be chosen at random, was chassis number OH 9138, registered PK 2339, and was the property of the company.

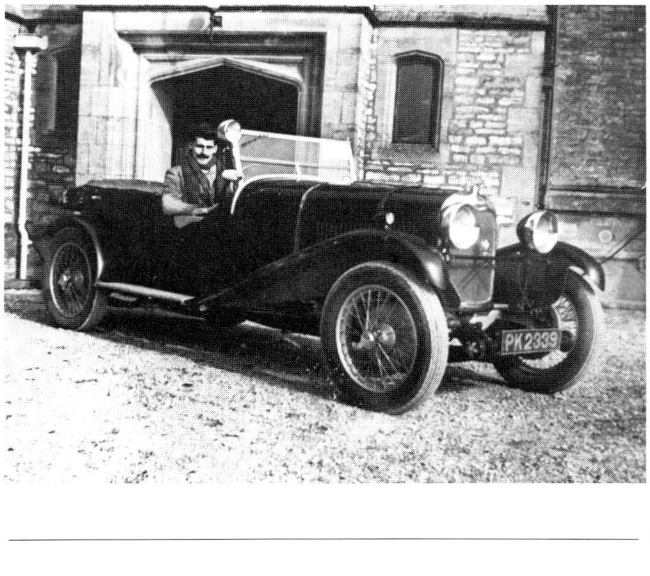

Possibly one of the last pictures to be taken of this famous car. It is seen here in 1950, when owned by Alan Hitch, who is at the wheel. Unfortunately all traces of this car were lost after Alan parted with it, and it is assumed to have been scrapped. Alan corresponded with Couper regarding the car's history, and is still in possession of a letter from him confirming that the car was to standard specification. However, pictures taken during the 1929 Brooklands Double Twelve, in which Couper had a class win, and the Brooklands six-hour race of the same year, clearly show the car to be fitted with an L/C engine, front chassis cross member and radiator. Could it be that Couper at that time had at his disposal two works cars? The car used in both the events described is generally accepted as being PK2339, but number plates were not fitted during racing, and the works swapped them about in those days anyway. Or was the car reinstated to standard Speed Model before the factory sold it? I doubt if we will ever know and sadly Mike Couper is no longer with us to solve the mystery. As can be seen, the car seems to have been to normal specification when this picture was taken. (Photo: Alan Hitch)

THE HIGH-CHASSIS 3 LITRE LAGONDA (TYPE Z3)

The 3 Litre Lagonda was first announced towards the end of 1928 and, as the 2 Litre Speed Model was a direct development of the 14/60, so the 3 Litre was developed from the 16/65. Two chassis lengths were offered; a short chassis with a wheelbase of 10ft 9in, and a long 11ft 6in chassis, both only available with luxury, rather sedate, saloon coachwork. However, like previous models, the 3 Litre could be purchased in chassis form for those requiring something perhaps a little more exotic in body styling, and several of the big names in the carriage trade produced coachwork to the whims and fancies of the customer, all of which, whether Lagonda built or not, were to the highest possible standards. The 3 Litre was a luxury motor car in every sense of the word; naturally it was expensive, considerably more so than its predecessors.

With the exception of the rear shock absorbers (now André-Hartford), the chassis was identical to the 16/65 but the engine, though similar in many respects, was virtually new. It was again six cylinders, OHV, but with a bore and stroke of 72 × 120mm (2931.5cc), RAC rating 19.28hp. The cylinder block was again monobloc cast in one unit with the crankcase, but was a completely new casting, as was the detachable cylinder head. The somewhat sober (no valve overlap) camshaft remained, and as before ran in four white metal bearings, a Roto-plunge oil pump taking its drive via a skew gear from its centre. The valve gear was mostly new, roller cam followers with spring-loaded push rods replacing the rocker-type follower of the earlier engine. The two hollow rocker shafts were separately fed with oil from each end of the engine, and the beautifully sculptured rocker arms were worthy of pride of place on anyone's living room mantelpiece. As before, the fully machined and balanced crankshaft ran in seven white metal bearings (bronze backed on later engines) and had hollow crankpins with aluminium end caps, the generator being driven from the crankshaft nose. BHB pistons, with fully floating gudgeon pins and bronze end caps were fitted. The camshaft was driven by a wide inverted tooth chain with a Weller spring tensioner. A cross shaft, driven via a skew gear on the camshaft nose, drove the water pump on the N/S end and the magneto on the O/S end, the magneto running

anticlockwise at three-quarter engine speed. The very early engines were fitted with a BTH magneto, but these were soon changed in favour of the superb Scintilla instrument. The first few production models had a cylindrical inlet manifold, and a single Zenith updraft carburettor, the exhaust manifold being similar to the 16/65. A two-bladed fan was fitted.

Very early examples of this model were fitted with an OH gearbox, but most production cars had the Z type and, in keeping with the sedate image of the car, the ZC set of ratios were chosen. All chassis were fitted with the Z type rear axle, and a CAV 12-volt lighting and starting system. Chassis and engine had the prefix Z3. Wire wheels were standard with 6.00 × 21 in tyres.

These were very sweet running and reliable cars and, considering the great weight and bulk of the machine, reasonable performers. *The Motor*, for instance, stated that the test car (PH 8669) climbed Priest's Hill near Staines with three up at a minimum speed of 48 m.p.h. in top gear from a 10 m.p.h. start.

Photographed shortly after it was unearthed, this is one of only three known surviving H/C 3 Litre cars. It is chassis number Z9381, engine number Z1126, first registered 28 March 1929, but without doubt a 1928 car. When found the chassis was fitted with a 1930s-style open touring body, but the manufacturer's plate identifies it as starting life as a Weymann saloon. The photographs were taken when the car was being dismantled prior to a long and tedious restoration. Fortunately, this very important car is in the hands of a capable Lagonda Club member.

The chassis frame of the H/C 3 Litre was virtually identical to the 16/65, and clearly visible here are the flat-topped chassis cross members and an OH gearbox. With the exception of a few very early cars, the Z box was normally fitted. Note the double drive at the rear corner of the gearbox. The drive still connected is for the speedometer, the other for the mechanically driven windscreen wiper. Its flexible drive is disconnected and resting on the flywheel case.

The nearside of the engine showing the cylindrical induction manifold and Zenith updraft carburettor; below it is the suction oil filter. The water pump is clearly visible at the front of the engine. The cast aluminium bulkhead is again identical to the 16/65. (Photos: Mike Hoare)

THE HIGH-CHASSIS 3 LITRE SPECIAL (TYPE Z3S)

The 3 Litre Special was introduced in March 1929. Basically the chassis remained as the standard car, but the engine was moved back some nine inches, as was the radiator, this now taking up a position slightly behind the front axle, so that the main weight mass was completely within the wheelbase. The petrol tank capacity was also increased to 20 gallons. Regarding the engine, the compression ratio was increased, and the ports enlarged and polished. Apart from these changes there were no major modifications, except for a slightly more free-flowing exhaust manifold.

Lucas electrics replaced the CAV systems, and all the production model Specials were fitted with the excellent Lucas P100 DB headlamps. However, a CAV windscreen-mounted spotlight was fitted, incorporating a mirror on its back. The lamp could be quickly removed and fitted to the nearside headlamp post for use in fog, an electrical plug and bracket being fitted for it in this position. Unfortunately, when so fitted, the driver was left without a rear-view mirror. A 'Setalite' was also a standard fitment, enabling the driver to pre-set the time the side and tail lamps came on for parking purposes when the car was unattended. A radiator stoneguard, mounted on a diamond-shaped frame, enhanced the frontal appearance of the car.

The H/C Special was also available in open form, this of course on the short 10ft 9in chassis, its Z type gearbox having a more sporting set of ratios, which were: first 12.88, second 8.05, third 5.15, top, and axle ratio, 4.1:1. Wire wheels with 5.25 × 21in tyres were fitted. The quoted maximum speed for the open car was just on the right side of 80 m.p.h. and the braking figures were very good, at 25ft from 25 m.p.h. This long-winged tourer was a very handsome motor car indeed. Obviously the cars were even more expensive than the Standard model, the Tourer being priced at £1,000, the Weymann Saloon at £1,100, while the chassis price was £835.

One of these 3 Litre chassis was made available to the PERR syndicate and one to Arthur Fox, both to be run for the Brooklands six-hour race. The bodies fitted to these chassis were quite interesting. Though being very similar to the Fox and Nicholl 1929 team of 2 litre cars, the 3 Litre had the sides of the body dropped, concealing the chassis from a point below the windscreen to the rear wheel arch. This styling was later adopted for both the 2 and 3 Litre models, but not until the 1931 model, introduced at the tail-end of 1930. Naturally, the engines of these two cars had further development work done on them, but the full extent is unknown. It is known, however, that Lea Francis pistons were fitted, also twin SU carburettors, these being bolted directly to the cylinder head, so deleting the external induction manifold. It has been stated that three of these cars were built, but again this is uncertain. The drivers nominated for the six-hour race were John Hindmarsh (PK 9160) and Frank King (registration unknown). The Hindmarsh car still exists, and it is

hoped that the restoration work required will soon be commenced.

Note Many 'authorities' on the motor car frequently refer to the 3 Litre as having a Meadows engine, and at this point it should be made clear that nothing could be further from the truth. The 3-litre engine was designed by the same hand as its predecessor, the 16/65 – none other than Arthur Davidson, who had joined the company way back in 1925 to design the 14/60 2-litre engines. Like its predecessors, the 3 Litre was built in its entirety at the Lagonda works in Staines.

John Hindmarsh poses with the H/C 3 Litre (PK 9160) prior to the 1929 BARC six-hour race at Brooklands. He won the 2000–3000cc class. Frank King, driving the second 3 Litre (number 11) retired with mechanical problems. Note the lower edge of the body sweeping down to conceal the chassis. This feature was later to be adopted on both the 2 and 3 Litre production models, but not until late in 1930. (Photo: Ivan Forshaw)

Production of the H/C 3 Litre commenced in April 1929. This is the first production Tourer; it was later registered PK 6368 and road tested by *Autocar*, the report appearing in the issue dated 29 March 1929. Note the side lamps, a perfect match to the P100 headlamps. The alternative mounting for the windscreen-mounted CAV spotlamp is also visible on the nearside headlamp post. There can have been few, if any, more beautiful cars on the road in the late 1920s or even today for that matter. (Photos: Quadrant/*Autocar*)

(Above)   Start of the 1929 Irish Grand Prix at Phoenix Park. Hindmarsh and the H/C 3 Litre (number 17) make a good start, but appear about to be cut up by the mighty blower Bentley, and car number 16 seems to have something of a problem already. Ivanowski in an Alfa Romeo was the race winner. (Photo: Ivan Forshaw)

The Lagonda showrooms at 9 Albermarle Street, Piccadilly, W1 in the late 1920s, the brand new cars within yet to find the first of no doubt many fortunate owners. (Photo: Ivan Forshaw)

Three Lagonda advertisements from the weekly motoring journals of the day. A few untruths, but who cared about the odd untruth in the roaring and enjoyable 1920s. However, to keep the record straight, the 3 Litre was far from standard, and the car was owned by the company.

14 The **Motor**   *July 16, 1929.*

FIRST BLOOD

First appearance of the New Lagonda 3-Litre 6-Cylinder "Special"—First in its class in the Brooklands Six Hour Endurance Race—a standard model driven throughout by its private and amateur owner— whilst the Lagonda 2-Litre team takes the Team Prize— a foretaste of further triumphs to come.

Mr. J. S. Hindmarsh in his new Lagonda 3-Litre Special. You can have identical models at the following prices:

Chassis	- - -	£835
Tourer	- - -	£1,000
Weymann Saloon	-	£1,100

LAGONDA

STOP PRESS NEWS.
Mr. Cooke's Special Lagonda awarded First Prize in Class 4, Concours d'Elegance, Brighton, July 4-5.

LAGONDA, LTD., STAINES, MIDDLESEX.
Telephones: Staines 122-123.   *Telegrams: "Lagonda, Staines."*
Lagonda Distributors (London) Ltd.,   Lagonda Distributors (Manchester) Ltd.,
9, Albemarle Street, W.1   Deansgate House, Deansgate, Manchester.

B10   KINDLY MENTION "THE MOTOR" WHEN CORRESPONDING WITH ADVERTISERS.

The General bestowing the
Cordon of the Legion of Lagonda
on the Terror of the Great
West Road

The
BRIGHTON CONCOURS D'ÉLÉGANCE
THREE CARS AWARDED FIRST CLASS PRIZES FOR ELEGANCE WERE FITTED WITH OUR COACHWORK.

Elegant
Original
Low
Comfortable
Coachwork.

MR. F. M. COOK'S SPECIAL LAGONDA
SPORTS SALOON AWARDED **FIRST**
IN CLASS FOUR.

THREE ENTRIES

THREE FIRSTS

G. WYLDER & Co.
Coachbuilders,
KEW GARDENS STATION, SURREY
'Phones : Richmond 2967, 2420.

Mr Cook's unusual Sports Saloon, mentioned in the 'Stop Press News' of the top advertisement. Both cars are H/C 3 Litre Specials.

Balloons will be balloons

Why was Leslie Wise ?
~ the answer is in the
front dickey

Portrait of M'King lapping the track on a stripped
Three litre special

Portrait of M'King lapping
a full litre Special

Above are some libellous
and fantastic comments
of our wild artist, made
at the recent highly suc-
cessful Lagonda Fête at
Brooklands.

LAGONDA
LTD.
STAINES, MIDDLESEX.
Telephones : Staines 122-123.
Telegrams : " Lagonda, Staines."

Lagonda Distributors (London)
Ltd. : 9, Albemarle Street, W.1.

Lagonda Distributors (Manchester) Ltd. : Deansgate House,
Deansgate, Manchester.

Chapter Five

LAGONDA

HIGH TO LOW

THE 1929 2 LITRE FOX AND NICHOLL RACING TEAM

A considerable amount of thought and preparation was put into the four 2 Litre cars that were developed for the 1929 racing season. Naturally, like the previous year's racing cars, the engines were highly tuned, but for this season the introduction of a new low chassis was an important development. This was achieved by creating a much greater drop between the stub axle and the spring platforms on the front axle beam; it was also formed in such a manner as to allow the brake perrot shafts to pass through the beam instead of being fitted below it, as on the H/C cars.

At the rear, packing blocks were placed between the top leaf of the rear springs and the axle spring platforms to reduce the height to that of the front. The two main chassis cross members were reduced in depth immediately inboard of the main side members, so that the floor could sit within the side members, and a front cross member, heavily dished in its centre as on the 1928 racing cars, to allow the crankshaft-driven generator to protrude between it and the radiator. The radiator and bulkhead were lowered by some two inches to give a lower body line, the rear of the bodies being cut short and raked to make room for a 25-gallon petrol tank. The tank was pressurised by a hand pump mounted on the

The first outing for the Fox and Nicholl cars was the 1929 Brooklands Double Twelve. But, in addition to these four cars, the works entered the very fast H/C 2 Litre, always assumed to be PK 2339 (but now seemingly fitted with an L/C engine), for Mike Couper to drive. This he did single-handed, winning the 2 Litre class prize at an average speed of 66.48 m.p.h. and covering over 1,595 miles during the race. Edmondson and Roberts were second in the class, with Jackson and Broomhall, and King and Wolfe taking third and sixth places respectively. PK 9201, the Rose Richards and Randall car, retired on the second day with a broken crankshaft. The outright winner was Ramponi driving an Alfa Romeo.

left side of the instrument board, obviating the need for a petrol pump. As on the 1928 cars, a scuttle-mounted reserve oil tank was fitted, its tap also mounted within the cockpit. The compression ratio was increased to 7.2:1, the ports enlarged and polished, and twin Zenith 35mm triple diffuser carburettors fitted. A very close ratio OH gearbox was used, and an OH rear axle fitted with a special straight bevel crown wheel and pinion, with a ratio of 4.0:1. Special quick-erect hoods and very small cycle type wings were fitted, as was a plain fairing over the front dumb irons. The chassis was also undertrayed, and again additional shock absorbers were fitted. The cars were registered PK 9201, PK 9202 and PK 9203 and finished black over cream. PK 9204 differed in some respects, the chassis being extensively drilled, and the body very similar in fact to the 1928 car. Aero-screens, plus a full width, fold flat, wire mesh screen were also fitted. This car also appeared from time to time with long wings, which in fact it wears at the moment. The original colour is uncertain, having been reported as black, green and sometimes grey. As it stands today it is black with red wings. Having spent many hours examining this car, I am convinced, along with the car's owner, that it was originally pale green, though possibly painted black and dark red during Jackson's ownership.

Though the four cars were prepared at Fox and Nicholl at Tolworth, and were, in fact, registered in Arthur Fox's name, PK 9201 and PK 9202 were owned by a syndicate under the name PERR. Arthur Fox owned PK 9203 and R. R. Jackson PK 9204, the PERR syndicate being Bill Edmondson, Cecil Randall, Arthur Pollard, George Roberts and Tim Rose Richards.

Mike Couper, goggles around his neck, stands by while Nottage (later Lagonda Chief Inspector) assists Couper's riding mechanic during a routine pit stop.

Couper at speed on the Brooklands banking. Clearly visible is the L/C radiator and front cross member. The absence of a starting handle also suggests that an L/C engine was fitted. (Photos: Bert Hammond Collection)

(Below) This superb photograph was taken alongside the Lagonda pits after winning the Sir Charles Wakefield class prize, Brooklands Double Twelve, 1929. Robin Jackson is at the wheel of car number 31 (PK 9204), Broomhall stands behind it, as does Frank King (with bald head), whilst Howard Wolfe can be seen at the wheel of the car second from left, race number 30 (PK 9203), with Tim Rose Richards (without helmet) and Cecil Randall standing behind it. Third from left is PK 9202, race number 25, with Bill Edmondson and George Roberts. Car number 32 is the works-entered H/C car, driven single-handed by Mike Couper, seen here with goggles around his neck. To his left, behind the car, can be seen Bert Hammond. (Photo: Ivan Forshaw)

PK 9203 outside the Fox and Nicholl service station.

Only one Lagonda was entered for Le Mans, 15–16 June 1929. This was Arthur Fox's 2 Litre PK 9203, driven for him by Tim Rose Richards and the Hon. Brian Lewis. Unfortunately, the car blew a head gasket and retired after 283 miles, the eventual winner of the race being a Speed Six Bentley driven by Woolf Barnato and Sir Henry Birkin. Bentleys also took second, third and fourth places. However, eight Lagonda cars were entered for the BARC six-hour race, held at Brooklands on 29 June. These were the four 2 Litre team cars and two 3 Litre cars, all entered in the name of A. W. Fox, plus a 2 Litre privately entered and driven by R. S. S. Hebeler, with Ian Hepburn as co-driver. The works H/C 2 Litre, still with L/C modifications,

was driven by Couper, again a single-handed effort.

Bentley stole the show, the winning car again driven by Barnato, but this time with Dunfee as his co-driver, the big car averaging 75.88 m.p.h. for the six hours. The Lagonda team, however, had nothing to be ashamed about, Hindmarsh winning the 3 Litre class, with the 2 Litre driven by Rose Richards and Randall a creditable ninth overall at an average speed of 63.98 m.p.h. The Fox team of Rose Richards and Randall, Roberts and Pollard, and Lewis and Jervis took the 2 Litre class prize, the Mobiloil Cup. Arthur Fox kindly presented this cup to the Lagonda Club in 1957, and it forms one of the premier awards for competitive events held within the club.

Start of the BARC six-hour race. The first ten laps were run with hoods up. Car number 18 is the 2 Litre of Jackson/Broomhall; the Rose Richards/Randall 2 Litre, number 15, is a little further down the field. (Photos: A. W. Fox and Ivan Forshaw Collections)

The 1929 Irish Grand Prix at Phoenix Park, Dublin, saw an entry of three Lagondas, all entered in the name of A. W. Fox. They were Robin Jackson's 2 Litre, Arthur Fox's 2 Litre thought to be driven by Euan Rabagliati (driver never positively identified), and a 3 Litre driven by John Hindmarsh. Jackson finished ninth overall at an average speed of 67.81 m.p.h. He is seen above in full flight during the course of the race while, opposite top, the driver of the 2 Litre, number 23, appears very concerned at the awe-inspiring sight of Thistlethwaite's vast Mercedes-Benz approaching fast on his nearside; the latter car was soon to blow a head gasket. The 2 Litre finished the race and covered some 68 laps, as did the Hindmarsh 3 Litre. The race winner was Ivanowski in an Alfa Romeo. (Photos: Ivan Forshaw Collection)

Both photographs below show the Fox and Nicholl Lagonda team after the 1929 Irish Grand Prix, seemingly with racing mechanics as the occupants.

Bert Hammond is at the wheel of the 3 Litre PK9160, and Donald Wilcockson (chief Fox and Nicholls mechanic) is at the wheel of the Bullnose Morris, presumably the race back-up car. The identity of the others is unknown.

Arthur Fox's 2 Litre PK9203 on the same occasion. Note the extra bonnet strap and twin sparewheels fitted for the Phoenix Park Race. (Photo: Tim Lee/Alan Elliott)

The Fox and Nicholl team *en route* to the 1929 Ards TT. Left to right, Bert Hammond, a mechanic (name unknown), Robin Jackson, Arthur Fox, Donald Wilcockson (Fox and Nicholls mechanic), C. A. Broomhall, Tim Rose Richards and Charlie Dodson. (Photo: Bert Hammond Collection)

The 1929 Ards TT saw no fewer than 67 cars leave the line at the fall of the starter's flag. Amongst these were three Lagondas: a 3 Litre driven by Hindmarsh and two 2 Litres, one driven by Rose Richards, the other by Jackson. Rose Richards was first away (right), but was flagged off at the finish. Jackson had problems and retired. The Hindmarsh 3 Litre finished 21st overall. It was originally intended that four Lagondas should run, but Dodson's mount was withdrawn prior to the start of the race. Twenty-two cars finished, with Carraciola the outright winner with his vast 7.1 litre, supercharged Mercedes Benz. Note the wire mesh screen fitted to Rose Richards' car for this race at his special request. (Photo: Bert Hammond Collection)

The L/C 2 Litre was a direct development from these Fox and Nicholl-inspired racing cars, and this is one of the prototype production chassis, the dropped cross members visible. It differs in some ways from the final production model, the most obvious of these differences being the petrol tank and the wheel nuts. The wheelbase was 10ft and the track 4ft 6in. (Photo: Ivan Forshaw Collection)

THE 2 LITRE L/C SPEED MODEL

The 1929 Fox and Nicholl team cars were in fact prototypes of the L/C 2 Litre Speed Model, but for the production cars the compression ratio remained the same as the H/C car, at 6.2:1, although the new position for the generator was retained. A single Zenith carburettor was fitted; however, twin systems were soon made available with a choice of Zenith or SU. On the team cars, and the first 40 or so of the production L/C cars, the sprocket previously used to drive the generator was omitted and the primary chain rerouted. This reversed the rotation of the camshafts and hence the firing order from 1–2–4–3 to 1–3–4–2. (Skew gears of the opposite hand were employed so that the rotation of the magneto was unchanged.) But for the 1930 models, introduced at the end of 1929, the sprocket was replaced and the original chain layout reinstated.

The 'light' OH gearbox and back axle were retained for the production chassis, with a final drive ratio of 4.2:1 for the Tourer and 5.44:1 for the Saloon, the ratio being changed on the open car to 4.4:1 from about the end of 1931. The lower radiator and bodyline was also a feature of the new car. For the production models, however, the attractive rounded back to the body was re-adopted, as only a 14-gallon petrol tank was fitted. As on the H/C cars, doors were fitted on the nearside only. The body designation was SML for the open car and LSMW for the saloon. Cycle type wings had become fashionable in the late 1920s and these were fitted as standard on the 1930 models but, unlike the fixed type fitted to the racing cars, the front wings, now mounted on the stub axles, followed the wheels when cornering, so reducing the hazard of mud splatter on the windscreen in wet weather. Fabric valances were also fitted to the inner side of the wings for the same purpose. The long wings were still available if preferred, but the rear wings now came down to almost hub height, again in an attempt to reduce spray, no doubt to the delight of all who followed.

This very fine example of the 1929 L/C Speed Model was seen at Prescott in 1979. The windscreens on this model were normally hinged at the top, and hence opened upwards. This car is unusual in being fitted with a fold-flat type, but this is believed to be original. What a pretty car it is, and a pity so few were made to designation SML. (Photo: Tony Wood)

The 1930 L/C Speed Model Tourer. This was the first Lagonda to be fitted with cycle type wings as standard. Long wings were still available if preferred. The step was soon to be replaced with running boards; body designation is T. (Catalogue Picture: Ivan Forshaw)

The 2 Litre L/C Speed Saloon. These fabric saloons were built by Lagonda under Weymann patents. The quality of the interior furnishings and fittings was superb (Type LSMW). A close-coupled saloon (CCS), almost identical to that of the H/C car, was also available. The price quoted in the 1930 catalogue for both models was £820: very expensive motor cars indeed in those far off days. (Catalogue Pictures: Ivan Forshaw)

The 2 Litre Special. It was originally intended that this car should be produced in addition to the 2 Litre Speed Model to cater for the competition driver. The car was considerably lightened. Note the absence of step, body valances, bonnet catches and so on, the bonnet being secured by a strap. The car was to be available only in chassis form, or with the T body as shown. However, only one was made, preference being given to the production of the supercharged 2 Litre which was being developed at the same time. Fortunately, the car still exists.

This photograph fully illustrates the elegance of the L/C 2 Litre. Note the stylish running boards, slim cycle wings and so on. The body is the later drop-sided type and was designated T2 (see Supercharged 2 Litre). This car was first registered in 1931. (Photo: Lagonda Club)

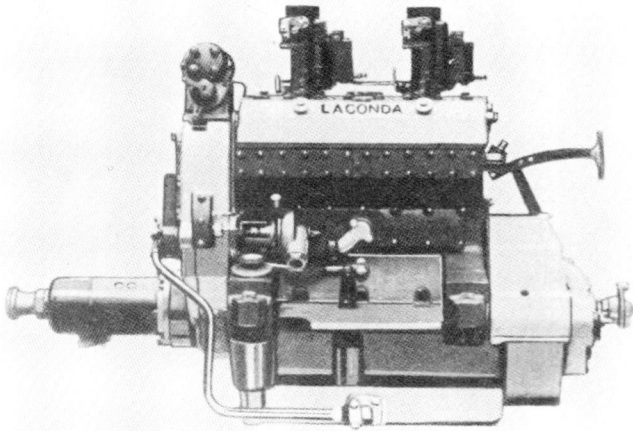

The engine of the Special had a modified cylinder head with vertical inlet passages, and twin vertical downdraught Zenith carburettors between the rocker covers.

A catalogue illustration of the 12.9hp 2-litre engine. Twin Zenith carburettors are fitted, but SU were also available.

Denis Flather at the wheel of L/C 2 Litre W330. The car had been a 21st birthday present from his father on 2 December 1931, but the desirable registration number was first issued in Sheffield during 1904. The T3 body on this car is finished black over white, and though with its quick-release radiator and petrol filler caps it has the appearance of the supercharged model 2 Litre (see Supercharged 2 Litre), the original owner has confirmed that this car was normally aspirated, as it is, in fact, now.

Denis Flather was a keen competitive motorist, and a successful one too. He is seen (centre) taking the final test in the 1935 RAC rally, in which he won a silver award. This photograph clearly shows the luggage boot of the T3 body. A superb tool kit was housed in its lid. Fitted suitcases were also available on this model at extra cost. Though Mr Flather parted with W330 prior to the war, he is still keenly interested in its well-being. He recently provided invaluable original photographs and technical information to the current owner to assist with the car's restoration. (Photos: Denis Flather)

W330 in 1984, seen here nearing the end of its superb restoration, with just the weather equipment to be completed. The small wheels are possibly a relic of the days when 21in tyres were almost unobtainable, a frustrating period when many an enthusiast, out of sheer desperation, had his car wheels reduced in diameter to suit available tyre sizes. (Photo: Peter Whenman)

Two illustrations from a Lagonda catalogue dated January 1932: a long-winged Tourer, with T2 body; and the Weymann Saloon, also shown with long wings, the Saloon now far neater, with the dropped bodyline, flush front door pillars and improved body mouldings. This model was available all fabric, or semi-panelled (metal below the waist line) at £25 extra. Cycle type wings were available on both cars at extra cost. The saloon bodies were designated W24 and W24P respectively. (Catalogue Photos: Ivan Forshaw)

This very desirable DHC by Carlton was first registered in 1932.
(Photo: Phil Ridout)

THE SUPERCHARGED 2 LITRE

The supercharged 2 Litre Lagonda was first announced at the Brooklands Lagonda Fête on 19 July 1930. The test and development car, registered PL 1240, still survives and gives reliable and enjoyable service to its owner. Naturally this car differed in many respects from the production models, retaining the light OH gearbox and back axle, for instance. However, these proved inadequate for the increased power of the supercharged engine, and all but the very early examples were fitted with the 'heavy' Z type axle and gearbox, as used on the 3 Litre, the final drive ratio being 4.1:1.

The supercharger was fitted vertically in front of the timing chest, the generator being moved forward to allow a bevel drive to be taken from the nose of the crankshaft, driving the supercharger at crankshaft speed. On the early cars, a Powerplus single rotor type unit was fitted, but most of the production models were supplied with a Cozette No. 9 and, like the Powerplus, blew at about 4lb per square inch. Later a Zoller No. 5 was made available with a boost pressure of 7lb per square inch, and was manufactured under licence by Lagonda. The higher pressure of the Zoller supercharger required some changes in the design of the inlet manifold and a Y-shaped manifold was developed. A single 1⅝in SU carburettor was used.

The crankshaft of new design was fully machined and balanced, the crank webs being thinner, but the crankpins being wider at 1¹¹/₁₆in, an increase of ⅛in on that of the unsupercharged engine crankshaft. Bolt-on balance weights were fitted. The crankshaft ran in five bronze-backed white metal bearings. As on the unsupercharged 2 Litre, the camshaft had a 236-degree opening period but was retimed to give a valve overlap of 15-degrees. An AC petrol pump was driven from the rear end of the inlet camshaft, the tachometer taking its drive from the rear of the exhaust camshaft. The compression ratio was reduced to 5.5:1. Alterations were also made to the exhaust manifold on later models, an olive and ring nut replacing the flange fixing for the down pipe.

The increased engine length of course meant that the radiator had to be moved forward. At the same time, the opportunity was taken to redesign its mounting, and all 2 Litres, supercharged or normally aspirated, were now fitted with trunnion mounted radiators, the base mounted radiators being prone to cracking under racing conditions. A tubular cross member now replaced the pressed steel one. This was mounted forward of the radiator, and on the supercharged models had an inverted U in its centre to clear the generator, as this protruded further forward, due to the increased engine length. Tension rods were fitted under the chassis side members and these were set, wire locked and sealed on assembly of the chassis, according to body weight. Breakage of the seals invalidated the warranty of the vehicle. These chassis and radiator modifications were also incorporated into the 3 Litre cars. Changes were also made to the coachwork: the body sides were dropped to envelop the chassis, a larger cut out for the driver's elbow, and a door was fitted on the offside rear in addition to the two on the nearside. PL 1240, the experimental car, was the first to be fitted with this T2 body. The supercharged cars were also available in saloon form, either fabric or semi-panelled, some of these being fitted with a luggage boot.

The bodies were designated W24 and W24P respectively.

Until the supercharged 2 Litre Lagonda appeared, motorists of experience viewed with mixed feelings the many efforts which were made to produce a usable road performance by this means. The Lagonda designers may be credited with producing one of the very few supercharged engines of the period to combine power, silence and extreme reliability.

At its inception the car was tested under the most rigorous conditions and proved capable, in full touring trim, of acceleration from rest to 70 m.p.h. in 22.4 seconds, with a maximum speed of over 90 m.p.h., and a minimum on top of 4 to 5 m.p.h. (These figures were taken from the supercharged 2 Litre catalogue of 1932.)

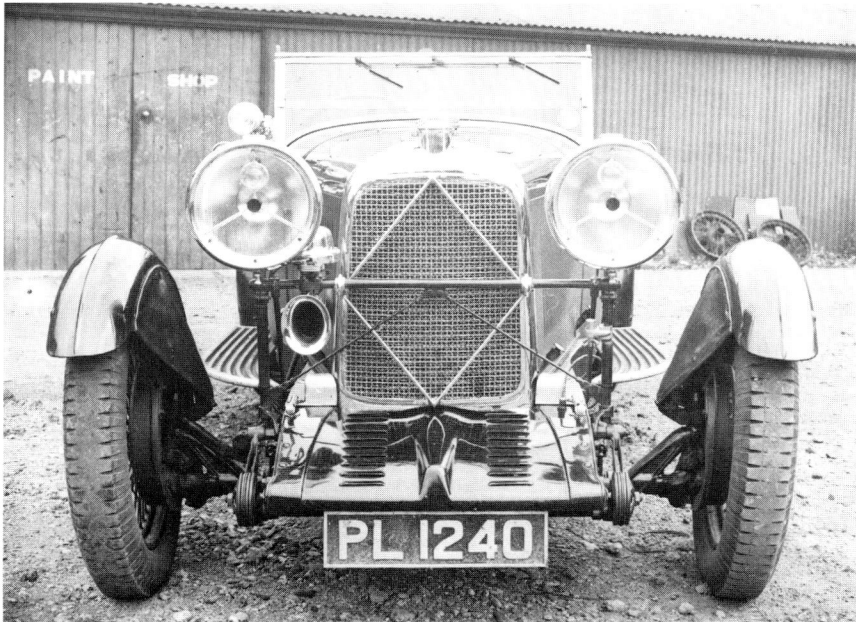

Two views of the supercharged 2 Litre Lagonda. This was the test and development car and is seen here at the Staines factory shortly after being road-tested by *Autocar* in the summer of 1930. The car had covered a considerable mileage before the press set their hands on it, hence its well-used appearance. This was the first chassis to be fitted with the T2 body. The car is still in service. (Photos: Quadrant/*Autocar*)

This truly magnificent supercharged 2 Litre Weymann Saloon was the subject of the *Autocar* road-test series no. 677, 20 November 1931. The car was registered PJ378. Unlike the open model on page 107, no record of this car exists in the Lagonda Club files. It is an unfortunate fact that many of these desirable sporting Saloons were destroyed in order to provide spares for the open cars; others had their bodies replaced with replica open touring coachwork, with the sad result that not one of these fine supercharged Saloons is known to survive today. The car shown has a W24 body, it was priced at £875, and was available with or without the luggage boot. The semi-panelled body W24P was £25 extra. (Photo: Quadrant/*Autocar*)

A 1932 supercharged Tourer with the T3 body. The rear luggage boot was fitted with superb quality leather suitcases, and an extensive tool cabinet was set within the bootlid. Single or double side-mounted spare wheels were optional. The 1932 catalogue gave the chassis price as £610 and the Tourer was £775. (Photo: Ivan Forshaw)

T. C. Mann with his supercharged 2 Litre on the Brooklands test hill – a JCC meeting in 1932. The chap on the left with his hand raised is Alfie Cranmer, Technical Director of Lagonda Motors. Conrad Mann also drove this car in the 1931 Monte Carlo Rally. Starting from Glasgow, he finished 34th overall. He won his class in the Mont des Mules hill climb, and also won the Condammi Cup for braking and acceleration tests. He retired in the 1931 Lands End Trial, but won a gold in the Lands End to John O'Groats in the same year. In 1932 he drove this same car in the Monte Carlo Rally, finishing 37th overall. (Photo: T. C. Mann)

Maurice Leo, with his 1930 supercharged 2 Litre, in full flight at the 1949 Vintage Prescott Meeting. (Photo: Richard Hare)

THE 2 LITRE CONTINENTAL

The Continental was the last of the four-cylinder range of 2 Litre models and was introduced in April 1932. Production ran concurrently with the Speed Model, the Continental being slightly more expensive, at £625 for the Tourer and £725 for the Saloon. The chassis and engine were identical to the normally aspirated L/C OH models, with the exception of smaller wheels, now 18in (tyre size 5.50 × 18in), and ribbed cast iron brake drums. A single SU carburettor replaced the Zenith instrument.

However, considerable changes were made to both the radiator and body. The radiator matrix was now separate from the shell and had thermostatically controlled shutters for temperature control. It was also raked, the bottom being some four inches further forward than the top. The bonnet was also changed and had an attractive curve at its rear end. The Tourer body was all steel, coach-built, and fitted with a fold-flat windscreen. The 14-gallon petrol tank was changed in shape, with a fairing blending it in with the protrusion of the chassis side members. The body was designated T4. The Saloon version was steel panelled below the waistline, and very similar in appearance to the Speed Model Saloon. Cycle type wings were fitted as standard to both models, but long wings were available if preferred. Due to the demand for a six-cylinder 2 Litre model, the Continental was superseded by the 16/80 after a production run of only four months, yet some 23 Continental models are known to survive, almost the entire production. (Photos: Lagonda Club and Roger Cooke)

Chapter Six

![Staines Lagonda England logo]

VARIATIONS ON A THEME

THE LOW CHASSIS 3 LITRE SPECIAL (TYPE Z3S)
First Series

Lagonda type designation is frequently the cause of confusion, and this is particularly so of the 3 Litre models. The 3 litre types Z3 and Z3S were originally *high chassis* cars, becoming *low chassis* models, yet retaining the same type designation. To confuse things further, the type Z3S, soon after its introduction in *low chassis* form, underwent fairly extensive chassis changes, and a trunnion-mounted radiator replaced the base-mounted type of its forebear, but it still retained the Z3S designation. For clarity, the *low chassis* 3 Litre Special type Z3S is headed 'first series' and 'second series' for ease of identification, but it should be noted that this was not the manufacturer's terminology.

Experience gained through the racing programmes of the 1928 and 1929 seasons led to the development of the L/C 2 Litre, and this experience was also applied in the development of the L/C 3 Litre Special. In fact, the special chassis was simply a lengthened version of the 2 Litre, its wheelbase being extended to 10ft 9in. But the 'heavy' Z type gearbox and rear axle, as used on the H/C 3 Litre, were retained, with a final drive ratio of 4.1:1 for the open models. Centre lock wire wheels were fitted as standard with a tyre size of 5.25 × 21in.

The engine also benefited from racing experience. Twin SU carburettors mounted directly on the cylinder

The 1930 catalogue illustration of the 3 Litre Special, low chassis. The twin three-branch exhaust manifolds, Scintilla magneto and superb Marles steering gear are all clearly visible. The large bulkhead-mounted Klaxon fitted on early models can also be seen. A large 12-volt battery on this chassis is mounted to the nearside of the gearbox. Normally two 6-volt batteries were fitted under the back seat, but the chassis shown is thought to be one of the prototypes. Some touching up is evident in this photograph, the artist responsible making something of a hash of the radiator.

head, as on the racing H/C 3 Litre, were fitted as standard to the L/C Special, as well as new twin three-branch exhaust manifolds. An AC mechanical petrol pump, driven by an extra lobe at the rear end of the camshaft, replaced the Autovac fitted to the H/C car, and the fan now had four blades to improve cooling.

These extremely quiet and smooth-running engines were exceptionally reliable and long-lived, and were manufactured to the highest possible engineering standards from the finest materials, as was the whole car. It was, of course, a rich man's toy, and at the time the most expensive car the Lagonda Company had produced. Even so, I have heard it said on many occasions that the Special was sold at a loss, subsidised by other models, and those with experience of the model find it hard to believe that a touring car of this quality could be produced for £1,000, even as long ago as 1930. It is without doubt a magnificent machine, and in its day was quite fast. Even today a good example can hold its own well with modern traffic, having a comfortable cruising speed of 70 m.p.h. and a maximum close on 84 m.p.h.

The nearside of the 72 × 120mm (2931.5cc) 3 Litre Special engine. The twin SU carburettors are finished stove enamel black, as is the AC fuel pump seen lower down at the rear of the engine. Almost immediately below it is the sump drain valve. Working forward from this valve is the large oil filler, its cap incorporating the dip stick, then the oil pump, oil suction filter, and, on the timing chest, a tachometer drive and crankshaft-driven generator. At the top of the timing chest is the water pump and, just visible, the magneto. The two external oil pipes to the valve gear can also be seen at either end of the cylinder block. The early engines are easily identified by the six camshaft cover plates. (Photograph: Ivan Forshaw)

The L/C 3 Litre Special in its earliest form. A four-seater, with fabric body fitted, it was designated T. Long wings were available, but few cars seem to have been fitted with them. Colour schemes were to customers' choice. The 1930 catalogue price was £1,000.

The 3 Litre Special Six Light Saloon, said to be of dual personality, having the inspiring performance of a fast sports car and the gentleness of an extra refined town carriage, but not the most handsome vehicle I have seen. Long wings were available. The car was priced at £1,100 and the body type was W26. (Photographs: Ivan Forshaw)

The 3 Litre Four Light Special Saloon. These fabric bodies were very light and rattle-free. The luggage boot was optional, and the car was perhaps better looking without it – six inches of interior space was also lost in the bodies so fitted. Long wings were available. Price £1,100, body type W24.

The 3 Litre Special Close Coupled Saloon. The car was a full four-seater but the two rear seats, to quote the catalogue, were made to disappear, leaving a large luggage platform. The boot also contained two superb fitted suitcases. Long wings were available. This model was far better looking in the flesh than in this illustration. It was priced at £1,100, body type CCS.

With the exception of the running boards, this is a good original example of the 3 Litre L/C Special Tourer. This car was first registered on 11 February 1930 and it still gives considerable pleasure to its owner who purchased it in 1950. (Photo: Alan Hitch)

A catalogue illustration of the 3 Litre Special instrument panel. The L/C 2 Litre panel was identical, and this photograph should be of interest to owners of either model who may be uncertain of the correct panel layout. This car is fitted with an enrichment control below the Ki-gas pump, but these were soon deleted.

(Below)   Lord de Clifford with his navigator Bert Hammond, and two other members of the crew, at the finish of the road section of the 1930 Monte Carlo rally. He finished 46th overall, but during practice for the Monte des Mules hill climb skidded over a cliff, fortunately without injury, though the car was said to be a write-off. This was one of very few L/C 3 Litre Specials to be fitted with Speed Model wings. Careful study of the photograph reveals de Clifford's signature in the lower right hand corner. (Photo: Bert Hammond Collection)

THE L/C 3 LITRE LAGONDA STANDARD CHASSIS TYPE Z3

After the introduction of the 3 Litre Special in March 1929, these cars, featured in the 1929–30 Lagonda catalogue, became known as the Standard 3 Litre, but many of the Special's modifications were incorporated in them. Lucas P100DB headlamps, for instance, are clearly visible in two of the catalogue illustrations.

The great dignity of the enclosed drive limousine – the body is of coach-built construction on the 11ft 6in chassis. A fabric limousine of Weymann construction was also available, both cars being full seven-seaters.

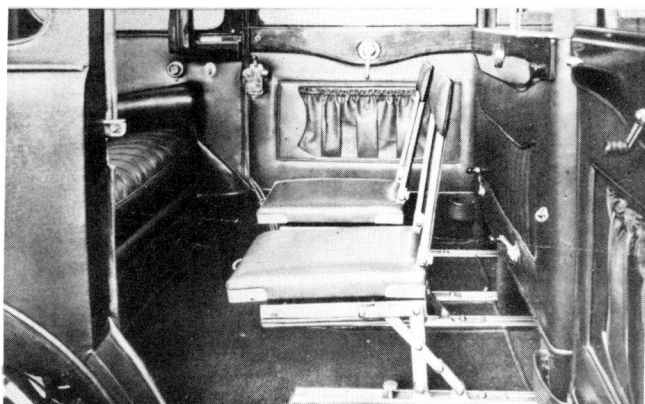

The interior of the enclosed drive limousine. The partition had two winding windows and the occasional seats, shown rear facing here, could be locked in any desired position. When not in use they slid neatly under the front seats. Upholstery was leather or Bedford cord, according to preference, the woodwork being solid walnut. Vanity boxes, smoking companions, down pillows and so on were standard fitments. A sliding roof, in the rear compartment only, now replaced the sun or shade roof of the early model.

The 3 Litre Standard Six Light Weymann Saloon. This large touring Saloon was on the 10ft 9in chassis and the catalogue quotes it as being fitted with the Special engine. The price of the 3 Litre had risen somewhat since its introduction, the standard Six Light Weymann costing £1,050 and the limousine £1,150. A coach-built tourer was also made available on the short chassis. This body was externally identical to the coach-built Tourer on the 16/65 chassis, but was now listed as a full six-seater, and featured pneumatic leather upholstery and the famous 'one man' hood. The car was priced at £945. (Catalogue Photos: Ivan Forshaw)

THE LOW CHASSIS 3 LITRE SPECIAL (TYPE Z3S)
Second Series

Both the normally aspirated 2 Litre and 3 Litre cars benefited from the chassis modifications incorporated in the supercharged car. The 3 Litre chassis length of course remained unchanged at 10ft 9in wheelbase, 4ft 8in track, but the Specials were now fitted with chassis tensioning rods, tubular front cross member, and trunnion-mounted radiator, the latter straddling the generator and now fitted with drain taps at the two lowest points. The engine was unchanged. The chassis price remained at £835, the Sports Tourer £1,000. Taut, precise, fast and elegant, the 3 Litre Special Tourer must rank as one of the most desirable and collectable vintage cars today.

Front view of the 3 Litre Special, with the deeper trunnion-mounted radiator and tubular front cross member visible. The headlamp stone guards were optional extras of the period, manufactured by Joseph Lucas especially for the P100 range of lamps. The car has the T body. It was first registered on 17 July 1930 and I purchased it in 1951, since when it has covered some 223,000 enjoyable miles. The photograph was taken at Brooklands in 1984. Note the deplorable state of the track – the result of successive governments turning a blind eye to the greatest motoring and aviation landmark in the world. (Photo: BP Oil)

No road-test was carried out on this revised L/C 3 Litre Special until 1931, and the demonstrator used had by then covered a considerable mileage. Even so, *Autocar* was most impressed, remarking on the car's performance and extreme comfort. This 1930 car is identical to that road-test vehicle, the two-door (nearside only) T type body seen to full advantage here. These cars lost little of their elegance with the hood raised. (Photo: Margaret Woods)

The sheer magnificence of the 3 Litre Special Tourer as seen from the balcony of the Brooklands clubhouse. (Photo: Geoffrey Seaton)

LONDON–NEW DELHI ON A 3 LITRE

A long and exciting association commenced in 1963 when David Crow became the proud owner of PL 1239, a 1930 3 Litre Special. After a full season of racing and rallying with the car in 1964, 1965 saw an overland journey from London to New Delhi. Preparation for the trip revealed badly scored cylinder bores, so a Lagonda M35R engine was installed. By early March, David and his companion Peter Surman were under way, the route from London taking them to Dover, Dunkirk, Madrid, Gibraltar, Algiers, Tunis, Benghazi, Alexandria, Beirut, Baghdad, Kabul, and Rawalpindi, arriving New Delhi on the 8th June. They had covered 11,057 miles, much of it over rough terrain and in appalling weather conditions. In all, a magnificent effort.

David Crow and PL 1239 in Spain while *en route* to New Delhi.

Journey's end, New Delhi, 8 June 1965 – David Crow at the wheel.
(Photos: David Crow)

PL 1239 as it is today, the original engine now refitted and the car nicely restored by a new owner but, sadly, carrying personalised number plates. (Photo: Clive Sherwood)

The photograph in this 1931 *Motor* advertisement shows the sleek lines of the 3 Litre Special Tourer. This car is fitted with the T2 body.

SUMMING up his impressions of the 3-litre Lagonda after an unusually severe trial, Mr. Alan C. Hess, the well-known motoring critic, says:

"May I say that I have never before submitted a big car to such a gruelling test nor have I ever heard of a big car putting up such a good performance under such deplorable road and weather conditions in a trial of this sort, and I am so enthusiastic about the performance of your 3-litre "Special" Tourer that I invite you to make what use you like of this letter."

We cordially invite you to gather your own impressions of this or any other Lagonda model by a trial at its wheel.

LAGONDA

2-Litre Chassis	£555
2-Litre Chassis, Supercharged	£610
3-Litre 6 Cyl. Chassis	£775
3-Litre Special Chassis	£835

Dunlop tyres. Cerric finish and Acetex Safety Glass standard to the All-British Lagonda

LAGONDA LTD., STAINES, MIDDLESEX

(Above)   The 1931–32 3 Litre Special Weymann Saloon. The whole character of the Z type 3 Litre can be summed up in two words: 'British Thoroughbred'.

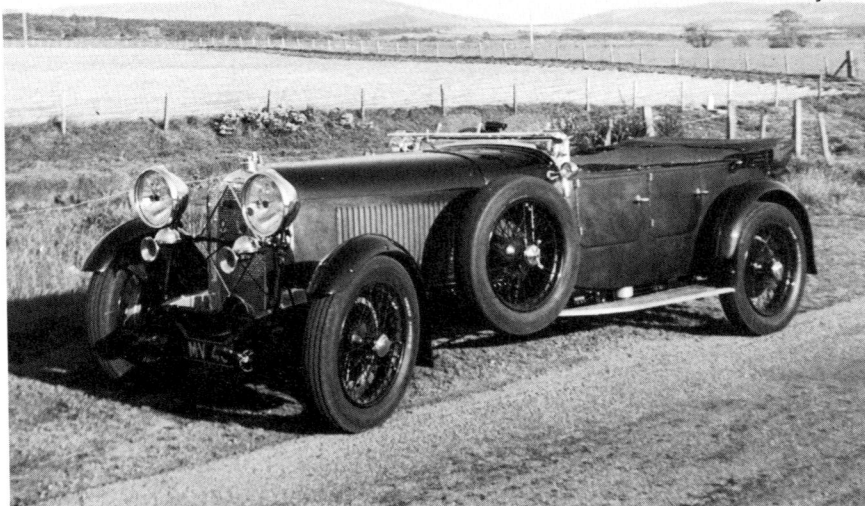

First registered on 23 November 1932, this extensively used but beautifully kept 3 Litre Special must be one of the last 3 Litre cars with the Z type chassis. A T3 body is fitted. The radiators on these late Z type cars were fitted with the racing type hinged filler caps. (Photo: Martin Holloway)

The 1931–32 catalogue illustration of the 72 × 120mm (2931.5cc) 3-litre engine. It is worth comparing it with the previous 3-litre engine illustration (page 113) as all the modifications are visible. These were: ram air engine breather intake, seen forward end of rocker cover; Vokes filters fitted to SU carburettors (Saloon models only); oil suction filter repositioned in front of the oil pump, to make room for an Auto-klean filter, which can be seen fitted to the forward nearside engine foot. Three cast aluminium camshaft cover plates replaced the six steel plates on the early engine. This engine was later uprated to 20.94hp (3181cc, 75 × 120mm). Externally the engine was virtually unchanged. However, these larger engines can easily be identified by removal of the valve cover, the valve spring length being longer, 2½in as opposed to 2in on the 72mm engine (measured with valves closed).

(Below) A 1932 3 Litre Special with a fully panelled T body. What an attractive and desirable motor car it is. (Photo: David Royle)

A very attractive 3 Litre Special by E. D. Abbott of Farnham, referred to as a Single Cabriolet Coupé. The body featured a disappearing occasional seat behind the front seats, and a large luggage area at the rear. The car is seen at the Abbott works prior to delivery in October 1931. (Photo: Farnham Museum)

Lord de Clifford (right) and Mr T. C. Mann (extreme left) with the works' 3 Litre during the 1932 RAC Rally in which they won a cup. Lord de Clifford also drove this car into 20th place overall in the 1932 Monte Carlo Rally. Careful study of the car reveals it to have a separate shelled radiator with winged badge, and close fitting stoneguard. Such cars are sometimes referred to as Selectors (see 3 Litre Selector and Selector Special). However, it is more likely that these radiators were fitted to all models for an interim period only, and were soon superseded by the more familiar controlled shutter type of radiator. This theory was strengthened when Mr Mann remarked that he had never driven one of the Maybach gearbox models. Certainly both the two surviving Selector cars known to me have temperature-controlled shutter-type radiators fitted. Note the makeshift anti-splash valances fitted to the wings, and the snow tyres fitted to the spare wheels. The body style was T3. (Photos: T. C. Mann)

Two very fine surviving examples of the 3 Litre fitted with the short-lived mesh fronted radiator. A standard chassis Saloon (above) at a *Concours d'Etat*; the judges are Ben Walker, left, and the late Don Roberts, centre. Seemingly, the car's owners need to cool their nerves during the procedure. (Photo: Richard Hare)

A magnificent 1932 3Litre Carlton-bodied DHC. Reputedly once the property of Edward VIII when Prince of Wales, this car won its class in the Lagonda Car Club's annual *Concours d'Elégance* in 1964. (Photo: Phil Ridout)

THE 3 LITRE SELECTOR TYPE ZMS
AND SELECTOR SPECIAL TYPE ZMBS

The Z type gearbox fitted to both the supercharged 2 Litre and 3 Litre models was a delight to the experienced motorist, but no box for the amateur. By the early 1930s, drivers were becoming less skilful, or less interested in driving as an art anyway, so Lagonda, like many motor manufacturers, started to experiment with easy, or self-change gearboxes. The simple solution would have been synchromesh, and by 1929 such a box had in fact been perfected in America. However, Lagonda chose the German Maybach *Doppelschnellgang* (double four fast-change gearbox). These were originally designed for the huge V12 7 Litre DS7 Zeppelin car, the engine of which weighed over a ton; naturally, the gearbox was also of considerable size and weight, and its mechanics frightfully complicated.

The fitting of this Lagonda manufactured Maybach gearbox to the 3 Litre chassis added two more models to the 3 Litre range, the Selector and the Selector Special, both cars costing £75 more than the normal gearbox model. With the exception of the modifications required for the mounting of this very heavy gearbox and its associated equipment, the 3 Litre chassis was unchanged, but due to the great additional weight, cracking of the frames soon developed, causing some concern and embarrassment to the company. Undaunted, Alf Cranmer called for a complete new chassis to be designed; this chassis was a great success. Designated ZM, it became the platform for the manual gearbox model 3 Litre as well as the Selector models, and later for the 3½ and 4½ litre cars, its length being reduced by 6in, from a 10ft 9in to 10ft 3in wheelbase for the Rapide models.

The new chassis frame was unusual as its side members were only parallel from the front to a point about 18in behind the rear engine mountings, and were then angled slightly outwards for the remaining length of the chassis. The two side members were no deeper in section, but all the joining cross members were tubular, the two main members being massive curved 3½in diameter tubes. The Z type rear axle was very similar to the previous one, its main difference being that the brake back plates were

cast aluminium and riveted to the axle tubes. The axle ratios were 3.66:1 for the Selector models, and 4.1:1 for the manual gearbox model Tourer. The front axle was completely new, and passed over the springs instead of below them as before. Most of the spring bushes were now Silentbloc. A new mechanical braking system with 16in chromidium cast iron drums, heavily finned to assist cooling, was fitted with single pairs of shoes to each drum, both front and rear. The radiator was also new and, though attractive, was a much cheaper radiator than the previous models. The shell was separate from the matrix, the latter being of the film type as opposed to the very efficient, but expensive, honeycomb core. Thermostatically-controlled shutters were fitted. The filler cap was of the quick-release pattern, and the badge changed to one of winged design. The engine was unchanged, all 3 Litre models since early in 1931 being fitted with the larger 75 × 120mm (21hp) engine.

The Maybach gearbox had two sets of ratios, four 'normal' and four 'emergency low', the desired set of ratios being selected by a central gear lever with four positions: neutral, normal, emergency low and reverse, the speeds being preselected by two small levers above the steering wheel, and the change effected by momentarily lifting the accelerator. With the centre lever back (normal) the ratios were: 3.66, 5.27, 6.95 and 10.61:1, which suited the car well, giving a maximum speed of 82 m.p.h.; with the lever forward (emergency low), the maximum speeds in the upper three ratios were 30, 42 and 62 m.p.h. Lagonda never publicised the fact, but if reverse was selected with the central lever, four low ratio reverses were also obtainable, by the use of the preselector levers. No doubt great fun was had by those who stumbled on the trick. Each of the two preselect levers was connected to an independent rotary valve, the valves being coupled to a pair of servo cylinders in the box. These servos were operated by a combination of partial vacuum from the engine via a reservoir, and atmospheric pressure.

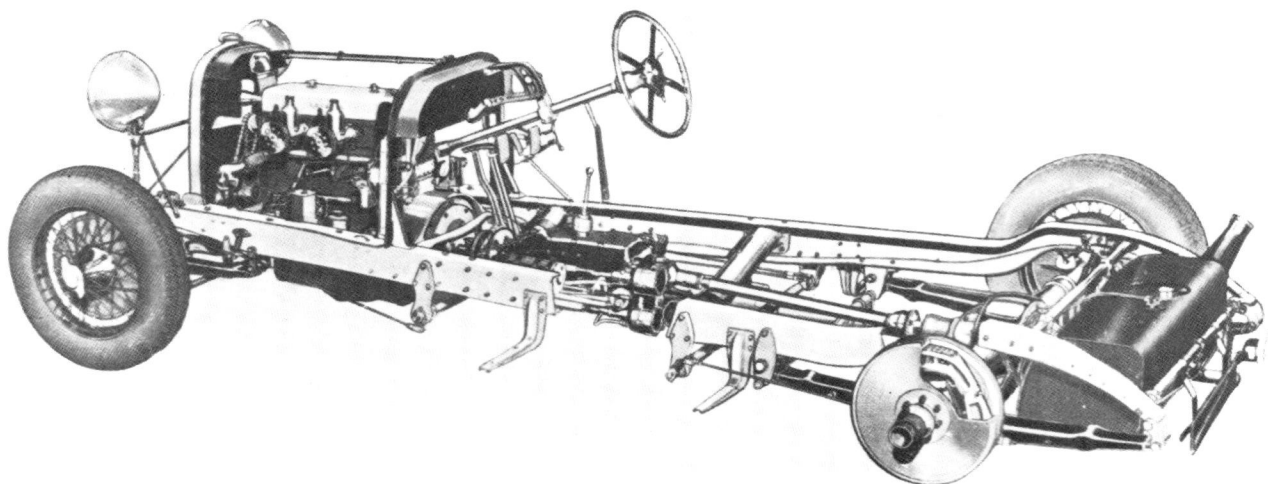

The 1932 Lagonda catalogue used *The Motor* illustrations for the 3 Litre Selector Special. This is the new ZM chassis of which the Maybach gearbox complete with its two servos can be seen; for clarity the maze of pipes and the vacuum reservoir associated with it have been deleted.

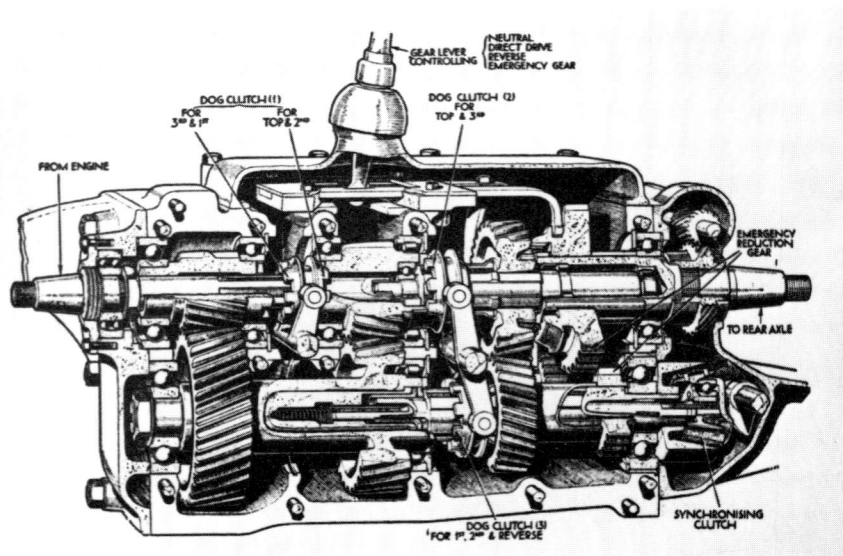

The Maybach gearbox, with half its case removed. The helical gears provide the indirect speeds; top was dog engagement, all being preselected. Twelve speeds were available, eight forward and four reverse. These complex gearboxes were manufactured under licence by Lagonda.

This 1932 3 Litre Selector Special is in the sort of condition the restorer likes to find a car, complete and original. The car is currently being restored, and with the rarity of saloons these days, this is a very worthwhile project. Coachwork was identical for the Selector Specials and the manual gearbox models. (Photo: Mrs Robby Hewitt)

Lagonda Equipment

"Extras" need have no place in the LAGONDA owner's vocabulary, as it is the policy of Lagonda, Ltd., to standardise any item of equipment as soon as its practical value to the motorist is proved. An example of this policy is found in the magnificent P.100 head-lamps supplied with most cars illustrated herein, and which are standard only upon one or two of the world's finest and most expensive cars. A quick-lift hydraulic jack is carried conveniently under the bonnet, and the small tools (complete even to a tyre pressure gauge) are neatly fitted in an oil and waterproof panel either inside the scuttle, or in the lid of the boot at the rear. Safety glass and centralised lubrication are standard to all models. "The equipment is positively lavish," writes Mr. John Prioleau in the "Observer".

THE 3 LITRE LAGONDA TYPE ZM

The ZM chassis of the manual gearbox model 3 Litre was almost identical to that of the Selector cars. The ZE/S3 gearbox was fitted and, though the ratios were the same as the ZE type, the ZE/S3 featured a silent (helical) third speed gear. (Photo: Chas K. Bowers)

(Above and left)   The ZM 3 Litre Tourer: this is a 1932 car with a fully panelled T2 body. This particular example was for many years the property of Mr Cecil Vokes, who used it extensively for testing his oil and air filters. Vokes owned many Lagonda models, but it is said that the 3 Litre was always his favourite. (Photos: Mrs Robby Hewitt and Geoff Seaton)

Three pictures from the 3 Litre sales brochure: top, a 1932 Tourer with a fabric T3 body; centre, the 1933 Saloon, built by Lagonda under Silent Travel patents, this body is the semi-panelled ST24A which was available with long, cycle or helmet wings, and with rear or side-mounted spare wheel; bottom, a 1933 Tourer with the T7 body. A large single door giving access to both front and rear compartments was fitted on the nearside, but the small rear door was retained on the offside of the car. During 1933 the wheel size was reduced from 21in to 19in. (Catalogue Illustrations: Ivan Forshaw)

A semi-panelled ST24 3 Litre Saloon with the popular cycle wings and ski running boards. The ST24 body had a peak above the windscreen with fresh air vents fitted in its lower face for demisting. A peak was not fitted to the ST24A Saloon. (Photo: Lagonda Club)

(Below) A similar car but with the attractive helmet wings. The furnishings of these cars were superb. (Photo: Chas K. Bowers)

(*Above*)   An attractive three-position Drop-head Coupé by Vanden Plas. (Photo: Chas K. Bowers)

Nothing seems to have been recorded about this exotic ZM 3 Litre, but though the attractive coachwork has a French flavour, it was in fact the work of Gurney Nutting. An almost identical body graced ZM 3 Litre registered KY 3510, and there may have been others. Where are they now? (Photo: Geoffrey Goddard)

The Lagonda Guarantee

Every new Lagonda is guaranteed for Nine Years in three periods of three years each. Before the expiry of each period, the purchaser is required to advise the Company in writing that he requires an extension of the Guarantee. He must then send his car at his own expense to the Lagonda Works at Staines for the necessary inspection on the date notified by the Company.

The Company will renew the Guarantee for a further period of three years, provided that the purchaser agrees to pay for any repairs and adjustments that the Company may consider necessary, and after these repairs have been completed.

The purchaser must at the time of purchase personally fill in and sign the Guarantee Application Card, and forward it to the Company. In exchange he will receive a signed copy of the Warranty, which must be produced for inspection at any time on demand.

A Guarantee can be assigned or transferred to anyone with the consent of the Company, and anyone desiring such transfer may obtain it by sending the Car at his expense to the Lagonda Works for inspection, and subsequently placing an order for any repairs and adjustments that the Company may consider necessary. The transfer fee is £5.

An extract from the Lagonda guarantee.

THE 3½ LITRE (TYPE M35 AND M35R)

The 3½ Litre Lagonda was unveiled in the autumn of 1934, production of this model running concurrently with the ZM type 3 Litre. The ZM chassis was used but reduced in length from 10ft 9in to 10ft 3in, as was the M45 Rapide (see M45R, page 185). In fact, the chassis frames of these two cars were identical with the exception of the forward cross member, the M35 forward member curving up to clear the crankshaft-driven generator of the 3½-litre engine. A Girling braking system was fitted, the shoes working within 16in finned chromidium drums. Andre-Hartford shock absorbers were fitted front and rear. The ZE/S3 gearbox with the ZE set of ratios was fitted, and like the ZM 3 Litre had the double helical 'Silent' third speed gear. M45R axles were used, but with a final drive ratio of 3.67:1. Standard wheels were 19in centre lock wire, with 6.00 × 19in tyres.

Though the external measurements of the 3½ litre cylinder block were identical to both the 72mm and 75mm litre engine, it is my belief that the 3½ litre block was a new casting. It is inconceivable that even the larger of the two 3 litre engines could have been stretched to a bore diameter of 80mm and retain a respectable rebore limit; the stroke of course was unchanged at 120mm, and again six cylinders. The engine was rated at 23.82hp (3619cc) with a compression ratio of 7:1, and for the first time Lagondas quoted a b.h.p. figure, this being given as 88 b.h.p. at 3,000 r.p.m. Alloy connecting rods replaced the steel rods fitted to the 3-litre engine, and the pistons were fitted with four rings above the gudgeon pin and one below; the gudgeon pin diameter was also increased. A larger rectangular breather intake replaced the funnel shape on the 3 Litre, and the rocker cover now had the oil filler fitted in its centre with 'Lagonda 3½ Litre' cast in its sides. Standard equipment was an Autoklean oil filter and twin SU carburettors fed from a 20-gallon petrol tank via SU electric pumps. The ZM type 3 Litre radiator was used.

Lagonda offered two bodies on this chassis, a Tourer (T9) identical to the M45 Rapide, and a completely new Saloon body (ST44), four-door, pillarless, fully panelled in aluminium. A rear-mounted spare wheel was fitted, this being partly sunk into the luggage boot lid, and fitted with an aluminium cover. A sun roof was optional. Chassis price was £550, the Tourer £695, and the Saloon £795. Maximum speed of the Tourer was quoted as 84 m.p.h. – little, if any, better than the 3 Litre, the increased body weight on the 3½ Litre chassis obviously taking its toll.

The maker's plates on early examples of the model were stamped M35, followed of course by the applicable body type designation, but most of the production cars were stamped M35R and, as there is no apparent difference between the two, it is reasonable to assume that all 3½ Litre cars were Rapides.

One of the younger Lagonda Club members casts a discerning eye over this very fine 3½ Litre Tourer. (Photo: Richard Hare)

The businesslike 3½ Litre Rapide Tourer. This is the T9 body and is externally identical to the 4½ Litre Rapide touring model.

The 3½ Litre Rapide Saloon (ST44), without doubt one of the most attractive closed cars available in the mid-1930s, and far lighter and neater than the Saloon version of its bigger engined brother (see M45R, page 188). (Photos: Chas K. Bower)

Chapter Seven

FILTERS, CLUBS AND ALL THOSE REVS

THE LAGONDA CAR CLUB 1932–39

Mr C. G. Vokes, the founder of the Vokes Filter Company, was a great Lagonda enthusiast; at one time he almost owned a set, from 2 to 4½ Litres. These cars were used extensively in his experiments into oil and air filtration, but he was also a keen competitive driver. During the winter of 1932, Cecil Vokes put the idea to Brigadier General Metcalfe that a Lagonda Owners' Club should be formed. The Brigadier General was delighted with the idea and offered some encouragement, with factory assistance, to members. The proposed club was adver-

tised in the motoring press, resulting in about a dozen Lagonda owners meeting at Vokes' Factory on a Sunday morning, and the Lagonda Car Club being duly formed. General Metcalfe became Club President, Cecil Vokes, Secretary and Treasurer, Mike Couper, Trials Secretary, and Major Bill Oates, Committee Chairman. The elected Committee members were C. C. L. Brown, E. d'C. Carr, A. D. Jaffe and P. J. Field Richards.

The first event was held at Hanworth Air Park on 28 March 1933, a gymkhana type of event, plus an air display

Some of Vokes' experimental oil and air filters fitted to the 75 × 120mm three-litre engine of KY 1700 when used as a mobile test bed. (Photo: Mrs Robby Hewitt)

LAGONDA HANWORTH RÁLLY

Great Success of a Meeting Held by One of the Newest of One-make Clubs

Visitors' cars, the latest Lagonda models, and the Hanworth Club's display aeroplanes under the shadow of General Metcalfe, President of the Lagonda Club, and the prime-mover of the Lagonda Company

THE Lagonda Club's first rally at Hanworth aerodrome last Saturday was altogether excellent, not in any sense too official, nor too impromptu, but just the right mixture of the two, aided by as perfect an afternoon as one could wish for and the presence of all the notables of the Lagonda Company, including General Metcalfe, who is a tower of strength in himself.

The rally part of the affair was won by Tong, who brought his Lagonda to the meeting from Lancaster, with Mrs. Lynd-Walker second, coming from Doncaster, and Mustchamp won the sealed time competition. There ensued an excellent potato race, competitors' passengers being compelled to exhibit tremendous activity in the rear seat, as the potatoes had to be dropped alternately from port and starboard. Inhabitants of saloons therefore, had a perfectly dreadful time, while one enthusiast on a blown sports car made too little allowance for speed on the bombsight and thoroughly missed the bucket. The competition was won by Tong in great style.

In the parking test, which came next, much good grass was cut to pieces while delighted drivers endeavoured to emerge at high speed from a pen facing one way, then reverse into another pen facing the other, causing great destruction of the boundary flags and shrieks of joy from the spectators whenever a man went astern at high speed and failed in his objective. This event was won by T. C. Mann, with C. T. Mann second, the variation of the initials being a considerable worry to the secretary.

After that musical chairs, played without music and without chairs, a Klaxon doing duty for the one, and upturned buckets with sharp edges serving for the other, was one of the best events of the afternoon and provided, as usual, plenty of fun before Mrs. Wilmot won, with Mrs. Dykes as runner-up in actual fact. At one time the success of this event was jeopardised by the reckless destruction of buckets by an official and his car.

Thereafter the air was full of the Hanworth Club's aeroplanes, varying from that practical but always humorous-looking affair, the Autogiro, to the projectile-like velocity of a neat Lockheed-Vega, with an attendant Planette which reminded some people very strongly of those early efforts in aviation at Brooklands, though in contrast to such it flew easily and well.

Tea and a dance ensued, during the first of which the prizes were distributed by Mrs. Metcalfe, assisted by lightning calculations with the sweepstake money by the honorary solicitor in making truly legal subdivisions, General Metcalfe himself paying a tribute to the undoubted success of one of the newest one-make clubs, and another tribute to Gordon-Crosby for the design of the club's badge, which is certainly excellent. Vokes, the secretary, deserved a special vote of thanks all to himself for doing an incredible amount of work in an infinitesimally brief space of time and keeping his sense of humour throughout, proceedings winding up with the pious hope that this would be the forerunner of many other Lagonda Car Club functions.

There is no doubt whatsoever that an afternoon spent in this manner, with mild forms of competitions which do not destroy one's car, and all the possibilities of discovering what "the other fellow" has done to his machine—one of the same type as one's own—is one of the pleasantest forms of club activity that any man can devise.

Beyond all possible question, too, the sight of so many different models and different types of one particular make of car gives the owner an increased sense of that *esprit de marque*, which is a very strong and a very sound feature of British motoring, in a way that could not easily be achieved in any other fashion.

Casque.

Autogiro joy-rides.

(Above) Spilling the spuds.
(Left) Parking

My bucket.

This report on the first Lagonda Club rally (28 March 1933) is reproduced by courtesy of *Autocar.* The aircraft are Percival Gulls.

followed by a dance in the evening. The club's first dinner was held at the Park Lane Hotel on 9 February 1934, over a hundred people attending. By this time the General was in hospital, and gravely sick, so Major Oates presided at the dinner in his absence. Gillie Potter was engaged to entertain the party, and the evening turned out to be a great success. From then on, this was a well supported annual event until the club was disbanded due to wartime restrictions at the end of 1939. Brigadier General Metcalfe died from cancer on 26 February 1934, and was succeeded by Sir Edgar Holberton, CBE, who took the title of Company Chairman and Managing Director.

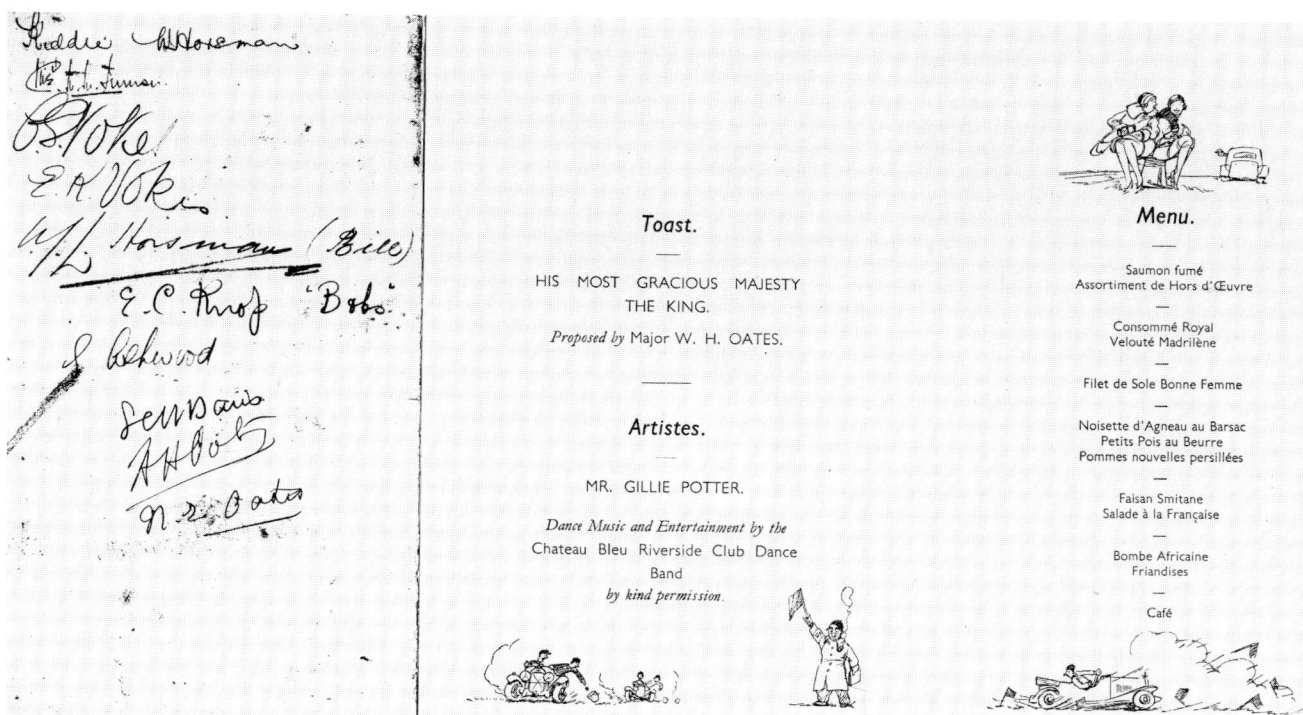

Toast.

HIS MOST GRACIOUS MAJESTY
THE KING.

Proposed by Major W. H. OATES.

Artistes.

MR. GILLIE POTTER.

Dance Music and Entertainment by the
Chateau Bleu Riverside Club Dance
Band
by kind permission.

Menu.

Saumon fumé
Assortiment de Hors d'Œuvre

Consommé Royal
Velouté Madrilène

Filet de Sole Bonne Femme

Noisette d'Agneau au Barsac
Petits Pois au Beurre
Pommes nouvelles persillées

Faisan Smitane
Salade à la Française

Bombe Africaine
Friandises

Café

The Lagonda Club's first dinner was held at the Park Lane Hotel on 9 February 1934. This is Cecil Vokes' menu bearing the signatures of some notable Lagonda personalities. (Picture: Phil Mayhew)

(Above)   Mr C. G. Vokes' stable of Lagondas lined up at his Alton farmhouse. They are, from left to right: 1929 3 Litre, now in the USA; 1932 3 Litre (said to be Vokes' favourite car), now owned by a Lagonda Club member; LG45 Tourer (alleged to have been hidden under a haystack in France for the duration of the war, bought by G. F. Carrington of Vokes Ltd, 1945), now in Sweden; 3 Litre Saloon (mostly driven by Miss Collin, Vokes' secretary), all traces lost after 1968; an M45 Saloon, not possible to identify. A 2 Litre also existed in this stable. The date of this picture is believed to be about 1945–46. (Photo: Mrs Robby Hewitt)

Looking remarkably like a 16/80 (see 16/80 Special Six, page 141) this was W. M. (Mike) Couper's L/C 2 Litre on test in Wales, prior to winning the 1932 Alpine Rally Glacier Cup. The car still survives, and though it has the four-cylinder, two-litre engine, it could otherwise well be a prototype for the six-cylinder model. (Photo: Lagonda Club)

THE 16/80 S TYPE SPECIAL SIX

The 16/80 was introduced in August 1932 to cater for the growing demand for six-cylinder engined cars of a moderate horsepower rating. It was unfortunate that 1930 and 1931 had been lean years for Lagonda, and it was vital that they cashed in on this six-cylinder market. In order to keep both development time and cost to a minimum, it was decided that the engines should be 'bought in', the chosen power unit being the six-cylinder 15.7hp (1991cc) Crossley. The engine dated back to 1928 so was well proven, and still capable of further development; it would also fit into the 2 Litre chassis frame with only minor modification. The Continental version of the 2 Litre chassis was chosen and, with the exception of the gearbox, the 16/80 chassis specification was as the Continental, even to its wheelbase. The radiator was also similar, though upright, and base-mounted; an attractive winged badge was fitted identical to that of the new ZM 3 Litre (see 3 Litre Type ZM3, page 127).

The Crossley engines were supplied fully assembled, but were completely stripped on arrival at Staines, every part being examined and measured before reassembly. All engines were then bench run before fitting to the chassis, always a Lagonda tradition. Lagonda engineers also extracted more power from these engines, as well as improving the cooling, by modification to the water porting arrangements.

Conventional in design, the Crossley engine was of cast iron, monobloc, the crankcase cast in one with the block, and with a detachable cast iron cylinder head, its ports being fully machined. The engine measured 65 × 100mm bore and stroke (1991cc), the overhead valves operated through tappets and push rods, with force fed lubrication. The camshaft ran in four plain bearings and was submerged in oil. Pistons of aluminium alloy, with fully floating gudgeon pins, these secured by circlips, and Duralumin connecting rods were fitted. The crankshaft ran in four main bearings which were pressure-fed from a submerged oil pump in the sump. A vibration damper was fitted to the crankshaft nose, but this was contained within the timing chest. A timing chain-driven intermediate shaft drove the generator, this in turn driving the magneto, usually a Scintilla, via a vernier coupling, these being mounted in tandem on an adjustable cradle on the offside of the crankcase.

On early engines the water pump was belt driven, and the fan was fitted to its spindle; the position of the water pump was later changed to a position on the offside forward face of the timing chest, and took its drive from the generator intermediate drive shaft. The fan remained belt driven from a pulley on the camshaft nose. Twin SU carburettors were fed from a 14-gallon petrol tank via an Autovac petrol lift, soon superseded by an SU electric petrol pump. Twin Y-shaped exhaust manifolds were fitted, the ports of two and three, and four and five being Siamezed. An Autoklean oil filter was operated from the clutch withdrawal shaft. Early examples of the 16/80 were fitted with a Lagonda-modified Crossley clutch, but most of the manual gearbox models were fitted with a Borg and Beck clutch.

A Z-type gearbox was fitted, with the ZD set of ratios. However, the excellent ENV Preselective (Wilson patent) gearbox was soon made optional, and a large number of these cars, both open and closed, were so fitted. Several very good examples of the 16/80 still exist. Some of these, however, are fitted with the OH type gearbox, and it is uncertain whether these boxes were original equipment or not, though all 16/80 models were fitted with the OH type rear axle. The final drive ratio for the manual gearbox model Tourer was 4.4:1, and 4.6:1 for the Saloon and preselector gearbox cars, both open and closed. The car carried the normal Lagonda warranty of nine years. Strangely, the 16/80 is never referred to as a 2 Litre, always the 16/80, yet at 1991cc it is closer to two litres than its predecessor at 1954cc. It is thought that the designation of 16/80 arrived from a combination of horsepower (15.7) and maximum speed, the manual gearbox models being capable of 80 m.p.h.

The 16/80 chassis, priced in 1932 at £475. Many of these chassis were fitted with extremely attractive coachwork by the specialist coachbuilders.

The 16/80 Family Saloon. This was a full five-seater of typical 1930s elegance. The coachwork was Lagonda, Type F7, and in this form priced at £650.

The 16/80 Four Door Panelled Sportsman's Saloon. These bodies were constructed under Silent Travel patents by Lagonda. Note the attractive helmet front wings and ski-shaped running boards. The Type ST24 was priced at £695. (Catalogue photos: Ivan Forshaw)

Seen at a Lagonda Club AGM, this beautifully turned out Tourer was first registered in May 1933. The body is a T5, and very attractive with the long wings. (Photo: Tony Wood)

Offside of the 16/80 engine. As can be seen, everything is easily accessible. The steering box is a Bishop Cam. This steering box became standard on all Lagonda models from 1931.

Nearside of the 16/80 engine, showing the twin SU carburettors, fuel filter and reserve fuel cock. These engines were very free revving and well capable of exceeding the safe rev. limit of 5,000 r.p.m., but the Duralumin connecting rods were likely to complain if the owner made a habit of it. (Photos: W. B. Wright)

This beautifully restored 16/80 Special Six is fitted with a replica T4 body on a 1932 chassis, but the art of the restorer today is such that few could identify it as not being the original Lagonda touring coachwork. When new, this car would have been virtually identical to the well preserved (ST24) Saloon shown below. (Photos: Peter Evans and the Hartop Collection)

This smart 16/80 Special Six is fitted with a T7 body. The car was first registered in 1934 under the name of Ben Travers of Rookery Nook, Burnham-on-Sea. The photograph was taken 50 years later. (Photo: Lionel Parker)

A very attractive 16/80 2 + 2 by Vanden Plas, though the line is somewhat spoilt by the unusual arrangement of the hood when folded.

A neat DH Coupé with three-position hood, again by Vanden Plas.
(Photos: Chas K. Bowers)

This 1932 Abbott Tourer featured a 20-gallon petrol tank. (Photo: Farnham Museum)

THE LAGONDA FACTORY 1933–34

An early 1930s photograph of Lagonda Motors. The front of the factory has now been moved back roughly in line with the pavement of the slip road on the left, and the Causeway increased in width. Though the gas works opposite still remain, the gas holder was demolished in 1986. Note the nanny walking with her employers, unfortunately a sight seldom seen today. The negative of this picture has been damaged.

A section of the engine machine shop. Extreme right, a 2-litre block on its side for machining, and, further to the left, a 3-litre block hangs on a hoist. In the foreground, a machinist inspects his work on a flywheel. (Photos: Lagonda Club)

The engine assembly shop. Mr Griffin, the foreman, is seen standing in front of a roof support, keeping a keen eye on things; no operation could take place or part be assembled into an engine without his blessing. In the right foreground, a 16/80 engine with the Crossley water pump and steel four-blade fan. Lagonda soon modified these engines by repositioning the water pump and changing the fan to one with two blades cast in aluminium.

Engine test: a 2-litre supercharged unit on the rig and a 16/80 engine stands on the trolley.

The sheet metal shop. Most Lagonda enthusiasts will be familiar with many of the items being manufactured here.

A section of the upholstery department, this section now considerably larger than when the last set of photographs was taken in 1921. Like today, only the finest quality hides were used in the manufacture of Lagonda upholstery. One of the machinists in the right-hand row was later to become Mrs Feeley (see LG45, page 217). (Photos: Lagonda Club)

Chapter Eight

THE BEST SMALL CAR
IN THE WORLD

THE LAGONDA RAPIER

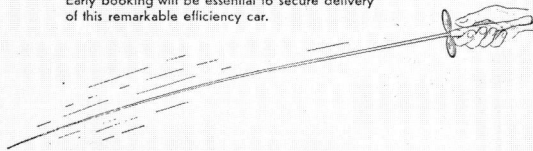

The motor industry generally was at a very low ebb by 1933, yet Brigadier General Metcalfe laid plans to add two new models to the wide range of cars that Lagonda was already producing. Bentley Motors had collapsed in 1931, so it made sense for the General to introduce the 4½ Litre to fill the gap that now existed for a quality high performance car, especially since a suitable chassis in the form of the ZM 3 Litre was in production and would require only minimal modification to accept a larger engine.

The second new model was a different kettle of fish, completely new from front to rear, the delightful little 10hp car later christened the Lagonda Rapier. However, the thinking behind its introduction can only be looked upon as misguided. Many manufacturers had by now attempted to produce the best small car in the world, but for reasons of cost all had failed. For Lagonda this was an especially dangerous path to tread; though the '10' was at the bottom of the Lagonda price range, it was still a machine for the well heeled, and such people preferred big cars. In addition, the company's finances were at an all time low. In fact, the company was so desperate that it endeavoured to obtain some financial backing for the Rapier and the 4½ Litre from the PERR Syndicate of racing enthusiasts. But in the event these negotiations proved abortive.

Irvin Thomas (Tim) Ashcroft was engaged by Lagonda early in 1933 and given the brief to design the last word in 1100cc motoring excellence, and to look sharp about it. With the aid of only a draughtsman assistant, he came up with a four-cylinder, twin overhead camshaft, all-alloy

LAGONDA
RAPIER

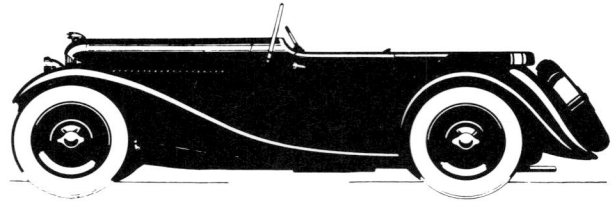

LAGONDA LTD.
STAINES, MIDDLESEX

engine with iron cylinder liners. The engine measured 62.5 × 90mm, bore and stroke (1104cc), rated at 9.69hp and had a proposed safe rev. limit of 5,500–6,000 r.p.m., a staggering figure for 1933.

To the disappointment of Ashcroft, the Lagonda board decided that an all-alloy engine would be prone to problems and far too costly. Unfortunately there was no time to go back to the drawing board, as by now Lagonda were committed to showing the Rapier at the Motor Show in the October of 1933. After much burning of midnight oil, a chassis was produced for exhibition, the engine of which was possibly mostly a mock up, and there was one complete car as a running demonstrator. Both these chassis differed from the eventual production models; it is fortunate, however, that both still exist.

BPC 44 (now registered CJB 765), the demonstration car, had a cast iron cylinder block and this almost certainly was a Meadows 4EJ, the remainder of the engine being to Ashcroft's design, including the cylinder head, though this was also now cast iron. The Meadows 4EJ engine was

rated at 10hp, and had a bore and stroke of 63 × 100mm (1247cc); to reduce it to 62.5mm would have been a simple engineering exercise to meet the Lagonda specification. The original design also called for a cast aluminium sump, but the castings were not available in time for the show. The show chassis and the demonstrator were therefore fitted with sumps prefabricated from sheet steel, camouflaged to look like aluminium castings. In order to stand the high loads to be imposed upon it, considerable care was taken with both the design and manufacture of the crankshaft, which for the size of the engine was quite massive. It was fully machined, balanced both statically and dynamically, and ran in three two-inch diameter white metal bearings in bronze shells. The connecting rods were equally robust, being of forged high tensile steel; the big ends also had a diameter of two inches.

A full flow filtration oil system featured adjusters for pressure and flow to the main bearings and camshaft skew gears. A gauze filter was used. The cylinder head

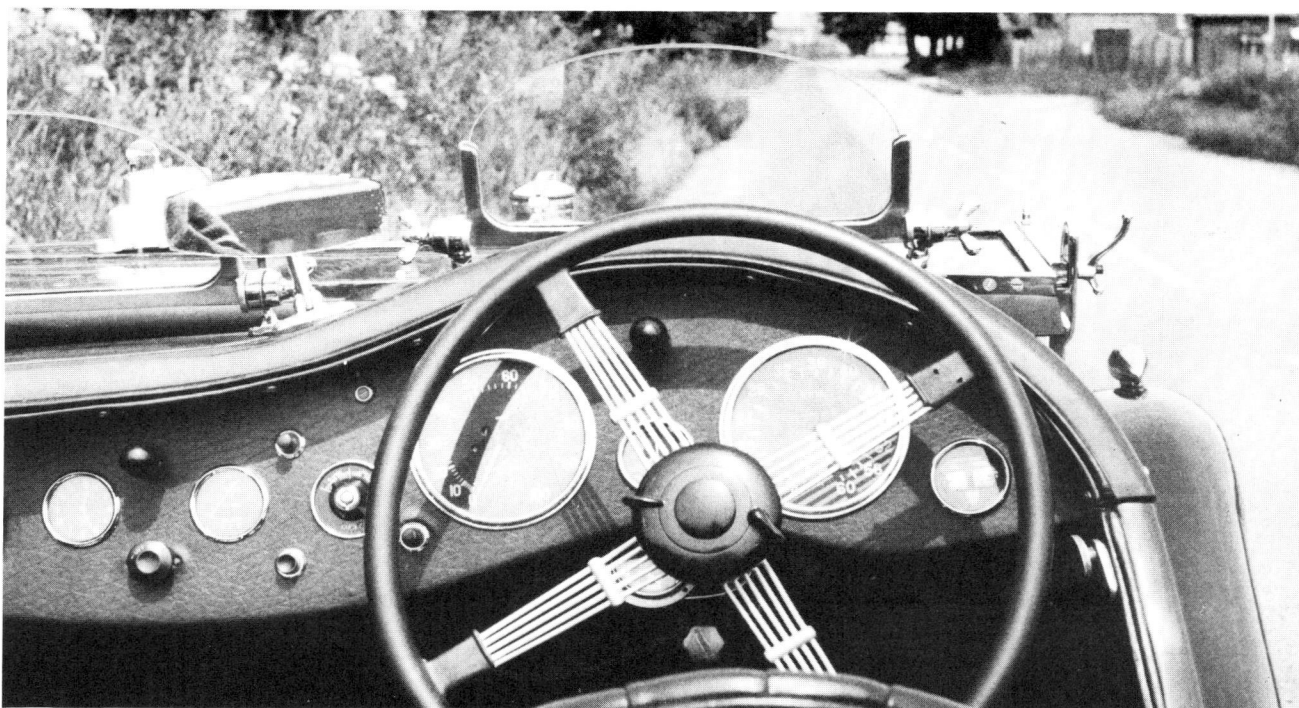

(Above) One can almost feel the excitement of the Lagonda Rapier from this superb photograph. The car is a short chassis prototype demonstrator. (Photo: Peter Cripps)

The Rapier chassis in its final production form.

had hemispherical combustion chambers, and could be removed without disturbing the valve timing. A compression ratio of 7.5:1 was chosen. Twin overhead camshafts had spring-damped double cams to promote smoothness. The cams operated the valves via finger followers which could be slid sideways for adjustment of valve clearances; adjustment was by shims. The camshafts were driven by a three-chain system in the form of a Y, with spring-loaded blade type tensioners, the oil pump taking its drive from the inlet camshaft. Twin Solex carburettors, each one having a separate manifold and feeding two cylinders, were fed by an SU electric pump from a rear-mounted eight-gallon tank. The exhaust manifold was on the nearside of the engine with the pipe well forward to reduce heat in the cockpit. A BTH GA4 magneto driven by a vernier coupling from the generator fired 14mm

The prototype Rapier exhibited in chassis form at the 1933 Motor Show. The two-seater body is by John Charles, for March. (Coachwork to the design of Earl of March of Kevill-Davies and March, Lagonda Agents.)

Prototype 1933 Motor Show demonstrator. The car was driven in the 1934 RAC Rally by Lord de Clifford. Originally registered BPC 44, but reregistered CJB 765 in 1941, it was once the property of Tim Ashcroft. (Photos: Tony Wood and Peter Cripps)

Rear and side views of the beautifully restored and very desirable 1933 Motor Show demonstrator. This short chassis car still retains its original engine. The prefabricated sump, hurriedly knocked up all those years ago, is clearly visible in the lower illustration; the capacity of these show model sumps was two gallons, not one gallon as often stated.

The attractive body is a one-off by Whittingham and Mitchell, built to the special order of Lagonda. Basically a two-seater, a seat does exist in the back for luckless extra passengers.

Originally the car was finished in Cambridge Blue but is now resplendent in bright red, and is seen here on completion of a long and arduous restoration. (Photos: Peter Cripps)

sparking plugs, and a vane type water pump was driven from an extension of the generator shaft. An adjustable thermostat was fitted in the outlet pipe between the head and radiator, the radiator itself being of the film type with a separate shell.

An ENV 75 preselector gearbox was coupled directly to the flywheel, and operated by rod and Arens cable. The rear axle was also ENV, with a final drive ratio of 5.28:1. The chassis was again a robust structure — its splayed side members were double dropped with seven cross members. An eighth member, rubber bushed at its ends, formed the rear engine mount. Semi-elliptic negative cambered springs were fitted and a Girling braking system with 13in drums. Centre lock wire wheels were fitted with 4.50 × 19in tyres. The wheelbase was 7ft 6¾in and the track 3ft 11¾in.

For the production Rapier the policy had been adopted that Lagonda should supply the chassis only, which was priced at £270, the coachwork to be provided by the traditional coachbuilders of the day. Lagonda Ltd imposed strict weight and price limitations on the coachbuilders, which led to many of the bodies being of inferior quality compared to the chassis upon which they were mounted. There was also some concern over the chosen chassis length as four-seater Saloons, DH Coupés and Tourers were envisaged, resulting in Lagonda agreeing to increase the chassis length by nine inches, this being inserted behind the bulkhead. Other chassis modifications were alterations to both the foot and handbrakes, and a new 'bent' draglink to improve the turning circle. The building of the production engines, which took on the form known today, was contracted out to Coventry-Climax. The chromidium iron cylinder head and block castings were extended forward to enclose the timing gears and chains; the water jackets now also enclosed the bores, and a water gallery was fitted on the nearside of the block, as was a full-flow oil filter and oil filler. SU carburettors replaced the Solex instruments, the manifold also being improved. Pipes were now fitted to drain excess oil from the cam boxes and return it to a two-gallon aluminium sump. A

Lord de Clifford entered a Lagonda Rapier in the 1934 Le Mans 24-hour race. The car was fitted with a special lightweight two-seater racing body, built by E. J. Newns of Thames Ditton, and the engine fitted had a shorter throw crankshaft, reducing the stroke to 88.3mm to bring it within the 1100cc class. A higher compression ratio was used. Co-driven by Charles Brackenbury, the car finished 16th overall, running on only three cylinders for the last three hours or so of the race. The car covered some 1,375 miles, averaging 57.29 m.p.h. for the 24 hours, and qualifying for the Rudge-Whitworth Cup, but still something of a disappointment – during tests at Brooklands prior to Le Mans the Rapier was found capable of 90 m.p.h., and a class win was hoped for. The car was registered BMG 2, and a chassis bearing these plates is currently being restored. Although it was common practice in those days to swap registration plates from car to car, and it is known that these plates were used on other Rapiers belonging to de Clifford, the Rapier Register is of the opinion that enough evidence now exists to confirm that this is in fact the Le Mans car. Regarding the production models, due to the increase in weight of the engine, Ashcroft's hoped for 80 m.p.h. never materialised, but most open cars were good for about 75 m.p.h. in standard form. (Photos: Rapier Register)

clutch was also fitted to allay wear on the gear bands.

The first two production models were displayed at the Westover Garage, Bournemouth, in February 1934, where the RAC Rally was to end. Lord de Clifford drove the prototype demonstrator in this event. The cars on show were a fixed head Coupé, finished in yellow and black, and a four-seat Tourer in red (BPD 239), both by Abbott.

Rapier sales were down on expectations, and in order to inject some punch into the demand for the car, a promotion was staged at Great Fosters Hotel, Egham, on 19 July 1934. Naturally, the press were invited, but to add a little colour to the proceedings, a few models and showbiz personalities also. On hand to demonstrate the cars were Sir Malcolm Campbell, the Hon. Brian Lewis and George Eyston. Lord de Clifford was also present with his Le Mans Rapier. The Lagonda representatives were Alf Cranmer (Technical Director), Frank King (Sales Manager) and E. H. Bolton (Works Manager).

Early in 1934, Lord de Clifford entered into partnership with Charles Dobson, of Dobsons Garage at Staines, specialising in tuned versions of the Rapier. This new firm became known as Dobsons and de Clifford Ltd. Three models were offered, a mildly tuned road car priced at £345, a semi-racer at £365, and a replica of de Clifford's Le Mans car in full race trim, complete with 18-gallon tank, at £515. It is doubtful, however, whether any of the last model were made.

Close-up of the radiator with its Lagonda and de Clifford Special badges.

The two-seater roadster with its attractive body by John Charles. Only six were made, and in order to keep within the 1100cc competition class, some were fitted with the 1087cc engine. The cylinder bores were reduced from 62.5mm to 62mm, but the standard crank with its 90mm throw was retained.

BMG 6 was the de Clifford Monte Carlo rally car. Somewhat dwarfed by the 3 Litre on the right, it is seen here at the Rapier Promotion Replay, 19 July 1984. (Photos: Phil Ridout)

Sponsored by Warwick Wright, the Rapier promotion was held at Great Fosters on 19 July 1934. This is the general scene on that historic day – in the foreground, BMG 6, the John Charles bodied de Clifford Special used for the Monte Carlo Rally the following year.

(Below)   A few of the celebrities at Great Fosters that same day. Left to right, elderly gentleman (identity unknown), Dorothy Boyd, Stanley Woodward, Enid Stamp Taylor, Alf Cranmer, Lord de Clifford, C. G. Vokes (of Vokes filter fame), W. R. Buckingham, the Hon. Brian Lewis, and Sir Malcolm Campbell entering a Warwick Wright Special (E. J. Newns' Eagle body). (Photos: Chas K. Bowers)

(Above)   Left to right, Stanley Woodward of Woodwright Publicity and Press Services Ltd (Lagonda Publicity Agents), Eddie Bolton (Lagonda Works Manager) and Sir Malcolm Campbell discussing intricacies of a Rapier chassis at Great Fosters Rapier Promotion, 1934. Campbell, who already owned an M45 Lagonda, added a Rapier fitted with four carburettors to his fleet.

Great Fosters again. Captain George Eyston at the wheel of the Lagonda Rapier de Clifford Special, BMG 6. (Photos: Chas K. Bowers)

(*Above and right*)   The scene at Great Fosters on the 50th anniversary of the Rapier Promotion, 19 July 1984. Sadly, few of the celebrities who witnessed the original event are alive today, but the cars live on, and with the enthusiasm shown for all models of the marque Lagonda, most will still be around in the year 2034. The Rapier Replay was a fine tribute from the Rapier Register to both the Lagonda Company and Rapier Cars Ltd. A well-organised meeting, blessed with perfect weather, made this a happy and memorable day. (Photos: Phil Ridout)

(Above)   The majority of Lagonda Rapiers were fitted with coachwork by E. D. Abbott of Farnham. This is their attractive Tourer at the Rapier Promotion in 1934, those far-off but memorable days when the sun always seemed to shine, the roads were clear, and the Rapier tank could be filled for under ten shillings (50p). The ladies of the day, however, were not usually seen smoking in public but, as a matter of interest, her packet of 20 Players would have cost 11½d (5p). (Photo: Chas K. Bowers)

An Abbott Drop Head Coupé. The hood could be fixed in the de Ville position (front seats only exposed) if required. (Photo: Colin Bugler)

(Above)   Abbot again: this is their Fixed Head Coupé; the hood pram irons, unlike the DHC, were purely ornamental. A Four Light Saloon was also made, but none are known to exist today. Abbot also produced Scud gliders and Flying Fleas, but it is doubtful whether they got very fat on the latter. (Photo: Phil Ridout)

The Abbott Four Light Fixed Head Coupé. This 1935 car was photographed at a Rapier Register meeting in 1958. Sadly, the original body has now been scrapped, and the car turned into a Special. (Photo: Rapier Register)

Lagonda Rapier Eagle two-seater. Originally these models were known as Warwick Wright Specials. The car shown here was first registered in 1935. (Photo: Tony Wood)

The Corinthian DHC was the most expensive body fitted to the Rapier chassis, and one of the most attractive. It was also unusual in having the spare wheel housed in the scuttle underneath the bonnet. Only two of these bodies were fitted to the Rapier chassis, with BLO 76 the sole survivor. (Photo: Geoff Seaton)

(Above) Lord Walpole with his Lagonda Rapier Abbott FHC in which he won a silver award in the 1935 RAC rally. (Photo: Lord Walpole)

A refreshing sight at the April 1984 VSCC Silverstone meeting was this Eagle Pillarless Saloon, the sole survivor of two that were built. This particular car is a de Clifford Special and was originally owned by Dobsons and de Clifford Ltd. Recently restored, the car is finished in its original black over green. (Photo: Phil Ridout)

About 13 Maltby bodies were fitted to the Rapier chassis. The DHC shown here is one of only two known surviving models by this coachbuilder. The most striking features of this body, strangely, were the superb polished wood door cappings and dashboard, each with its 27in long rapier, the nickel-plated blade of which was set flush, while its timber handle and guard were raised. The dashboard was similarly treated with two rapiers point to point. (Photo: Tony Wood)

THE ECCLES RAPIER

Specially built in 1935 to the order of Roy Eccles for Brooklands racing, the Eccles Rapier must surely rank as the ultimate Lagonda Rapier. The engine for this car retained the standard diameter bore but, to keep within the 1100cc class, a shorter throw crankshaft was used, the bore and stroke of 62.5 × 88.3mm giving 1080cc. However, a giant Zoller supercharger was fitted, this taking its drive off the generator.

The first of many successes for Eccles came at the Brooklands August Bank Holiday meeting when he won the Second Short Handicap at 104.67 m.p.h. Two good years followed, the car being driven by both Roy and his wife Marjorie at Brooklands and elsewhere, both of them knocking up victories. Perhaps the most noteworthy events were the First August Mountain Handicap, when a dead heat was recorded (only the second in the history of mountain circuit racing), King-Clark's blown MG going over the line level with Roy Eccles' Rapier; and in the Third Mountain Handicap, Marjorie Eccles on scratch finished second to Clayton's Amilcar, which also started on scratch. At the 1937 Easter Meeting, the Second Mountain Handicap was won at 69.74 m.p.h., beating the ERAs of Bira and Connell. Roy Eccles' last race was the closing meeting at Brooklands for the 1937 season, winning the second Campbell Circuit Handicap at 67.19 m.p.h. Roy died suddenly the following January, aged only 36.

For the Dunlop Jubilee Meeting, Brooklands, 24 September 1938, Marjorie Eccles entered the Rapier Special for the First Dunlop Jubilee Trophy Race. This was over ten laps of the Campbell Circuit and, driven by N. S. Brockelbank, the car was in fifth position on the first two laps, but retired on the third.

(Above)   The 1935 British Empire Trophy Race, Brooklands. Roy Eccles' first race with the Eccles Supercharge Special, number 16 (Eccles Rapier), with Lord Avebury, 1100cc Alta, number 17 alongside. Behind the Rapier is Donald Letts' 1100cc MG Magnette number 12 with, in the background, an R Type MG. The Rapier retired after the 49th lap, the race being won by Dixon's Riley at 74.47 m.p.h. (Photo: Geoffrey Goddard)

The Eccles Rapier takes the Esses at a VSCC Prescott Hill Climb in August 1975. (Photo: Tony Wood)

The mysteries of 'The Robinery' revealed (Robin Jackson's tuning sheds). The Eccles Rapier (centre) displays its giant blower, while a mechanic works on a 1500cc Alta. Nearer the camera is a Q Type MG and, just in the picture, a Bugatti. (Photo: Geoffrey Goddard)

Chapter Nine

BIG IS BEAUTIFUL

THE 4½ LITRE TYPE M45

As previously mentioned, two new Lagonda models were unveiled during 1933: the Rapier, and the exciting 4½ Litre car, usually referred to nowadays as the M45. Unlike the Rapier, the M45 was an immediate success; this elegant sporting machine, almost as fast in closed form as open, was now the largest engined British sports car available and had few competitors capable of approaching its performance. Both Daimler and Rolls Royce were, of course, still building larger engined cars, but it would take a lot of imagination to refer to them as sporting. The M45 was a fast, rugged, 'he-man's' motor car, and one that soon found favour amongst the rich sporting fraternity of the day.

Surprisingly, little was new about the M45. Its chassis was the 10ft 9in wheelbase ZM 3 Litre, suitably modified to accept the 4½ litre Meadows engine, itself dating back to 1928. The chassis modifications amounted to an extra tubular cross member fitted between the front dumb irons at their most forward point, a similar cross member to form a mounting for the rear of the gearbox, and the 3½in diameter forward main cross member, altered in its centre to give clearance for the intermediate drive shaft Hardy Spicer fabric couplings. A Clayton-Dewandre servo was incorporated within the braking linkage; this had in fact been an optional extra on the ZM 3 Litre and, in addition to the normal set of André-Hartford friction dampers, a set of André tele-controls was fitted, their adjustment controlled by screw plungers mounted on the steering column, with pressure gauges for both front and rear pairs. A Meadows T8 gearbox was fitted, and the final drive ratio for the Saloon, Coupé and a few of the Tourers was 3.67:1, most Tourers being fitted with a 3.31:1 rear axle. Centre lock wire wheels with 6.00 × 19in tyres were fitted as standard.

The chosen engine was the six-cylinder OHV Meadows 6ESC, with a bore and stroke of 88.5 × 120.65mm (4453cc) rated at 29.13hp and producing some 108 B.H.P. at a mere 3,100 r.p.m. on a compression ratio of 6.1:1. The crankcase and sump units were of aluminium alloy, whilst the cylinder block and detachable head were of chromidium cast iron. A feature of the design was that no water passed across the head face, three external transfer ports being fitted to interconnect the block and head. The crankshaft was both statically and dynamically balanced, and ran in four white metal bearings in bronze shells, a Lanchester type vibration damper being fitted to its nose. The connecting rods were fully machined and had split small ends; aluminium split skirt pistons were fitted. The camshaft also ran in four bearings, and operated a conventional overhead valve gear through push rods. A force-feed lubrication system fed the main and big end bearings, but the supply to the valve gear and timing chains was metered by the oil pressure relief valve. Twin ignition systems, coil and distributor on the exhaust side and a BTH CE6/S magneto on the inlet side fired two plugs per cylinder, the coil system timed 2 degrees in advance of the magneto. A Meadows clutch was fitted, but with a Lagonda clutch stop and, when correctly adjusted, made fast and smooth gear changes possible for the average driver. Twin SU carburettors fed by twin SU electric fuel pumps were standard equipment. The radiator had a detachable shell with thermostatically controlled shutters, the cooling being assisted by a water pump and four-bladed fan.

A Lagonda inspector was posted to Henry Meadows to certify that the engines were built to approved standards, and the usual procedure of bench testing was continued before fitting to the chassis. Even so, these engines lacked the refinement and smoothness associated with Lagonda designed and built engines. They were also prone to oil leaks, and vibration at the high end of the r.p.m. scale, but they produced enormous torque and coupled to the taut ZM chassis made a desirable combination – the brashness of the engine somehow added charm to the vehicle. The M45 today ranks as one of the most desirable PVT cars, and many fine examples still exist, though mostly in open form. Chassis that orig- inally carried saloon coachwork have been fitted with replica touring or racing style bodies, and many others have been destroyed in order to provide spares for the open cars. Fortunately, about a dozen of these beautifully appointed sporting saloons are known to exist, three of these currently being restored. Perhaps the tide has at long last turned with the realisation that a car fitted with its original coachwork, be it open or closed, is far more desirable than a replica, however good it may be.

T. C. Mann drove this works prototype M45 in the 1933 Monte Carlo Rally. Starting from John O'Groats he finished 33rd overall and also broke his own 1932 class record in the Mont des Mules hill climb. He is seen here extreme right, at Monte Carlo. The car could easily be mistaken for a T3 bodied ZM 3 Litre, but note the chassis cross member covering the aperture in the radiator: the generator would protrude through had a 3-litre engine been fitted. (Photo: T. C. Mann)

APJ 367 was another of the works pre-production cars, and the only 4½ to be fitted with the T6 body. Lord de Clifford drove this car on a reconnaissance of the 1934 Monte Carlo rally route from the Athens start point. This car later spent many years in the police force, most of its time on the skid pan at the Hendon Police College. Happily, it is once again in private ownership. (Photo: Quadrant/*Autocar*)

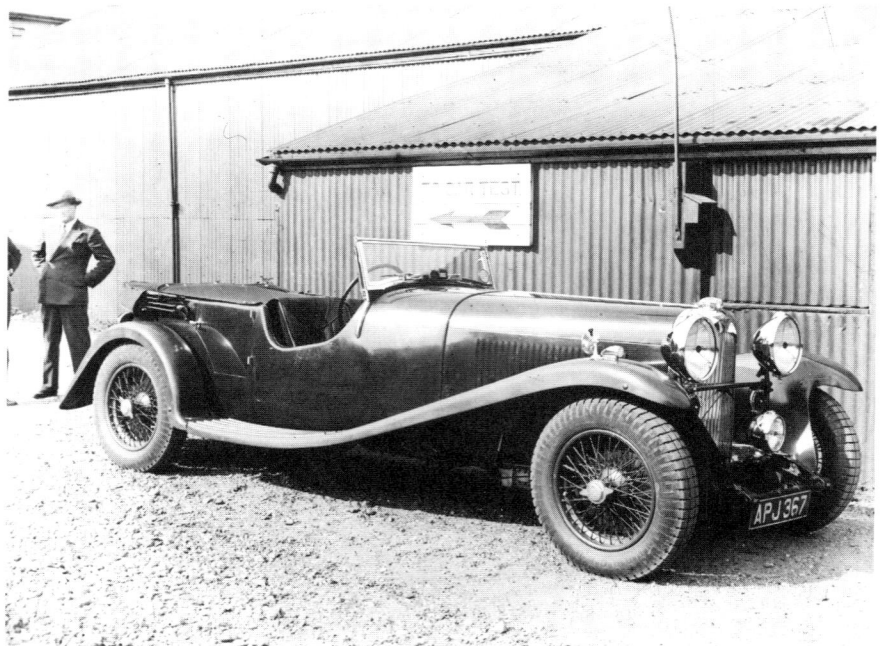

Lord de Clifford with an admiring and perhaps sympathetic crowd during the 1934 Monte Carlo Rally, in which he rebuilt the steering in Vienna after hitting a rock, was pulled out of the mud no less than three times in Bulgaria, and finally had to retire on the Greek border with a broken crankcase after an argument with a boulder. The car, registered AMT 77, was a T7 bodied M45 from his own stable. (Photo: National Motor Museum)

T. C. Mann sorts out a problem on his way to Monte Carlo in 1936. He was later bogged down in severe snow drifts and did well to finish 60th overall. Mr Mann bought this car new in February 1934 and still owns and uses it. The T5 body was fitted to his special order. Two other similar bodied M45s are also known to exist; sadly one of these has been hideously disfigured about its rear quarters by some misguided owner. (Photo: T. C. Mann)

Correct in every detail, this beautifully restored M45 was first registered in August 1934. The car deservedly won its class in the 1984 Lagonda Club's *Concours d'Elégance*. (Photo: Phil Ridout)

These 1934 catalogue illustrations show the 10ft 9in wheelbase 4½ Litre chassis (bottom), priced at £675, and the two standard production Lagonda bodies available on this chassis. Top, the four-seat Tourer (T7 body) priced at £825 and, centre, the Sports Saloon (ST34) priced at £950. (Catalogue Illustrations: Ivan Forshaw)

(*Above*) The graceful wings and general balanced proportions of the T7 bodied M45 are clear in this side view. Equally impressive was the performance with a maximum of 97 m.p.h., and acceleration from rest to 50 in ten seconds; exciting figures at the time and respectable even today. Note the spare wheel cover, an item seldom seen on these cars nowadays. The example, a factory demonstrator, is seen at the Staines Works in 1933. (Photo: Quadrant/*Autocar*)

This 1934 M45 chassis carries replica T8 touring coachwork. The T8 body had two large doors to the front, as opposed to the one on the nearside and small offside rear door only on the T7. (Photo: Roger Cooke)

Two views of the M45 Saloon (ST34). The *Autocar* spoke of it as 'a car so fascinating that to overrate its virtues is hardly possible'. These beautifully appointed cars were upholstered in the finest quality hides and featured sunray pleating on the door panels, ebonised solid walnut interior woodwork, door cappings inlaid with pewter, and, of course, 'his and hers' vanity boxes. In performance these heavy saloons gave little away to the open model, acceleration figures being identical and the top speed in excess of 90 m.p.h. (Photos: Chas K. Bowers and Geoffrey Seaton)

Nearside and offside views of the Meadows engine. (Photos: M. B. Jones and C. S. Heaton)

First registered in October 1933, this M45 has the appearance of the standard T7 Tourer but in fact it has no forward doors, having two small doors to the rear only, possibly built in this manner to the requirements of the original owner. (Photo: Major A. J. Loch)

A handsome two-seater by Wylders of Kew Gardens. Built to the order of one Honourable Arthur Ryder Bastard Owen, who first registered it on 7 April 1934. He only kept the car a few months, however, as it was put up for sale by Abbey Coachworks with a mere 5,000 miles on the clock, and advertised in the *Motor* dated 18 September 1934 (possibly explaining why the car is often reported as Abbey bodied). It was purchased by a Huddersfield mill owner who used it during the summer months until the outbreak of war. The car was not used again until bought by the present owner in April 1977, still in mint condition, the mileage to date some 19,500 from new. (Photo: C. S. Heaton)

Entered in the 1934 Eastbourne *Concours d'Elégance* under the name of Major Cohn, this dark red Lancefield Drop Head Coupé won its class as a Saloon with the hood up, and took second place as a Tourer with the hood down; the kitchen sink was no doubt in the boot. The car is now in the USA. (Photo: Lagonda Club)

(Left and below) A very fine Drop Head Coupé by Freestone and Webb. It was purchased in chassis form by a Mr Erhardt late in 1933, who himself drove the chassis to the Freestone and Webb works for the coachwork to be built and fitted. The car was first registered in the above name during May 1934, and is still in regular use by a member of the same family. Note the unusual side opening boot lid, shown open in the upper picture. (Photos: Phil Erhardt and Geoffrey Seaton)

An All-weather Tourer by Vanden Plas. These touring bodies featured wind up windows as opposed to the detachable sidescreens normally supplied with touring coachwork. (Photo: Peter Cripps)

An exotic two-door Sports Saloon by John Charles, built on Silent Travel principles to a design by Brainsby Woollard. The car was registered AYV 1 during May 1934, but after the war spent many years as a hen house. The photograph shows the car as it is today, beautifully restored to its former glory by its current owner. Two four-door versions of this body were also built, one being shown on the John Charles stand at the 1934 Olympia Motor Show. (Photo: Peter Biggs)

A smart saloon by Park Ward, a stock design by this company and one that graced many a Derby Bentley chassis.

Perhaps the most desirable was this magnificent sporting two-door saloon by Freestone and Webb. (Photos: Lagonda Club)

A stylish Fixed Head Coupé by Barker on the M45 chassis. (Photo: National Motor Museum)

An Extract from a Lagonda Sales Brochure

Swift silence; safety and perfect comfort at high speeds, and performance that is attained, only by high class cars – *that* is the Lagonda.

Built, complete to the last detail, under one roof, the Lagonda is a thoroughbred, with a proud heritage of the soundest British engineering principles and craftsmanship.

If you seek standardised, mass-produced cars, or sensational novelties in design, waste no time with this catalogue, for every Lagonda is individual, built by experts who have pride in their craft, and created on proved lines to embody every feature that contributes to its essential swift, silent comfort and to dependable safety.

If the best British workmanship and the finest materials appeal to you, and if character, sweet running and a high maximum speed, together with the car as a whole looking the thoroughbred it has proved itself to be, are qualities that attract you, there is no need to look further; you will find them all in this British car that over a quarter-century of experience has produced.

You will be welcomed at any time you care to visit our Works to see Lagondas in all stages of construction, and because the only satisfactory way to judge a car is to drive it, you are cordially invited to try any model you wish.

THE TOURIST TROPHY 4½ LITRE LAGONDA

For the 1934 Tourist Trophy, Lagonda Ltd built three 4½ Litre (M45) competition chassis to the special order of Warwick Wright. These chassis were built under the watchful eye of Arthur Fox, who was responsible for running the cars as a team.

The wheelbase of these chassis was shortened by 6in giving a wheelbase of 10ft 3in. The 3½ Litre (M35) was in fact being developed about this time also, and like these special M45 racing chassis had a wheelbase of 10ft 3in; it may well be that the 3½ Litre chassis side members were used. Again, like the M35, a Girling braking system was fitted, but with ducts mounted in the backplates to improve the cooling. The road springs were special, and of negative camber. Bronze bushes also replaced the Silentbloc type used on the production chassis. André-Hartford friction shock absorbers, together with a set of Luvax hydraulics, took care of the damping. Bishop steering gear was retained, but the box was mounted further forward on the chassis, and braced to counteract the heavy side loads imposed during high-speed cornering. A Meadows T8 gearbox, and a straight bevel rear axle, gave ratios of 8.94:1, 5.75:1 and 4.05:1, with a top

and final drive ratio of 3.14:1. Centre lock wire wheels were fitted with 6.00 × 19in Dunlop racing tyres.

Though the Meadows 6ESC engine was no newcomer to racing (Invicta used this engine reasonably successfully), it was not designed with racing in mind, so with the increased brake horsepower, together with the reliability required for long-distance racing, further development was important. To meet such heavy demands, the crankcases for these engines were cast in RR50 alloy, and the crankshaft big end journals increased in diameter from 2in to 2⅛in. The split small end connecting rods were discarded, new rods being manufactured with plain small end eyes, the gudgeon pins now being merely located by a bolt. Martlett H/C lightweight pistons, together with a thinner cylinder head gasket, raised the compression ratio to 7.6:1. A weak point on the Meadows engine was the joint between the crankcase and cylinder block, and some improvement was made in this area by increasing the diameter of the two most forward studs, surprisingly not all of them. Of course, the Rapide engine, a direct development from these racing engines, had all the studs increased in diameter.

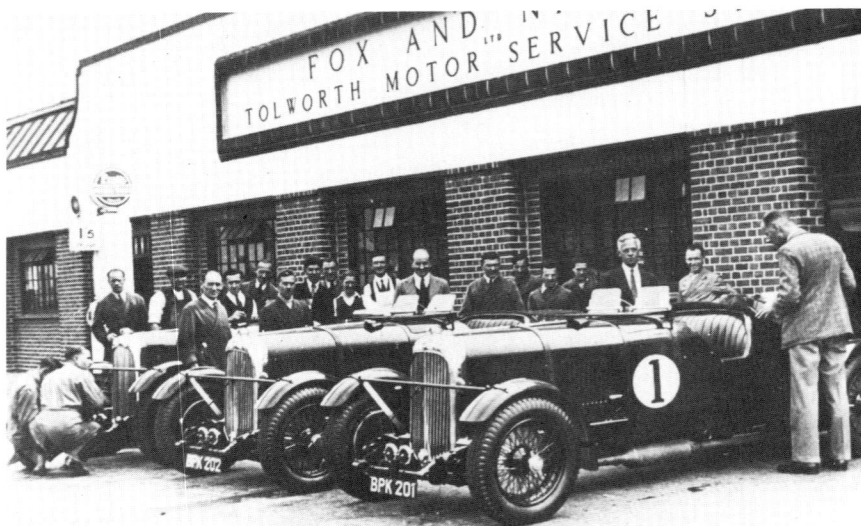

Fox and Nicholl staff pose with the M45 team prior to departure to Ulster, September 1934. With them is John Hindmarsh standing by the wheel of his mount, BPK 202. (Photo: Fox Collection)

Other modifications were lightened valve gear, special valves with split collets to retain the springs, a Scintilla Vertex magneto replaced the coil system, and a horizontal Scintilla magneto was used in favour of the BTH instrument fitted on the production engine. The sump baffles were modified in an attempt to retain the oil around the pump during heavy braking, and an oil temperature bulb was also fitted. Like the production engine, twin SU carburettors fed by twin SU pumps were retained, but two standby pumps controlled by a separate switch were also available in case of emergency. The fuel tank capacity was increased to 27 gallons. The standard M45 radiator was fitted, but mounted in a raked position, and the thermostat discarded in favour of a manual control for the shutters.

The stark four-seat doorless bodies carried no ornamentation of any sort, other than a fin down the centre of the spare wheel fairing. They were designed by Arthur Fox, and possibly built in the Fox and Nicholls workshops, or by Wylders of Kew. The three cars were finished in bright red.

The chassis numbers of the team cars were Z11118, 11079 and 11078, and registered BPK 201, 202 and 203 respectively. All three still exist, and are still very active. E. D. Abbott of Farnham produced a replica body of the Fox and Nicholl cars on an M45 Rapide chassis, which suggests that they may also have been responsible for the coachwork on the team cars. This is mere conjecture, however.

Fifty years on, almost to the day, the cars unite opposite the old Lagonda Causeway works (now Petters) to celebrate the 1934 Tourist Trophy, the only time all three cars ran in a race together. This nostalgic gathering was followed by them being driven in convoy to the site of the Fox and Nicholl service station at Tolworth. The event was organised by Denis Jenkinson, seen second from left in the lower picture talking to Arnold Davey, Registrar of the Lagonda Club. (Photos: Geoffrey Seaton)

THE 1934 RAC TOURIST TROPHY

Forty cars were on the line for the start of the 1934 RAC Tourist Trophy. Amongst these were the three 4½ Litre Lagondas, entered in the name of Arthur Fox. They were BPK 201 (race number 1) driven by the Hon. Brian Lewis, BPK 202 (race number 2) John Hindmarsh, and BPK 203 (race number 3) John Cobb. Ahead of them were 35 laps of the gruelling Ards circuit. The TT was always an exciting race, but few more so than this one. On the 25th lap Lewis brought the crowds to their feet when he mounted the pavement opposite the stands to overtake Eddie Hall's 3½ Litre Derby Bentley (Rolls Bentley), the start of an hour long battle between these giants of the sport until the 33rd lap, when the tyres of the Lagonda gave out, forcing a pit stop. With only two laps left to go, all hopes were lost of catching Hall again, or indeed the flying MG of Dodson. The race was won on handicap by C. P. J. Dodson, MG Magnette; 17 seconds behind came Hall's Bentley (first in its class); fourth, fifth and eighth the Lagondas of Lewis, Hindmarsh and Cobb (second, third and fourth in their class respectively). Seventeen cars finished.

John Hindmarsh approaching Quarry Corner.

A relaxed John Cobb leads C. Penn-Hughes, Aston Martin. (Photos: Martin Whitehead and the late Lt. Col. Darrell Berthon)

THE 4½ LITRE RAPIDE (TYPE M45R)

Introduced in September 1934, the M45 Rapide had a chassis frame virtually identical to the 3½ Litre (M35), except of course for minor alterations in order to accept the 4½ litre Meadows engine. The equipment, however, was far more comprehensive, including such refinements as Smiths 'Jackall' jacks, Luvax hydraulic shock absorbers, in addition to a set of André Telecontrol dampers, and a grouped chassis lubrication system as on the earlier OH and Z type chassis. Like the M35R, Girling brakes were used, but the drums were cadmium-plated, as were the road springs, the leather gaiters being discarded. Also discarded were the Silentbloc bushes in the spring eyes and hangers and a return was made to bronze bushes.

Full advantage was taken of the development in the Meadows engines of the three Tourist Trophy cars, and almost all the modifications were incorporated in the Rapide engine, including the uprating of material specifications of the crankcase. In addition, the crankcase to cylinder block studs were all increased in diameter, the oil filler was moved to the top of the rocker cover, and this now had Lagonda Rapide cut in its sides. The lubrication system was improved by the addition of a Tecalemit full flow filter with a felt element, and the engine breather moved to the top of the timing chest. The engines were assembled at Staines, and now also incorporated many parts manufactured there.

In order to cope with the increased power output of this engine, the back axle differential assembly carrier was more robust, and the ratio 3.31:1 used. The T8 gearbox, though, was unchanged, and the resulting overall ratios were 3.31, 4.2, 6.6 and 10.3 to 1. For the first time on a Lagonda a freewheel was fitted, the unit being mounted on the rear of the gearbox with a short lever to operate it protruding through the floor. The freewheel was not a success; many customers refused to have it fitted, others soon had it removed, and only one Rapide is known to be now so equipped.

Initially, the only Lagonda-built body available on the Rapide chassis was the four-seat Tourer (T9), externally identical to the M35R, but more lavishly equipped. Eventually, a Lagonda-built Saloon was included in the model range, and the Tourer body updated (T10).

The performance of the M45 Rapide was, of course, remarkable for the period, and it was the fastest production car available irrespective of price, the Tourer being capable of a genuine 100 m.p.h., with acceleration figures that would satisfy a modern car enthusiast. Every car was fully run-in prior to delivery.

Nearside of the 4½ Litre Rapide engine. Note the hand-scraped aluminium castings, the work of craftsmen, sadly often buffed away by today's 'enthusiasts'. (Photo: Chas K. Bowers)

These 1935 catalogue illustrations show the 10ft 3in wheelbase 4½ Litre Rapide chassis, priced at £675 and, centre, the four-seat Tourer (T9) priced at £1,000. This was the only Lagonda-built body available on the M45 Rapide chassis at the time of its introduction. The Saloon by Gurney Nutting (top) was also shown in the 1935 catalogue, priced at £1,250, but it is not known whether any were actually made. (Catalogue Illustrations: Ivan Forshaw)

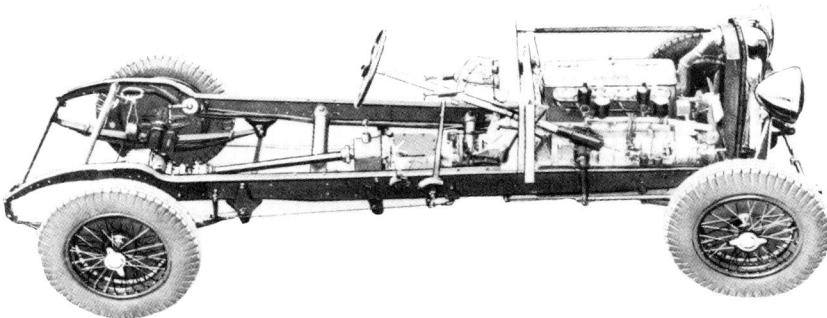

(Above) The M45 Rapide Tourer (T9). Note the neatly concealed hood when folded and the cadmium-plated brake drums.

Eventually, a Lagonda-built saloon body (ST54) was produced for the M45 Rapide chassis, but was a little heavy looking. The car was priced at £1,125. (Photos: Chas K. Bowers)

(Above) The last of the open M45 Rapides were fitted with a T10 body. In addition to the valanced wings, there were several detail modifications, not least the unusual tread arrangements on the running boards. The price was unchanged at £1,000. The photograph shows the car at Brooklands for high-speed testing in April 1935. (Photo: Quadrant/*Autocar*)

The Tourist Trophy Replica by E. D. Abbott had a few more creature comforts than the original examples. This car is now in India. (Photo: E. D. Abbott)

Lagonda magnificence. Reflections in the radiator of the 1934 RAC Tourist Trophy, and 1935 Le Mans M45, BPK 203. The current owner also owns sister car BPK 201. (Photo: Mrs Robby Hewitt)

LE MANS 1935

1934 was a bad year for Lagonda; by June 1935 and, of course, Le Mans, the receiver was well and truly established in the Causeway works. Prior to this, however, the three 1934 Tourist Trophy cars were offered for sale, presumably by Warwick Wright, though it is thought Lagonda had an interest in them. About this time, Arthur Fox was looking for a suitable car to run at Le Mans, and bought BPK 202. Ex-Bentley boy, Dr J. D. Benjafield, had similar ideas and bought BPK 203. Race preparation was carried out by Fox and Nicholl at Tolworth, both cars also being entered for the race in the name of A. W. Fox. The nominated drivers were John Hindmarsh and Luis Fontes, BPK 202 (race number 4), and Dr J. D. Benjafield and Sir Ronald Gunter BPK 203 (race number 14).

Some modifications were made to the cars, but these were mostly to meet race requirements and included an additional bonnet strap and, of course, a regulation lighting set. Spotlights were also fitted and, for identification at night, these were mounted on the offside of 202 and the nearside of 203. A single aero-screen and a full-width wire mesh screen were fitted, the latter being

folded flat for the race. Some creature comforts were also included, these being ventilators mounted low down on the scuttle sides, and a rack on the panel containing segments of Wrigley's chewing gum. The extent of tuning is unknown, but a blister appeared on the bonnet side panel, presumably to allow a freer air flow to the carburettor intakes.

Few motor races could be more of a test of man and machine than the 24-hour race at Le Mans, and few could present such excitement, frustration and disappointment. Those at both Staines and Tolworth had experienced a fair share of these in the past, but hopes were high for 1935. The cars were fast, reliable and, with the exception of Fontes, the drivers old hands at their craft; the young Fontes of course was no amateur either.

Saturday 15 June was wet and though there was some improvement when the flag fell at 4 p.m., the weather remained showery for most of the race. The Hon. Brian Lewis was first away in a supercharged 2.3 Litre Alfa Romeo, but Hindmarsh was second off the mark, closely followed by Benjafield, both cars soon settling down to consistent lap speeds. The first excitement came shortly after 9 p.m. when Hindmarsh clipped the tail of Fothringham's Aston Martin after it had turned over at the exit from the notorious White House corner, fortunately without serious injury to its driver. The Lagonda suffered a smashed headlamp; this was covered, and within seconds Hindmarsh was back in the fray, but it was soon apparent that more serious damage had been inflicted. The car was steering badly, the brakes were pulling to one side, and, in all, it was something of a handful on the slippery road. At 10 p.m. the Hindmarsh/Fontes car was two laps behind the leader, Sommer's Alfa Romeo, the Benjafield/Gunter car running faultlessly in sixth place, but by 11 p.m. there was a change of fortune – Sommer went out with fuel problems, putting the Hindmarsh/Fontes Lagonda into the lead. During the small hours a lengthy pit stop was made to have the brakes and steering attended to, so by 4 a.m. the Hindmarsh/Fontes Lagonda was down to fourth position. However, consistently good lap speeds put them back in the lead by 10 a.m. and all fingers were crossed in the Lagonda pit as the Benjafield/Gunter car was now in striking distance for second place; but it was not to be. Next time round found Benjafield in

trouble with his gearbox which had locked in top and, though a lengthy pit stop was made, nothing could be done. So, relying on the great power of the engine, Benjafield set off to complete the race in top gear. The other Lagonda was still leading the pack, but some nail-biting moments arose when Fontes made an unscheduled stop to report low oil pressure. A hefty oil leak was soon diagnosed, but it was against the rules to replenish the sump. He was therefore sent on his way with the oil pressure diminishing rapidly, but instructed by Arthur Fox to continue. Further excitement occurred when it was announced over the loudspeakers that the lap scoreboard was wrong and that the Helde/Stoffel Alfa Romeo was in the lead, but this turned out to be a mistake to the relief of all concerned in the Lagonda pit. Despite the oil problems, the Hindmarsh/Fontes Lagonda romped home a clear winner by 8.5km, averaging 77.86 m.p.h. during the 24 hours, and covering some 1,868.74 miles. The Helde/Stoffel Alfa Romeo was second, and the Martin/Brackenbury Aston Martin third overall, the Benjafield/Gunter Lagonda coming thirteenth overall. Of the 58 starters, 28 cars finished, 22 of these British (there must be a moral in this somewhere). When the engine of

BPK 202 at the pits prior to the start of the 1935 Le Mans 24-hour race. (Photo: Mrs Robby Hewitt)

BPK 202 was examined after the race, it was found that almost all of its 3 gallons of oil had been lost. The main prize for the race was the eighth *Coupe Annuelle*, the *Coupe de la Revue des Usagers de la Route*; this Arthur Fox kindly donated to the Lagonda Club.

(*Above*) Start of the 1935 Le Mans, the track still waterlogged from heavy rain for most of the day. John Hindmarsh (number 4) makes a quick get-away, with J. D. Benjafield (number 14) close on his heels. The Benjafield car was a late entry and took the place of a non-starter. (Photo: Mrs Robby Hewitt)

Luis Fontes during the final lap of the race, looking quite relaxed despite the worry of a failing engine. (Photo: National Motor Museum)

Their finest hour. The bespectacled 21-year-old Luis Fontes, with co-driver John Hindmarsh, surrounded by well-wishers as they toast their glorious Le Mans victory. Hindmarsh was, of course, very experienced, and a regular driver for the Fox and Nicholl racing team. Fontes, however, was little known until the spring of 1935 when he achieved fame at Brooklands by winning the JCC Jubilee Day International Trophy Race in the ex-Lewis ex-Cobb 2.3 Alfa Romeo, hired from Thomson and Taylor just the day before the race, but promptly bought after his success. Despite the unusual heat of this spring day, Fontes had driven the entire 250 miles of the race in a relaxed but confident manner, at the high average speed of 86.96 m.p.h., beating the favourites Freddy Dixon and Eddie Hall, who came second and third respectively. The great achievement of these men with the Lagonda at Le Mans never received the credit or publicity it deserved, partly due to the receiver being firmly in residence at the Staines factory by this time. Had the event taken place just a few weeks earlier, the fortunes of Lagonda Motors Ltd may well have been very different.

Ironically, both these fine drivers lost their lives in flying disasters, Hindmarsh when testing the prototype Hawker Hurricane over Weybridge in 1937, and Fontes when he was serving with the RAF during the war. (Photo: Quadrant/*Autocar*)

Though the 4½ Litre models were selling well, the profit on them was far too small to outweigh the losses that were being incurred on some of the other cars. The 3 Litre, for instance, even though a little cheapening was evident on the later models, was ridiculously underpriced. The demand for the 16/80 was disappointing, being frowned upon by the enthusiast of the day, and the Rapier could only have been a viable proposition had it sold in vast numbers. The introduction of the Rapier was, of course, an attempt to attract those with a shallower pocket than the usual Lagonda clientele, though it was still not a cheap car in the true sense of the word. However, many old and valued Lagonda customers resented this little newcomer assembled from parts made elsewhere, and had no intention of driving a large expensive machine bearing a similar badge, so turned to other manufacturers to provide their thoroughbred transport.

Production of the Rapier chassis was spasmodic, being largely dependent on the company's finances, or lack of them, at the time. Some of the Lagonda employees in fact talk of periods when the wage bill could not be met until a few more cars had been sold. Estimated sales for 1934 were some 500 complete chassis. Engine assemblies had been ordered from Coventry Climax, along with many chassis components from other manufacturers, to fulfil this programme, but in fact only about half of these had been sold by the end of the year. The result was that at times the factory was overflowing with unsold Rapier chassis. Due to a hard winter, and the newly implemented speed limits, sales for sports cars slumped further in 1935 and, by mid-April, a receiver had been appointed. Production of all models came to a halt and an extensive advertising programme was embarked upon in an attempt to shift the backlog of vehicles. However, it was all to no avail and the company was put up for sale by tender, tenders being opened on 18 June 1935.

The Rapier had been produced at a rate never before seen at Staines, as many as twenty a week at times. With its relative cheapness and bought-in engine and components, many, even to this day, believe it to have been out of keeping with the traditional policies of the company and entirely responsible for its downfall. Such arguments are perhaps a little unfair; certainly it played a major part, but the other factors should also be considered, plus the depressed state of the economy at the time.

In the normal course of events, the Lagonda win at Le Mans might well have put the company back on its feet, but it was all too late. There was no money to advertise this achievement, and little point in doing so, as only a skeleton staff remained. So, had the order books started to fill, it would have been impossible to produce any vehicles; by this time the receiver was in, and attempting to sort things out.

The highest tender was from a consortium headed by a Mr Alan P. Good, who outbid three others, including one from Rolls Royce. Alan Good became Chairman of the new company, with R. G. Watney as Managing Director and W. O. Bentley as Technical Director, who took office in August 1935. The company was registered in the name of L. G. Motors (Staines) Ltd.

(Above) The service department as it was in 1932. In the left foreground can be seen a Continental Tourer, while on the right work proceeds on a 2 Litre. In the centre of the picture the taller man of the two is the Service Manager, Mr J. E. Davies, who held this responsible position from 1920 until joining the services in 1940. After the war, Lagonda offered for disposal their entire stock of spare parts for the 16/65, 2 Litre, 16/80 3 and 3½ Litre cars. These were purchased by Mr Davies who set up business at 273 London Road, Staines, specialising in the sales and service of these cars. Later service was also available on the full range of 4½ Litre models.

Mr Davies in later years. Due to the war, the Lagonda Car Club was disbanded at the end of 1939, but was re-formed in 1947 by Mr and Mrs J. E. Davies, who held the first meeting at their home at Shepperton on 29 June 1947, Mrs Davies being nominated as Secretary. (Photos: Mrs V. E. Davies)

Service

Lagonda is proud of its Service Department – embracing not only the fully equipped Service Depot at Staines, but a competent staff of travelling and resident Service Representatives up and down the country. The work of the Service Department is best described in the words of users of the Depot:–

"Having to call at your works a few days ago I was greatly impressed by the kindness and courtesy shown me by the Foreman and his assistants. Nothing was too much trouble. From experience of other firms, I had anticipated kicking my heels round Staines for most of the day. Nothing of the kind. Instant attention, a thorough test, and a touch-up here and there, and I was back in town for lunch. When showing the car to my admiring friends I do not forget to mention SERVICE."

"You are to be congratulated on your very capable and courteous staff." – "Excellent service: I think Lagonda deserves to prosper on that account alone." – "After being into your depot several times I write to thank you for the courtesy, rapidity and high efficiency that is invariably shown; I have not met its equal either at home or abroad."

These are extracts from letters which do us good in more ways than one!

An extract from the 1932 Lagonda catalogue.

Chapter Ten

LAGONDA

OUT OF THE ASHES

Alan P. Good, Company Chairman.

(Far left) R. G. Watney, Managing Director.

(Left) W. O. Bentley, Technical Director, the position held for so many years by Alfred H. Cranmer in the old company. (Photos: Arnold Davey)

The Lagonda press announcement, August 1935.

LAGONDA

Announcement

Many people will be glad to learn that a new Company has been formed with a capital of £250,000, of which £179,000 has been subscribed, which will continue to manufacture Lagonda cars. The new Company has Mr. A. P. Good as Chairman, Mr. W. O. Bentley as Technical Director, and Mr. R. G. Watney as Managing Director. The Works at Staines are being extended and reorganised to facilitate production. The Service Department is being enlarged, and will have modern equipment for repairs and Guarantee work.

The motoring public may confidently expect that Lagonda Models for the coming season will be in the front rank of exclusive British cars. Following upon the outstanding performance of the winning Lagonda car at the Le Mans Race, there will be many who wish the new Company every success.

A 4½-litre Lagonda will be developed and continued for the coming season. The car's already remarkable performance will be further enhanced by altogether improved suspension, more silent running, lighter steering, more attractive and comfortable coachwork. Owners are reminded that the current Guarantees on Lagonda cars are valid, although another concern, Rapier Cars, Ltd., 195, Hammersmith Road, London, W.6, has acquired all interests appertaining to the 10 h.p. Rapier Car.

LAGONDA MOTORS, Props. L.G. Motors (Staines) Ltd., Staines, Middlesex

Telephones : Staines 1122 (4 lines)   Telegrams : Lagonda, Staines

The Lagonda announcement on page 198 clearly outlines the policy of the new company: the 2 and 3 Litre cars, along with their derivatives, the very models that had gained such high esteem for the company, in addition to the Lagonda Rapier, were no more. Gone also were most of the key men who had worked so hard to build up the firm from its pioneering days; the few who were given positions in the newly formed company seemed to find the management difficult to work with and most soon found employment elsewhere. W. O. Bentley, his contract with Rolls Royce now expired, was persuaded by Alan Good to take over the position of Technical Director, with R. G. Watney from Rootes as Managing Director. W. O. also brought along a few of his engineering colleagues, and some were said to be unapproachable. At the time of the takeover some 200 or so Rapier chassis, engines and components were cluttering up the factory, and these were purchased by Rapier Cars Ltd, a new company set up by Major W. H. Oates, Tim Ashcroft and Nevil Brockelbank. They also bought from Lagonda the lease of 195 Hammersmith Road, the new company

being registered on 7 August 1935, with Rapiers back in production by the end of the year. That address proved unsatisfactory as a factory but suitable premises were soon found at Kew, the Hammersmith Road base being retained for use as a design office and service department.

Technically, the cars assembled by this company were still Lagonda Rapiers, as they were built from parts purchased from L. G. Motors. The first of these was available for sampling in November 1935, but it can have been little different from the Lagonda product, as the only changes were the radiator badge, and the deletion of Lagonda's name from the camshaft covers. It is estimated that about 45 of these Rapiers were made.

Rapier Cars Ltd marketed the cars complete with body, almost all being fitted with coachwork supplied by Ranalah. These were a four-seat Tourer, a Drop Head Coupé and a Saloon, priced at £375, £410 and £415 respectively. A two-seater was also available, but only one is thought to have been built; this car is still in service. The Rapier was still available in chassis form, this being priced at £270.

John Charles Ranalah bodies were fitted as standard on the Rapier Car Company's output of chassis. Available were a smart four-seat Tourer; a Drop Head Coupé and a four light Saloon; only three of the last model are known to have been built. About 13 DH Coupés and 18 four-seat Tourers can be accounted for. One two-seater was made, this possibly to special order.

A Ranalah-bodied Rapier at Wookey Hole, Somerset in 1936. The car, believed to have been a demonstrator, still exists. (Photo: Mrs E. Humphreys)

The Ranalah four-seat Tourer was a nicely balanced motor car. This restored example was seen at the Lagonda Rapier Promotion Replay in 1984. (Photo: Geoff Seaton)

This 1936 Ranalah two-seater is thought to have been the only one built. Recently the subject of a six-year rebuild, it is seen here at the Rapier 50th Anniversary Parade at Silverstone on 14 April 1984. (Photo: Jean Wood)

(Above)   The majority of Rapiers seem to have been registered during 1936; this example of that year is one of only two that were fitted with coachwork by Bertelli, and the sole survivor. It is seen here at VSCC, Oulton Park in 1975. The car is now in Australia. (Photo: Tony Wood)

The supercharged Rapier at Brooklands during its road test by the *Motor.*

Sales figures for the Rapier were disappointing and, in an attempt to widen the market, Rapier Cars introduced a supercharged model for the 1937 season. Certainly some successes had been achieved at Brooklands and elsewhere by Lagonda Rapiers modified in this form by their owners, the most notable of these being Roy Eccles' purpose-built track car.

On the production Rapiers, Alan Lamburn was responsible for the design modifications and a Centric supercharger was chosen, giving a boost pressure of 7 p.s.i., fed by a single Arnott carburettor. The blower was driven by an enclosed chain, the magneto and generator having been moved rearwards to allow the driving sprocket to be interposed. A thicker cylinder head gasket lowered the compression ratio, but structurally no modifications were required as these robust little engines performed quite happily in this form. The chassis was unchanged with the exception of the gear change lever being moved to a central position, and there was a new final drive ratio of 5.57:1. Surprisingly, very few of these fast little cars were sold, possibly less than half a dozen and, considering the lack of demand for the Rapier generally, it was no surprise when the company went into liquidation. This was in March 1938.

Major Oates continued to lead an active life until the age of 89. Tim Ashcroft, however, died quite young during the 1950s; his grave is now maintained by the Rapier Register.

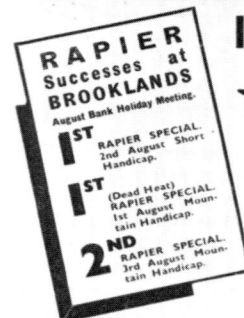

A Rapier advertisement from *Motor.*

Designed specifically for the Phoenix Park races, this was the last Rapier to be built. It is seen here before practice for the Leinster Trophy Race at Tallaght, Co. Dublin in 1937, with motor cycle ace Manliffe Barrington at the wheel. (Photo: Rapier Register)

THE 4½ LITRE TYPE M45A

The M45A was an amalgamation of the standard M45 and the Rapide; it was again the ZM type 10ft 9in wheelbase chassis but, in order to increase the interior body dimensions, the engine was moved forward to a position similar to that of the Rapide models. As on the Rapide, a Girling braking system was used, but the engine remained as the standard M45, though the Rapide-type rocker cover was fitted, with the oil filler in its centre. The only other changes were the radiator, now as fitted to the Rapide and, perhaps a retrograde step, the smaller and cheaper Lucas 'Long Range' headlamps replacing the P100 lamps of the previous models.

The four-door pillarless Saloon (ST64), though similar to the ST34 body fitted to the standard M45 Saloon, was a little more roomy and had a larger and more rounded boot, flush door hinges, improved body mouldings, and many detail changes, including the shape of the windscreen. Also restyled were the wings, which now had a ridge along the centre and were valanced.

The M45A was originally intended to be the new model for 1936, though two had been delivered before the old company went into liquidation. However, the new management were soon off the mark in announcing this 'new' Lagonda to the press in order to get a car back on the market without too great a lapse of time, but behind the scenes frenzied activity was taking place at Staines, with W. O. Bentley and his team busy designing and building the LG45 model Lagonda for 1936.

The handsome but short-lived M45A – no more than ten examples were built. (Photo: Chas K. Bowers)

After Mr A. P. Good had established himself at Staines, one of his first priorities was to have the place tidied up a little, at least in the areas the customers saw. This photograph was taken towards the end of 1935; it is in fact the same service department as the one shown on page 195, cleaned and decorated, but taken from a different corner of the building. In the foreground, and just left of centre, are a couple of 4½ Litre (M45) Saloons: a large, probably Park Ward, 4½ Litre Limousine, with an M45 Gurney Nutting Airflow Saloon to its left. On the right of the M45 in the foreground are a pair of enamelled P100 headlamps belonging to an engineless 3 Litre, and next to them, a 2 Litre, sporting polished aluminium Ace wheel discs.

The kit store – this was an annexe off the service department, and contained upholstery for the cars under manufacture, with the customer's name above each set. (Photos: Mrs V. E. Davies)

THE 4½ LITRE (M45) TOURIST TROPHY CARS, 1935

Encouraged by his win at Le Mans with BPK 202, Arthur Fox added the remaining Tourist Trophy car, BPK 201, to his stable, and ran both at Ulster in the 1935 TT. Race preparation led to considerable further development of the engines of these cars. The compression ratio was raised to 7.75:1, and a new exhaust and carburettor intake system devised, but the standard SU H5 carburettors were retained, though fitted with richer needles. The details of Fox's intake system were a well-kept secret; presumably it was a ram air device of some sort, though

the very large bulge that appeared on the bonnet side to house it had no inlet. The new management at Lagonda were keen to keep the Fox and Nicholl association alive, and made available to Fox the engine test facilities at Staines, where further experiment and tuning was carried out, with alterations to ignition timing, tappet adjustments and so on. The final result was that the brake horsepower figures were improved at all power settings, and the engines as raced produced over 140 B.H.P. at 3,800 r.p.m.

BPK 201 (race number 2) with BPK 202 (race number 1) during scrutineering at Ulster, September 1935. Arthur Fox's exhaust system is in evidence – it not only improved the car's performance, but perhaps also its appearance. Earl Howe's brace of eight-cylinder Bugattis can be seen in the background, number 4 driven by the Hon. Brian Lewis and number 5 by the Earl himself, who finished third overall, Lewis retiring with clutch slip. (Photo: Mrs Robby Hewitt)

THE 1935 RAC TOURIST TROPHY RACE

As in the previous year, the race was 35 laps of the Ards circuit, but there was a smaller entry, with only 35 cars on the line at the fall of the flag. Among these were the two 4½ Litre Lagondas entered by Arthur Fox, BPK 201 (race number 2) driven by Charlie Dodson, and BPK 202 (race number 1), John Hindmarsh. A Lagonda Rapier was also entered, driven by R. Davies Millar. Freddie Dixon made a fast start with his Riley, and was soon in the lead on handicap, followed by Hall's Derby Bentley, and the two big Lagondas. The seventh lap saw the Rapier go out with big end failure due to a fractured oil pipe, but shortly after midday Hindmarsh was in the lead with Dodson not far behind, the position soon to be lost due to the large car's hunger for tyres, and an inevitable pit stop. Meanwhile, great excitement occurred in the Singer camp, as three cars crashed almost simultaneously, due to steering failure, the fourth one then being withdrawn before it suffered a similar fate. By about 4 p.m. Hindmarsh was slowing up, resulting in a lengthy pit stop to clear a fuel blockage and change another set of wheels. Though he managed some very good lap times after this, he never caught up with the leaders. The race ran out with Freddie Dixon the winner on handicap, the Riley averaging 76.90 m.p.h.; Eddie Hall was second (first in his class); and Earl Howe's Bugatti third (second in class). The Hindmarsh Lagonda finished seventh overall (third in class), and Dodson eighth overall (fourth in class).

Arthur Fox subsequently sold the two 4½ Litre TT cars, but the special inlet and exhaust systems were removed beforehand.

John Hindmarsh preparing to refuel BPK 202. A mechanic in the pits waits to pass over a churn of petrol. Note the large bulge on the bonnet concealing Arthur Fox's carburettor intake system. (Photo: Mrs Robby Hewitt)

A stronger organisation with Mr. W. O. Bentley as technical Director has developed, and introduces for 1936, a new $4\frac{1}{2}$-litre Lagonda which will particularly appeal to knowledgeable motorists requiring a car possessing the rare and very attractive qualities peculiar to a high calibre British car. Here is a car which in recent years the market has so sadly lacked.

L. G. MOTORS [STAINES] LIMITED, MIDDLESEX, ENGLAND.   Telephone: Staines 1122 (4 lines)

Chapter Eleven

THE INTERIM YEARS

THE 4½ LITRE TYPE LG45

The Lagonda model range for 1936 was unveiled late in September 1935. Designated LG45 (an abbreviation of L.G. Motors and 4½ litres), the car was offered with three Lagonda body styles, or in chassis form only for those preferring bespoke coachwork. Development of the car was to continue during production, the modification state being referred to as Sanctions, the applicable Sanction number appearing on the maker's plate following the engine number. The first Sanction (S1) amounted to approximately 100 cars.

Sanction 1 Chassis

Based on the 10ft 9in wheelbase ZM type chassis, the car was the best of both worlds, namely the Rapide and the M45A. The chassis was extensively modified, the main cross members being moved forward in order to increase the length of the rear floor wells, the gearbox now fitted between these two members. Softer road springs were fitted all round, these damped by Luvax linked hydraulic shock absorbers, one of which contained

The superb drawings by Connolly on this and the following pages are taken from a Lagonda LG45 catalogue, and are reproduced by courtesy of Ivan Forshaw.

a pump and monitored the road surface, increasing the damping effect at all wheels when a rough road was encountered. In order to improve soundproofing and insulation, the cast aluminium bulkhead used on previous models was replaced with two prefabricated bulkheads, the gap between them housing the batteries and ancillary equipment. Chassis lubrication was a Tecalemit one-shot system, operated by full depression of the clutch pedal and supplied from a reservoir mounted under the bonnet.

The Girling braking system was retained, as was the Smiths 'Jackall' system fitted to the M45 Rapide but, with the exception of a very few cars, the jack pump and controls now lived in a dummy wheelcase fitted on the nearside of the car. Again, a Meadows gearbox was fitted, but it now contained Lagonda designed and manufactured synchromesh third and top-speed gears. Designated G9, the ratios were 11.49, 6.15, 4.76, with a top and axle ratio of 3.58:1. Ratios of 3.66 and 3.185 were also used. Road wheels were reduced to 18in, and carried 6.00 × 18in Dunlop tyres. The radiator was as the Rapide, and the dumb irons were modified to accept bumpers, while at the rear the 20-gallon petrol tank grew another filler neck so that it could be filled from either side of the car.

Basically, the engine was the 88.5 × 120.65mm bore and stroke (4453cc) Rapide, but with a lower compression ratio at 6.8:1, and slight alterations in valve timing. The horizontal Scintilla magneto on the inlet side was retained, but the coil ignition set on the exhaust side was replaced with a Scintilla Vertex magneto, mounted in the space previously occupied by the distributor, and again driven from the generator. Automatic advance and retard was fitted for both magnetos, but the system could also be manually operated if desired. The twin SU H5 carburettors were fitted with sliding jets for mixture enrichment, their control mounted on the panel. A large cylindrical air cleaner/silencer was connected to the carburettor air intakes by a tapered cast aluminium branch pipe, while on the other side, the exhaust system featured three silencers. The Meadows clutch was discarded in favour of a Borg and Beck clutch; no clutch stop was fitted. Modifications were also made to the water pump.

Sanction 2 Chassis

Introduced in about May 1936 (approximately 24 chassis were constructed). Specification was as for Sanction 1, but with the generator fitted offside of the engine, and two Scintilla Vertex magnetos were fitted on the nearside, number one (forward) firing inlet sparking plugs and number two (rear) firing exhaust plugs. Chassis lubrication was now fed with hot oil from the sump.

Sanction 3 Chassis

Introduced in July 1936, this Sanction formed the majority of the production. It was as the earlier Sanctions but with a new cylinder head to the design of Harry Weslake, incorporating the induction manifold cast completely within it. Carburettors were bolted directly to the side of the head and there were slightly smaller exhaust valves, and larger inlet valves. A spring-loaded damper was fitted to the engine mounting to reduce 'flutter' when pulling hard at low engine speeds. There was a G10 gearbox with synchromesh gears, second, third and top, and optional centre or right-hand change. There were Bowden cables at the rod ends to the brake compensator. An anti-roll bar was fitted between the rear shock absorber levers.

Sanction 4 Chassis

These were the last twenty or so of LG45 production and their specification was as for the other Sanctions, but with modified camshaft and valve timing, and slight alteration to the ignition timing.

The three Lagonda body types available were a Saloon, Tourer and Drop Head Coupé, the Saloon and Tourer both being updates of previous models. However, the Coupé was completely new, built to the design of the young Frank Feeley, who had recently taken the position of Chief of Body Design and was soon to revolutionise Lagonda body styling. W. R. Buckingham, who held this position with the old company, had now been upgraded to Works Manager. Though there were a few changes to body detail from Sanction to Sanction, on the open models it takes a very experienced eye to identify one

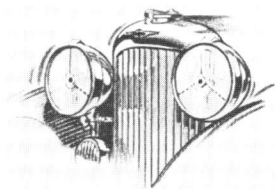

The earliest examples of the LG45 Saloon were very similar to the M45 Rapide, but fitted with a side-mounted spare wheel and cover, with a matching cover on the nearside for tools and Jackall system. Body style SB1.

Clearly evident on this chassis illustration are the twin fuel filler necks, double bulkhead and large air cleaner for the carburettor intakes.

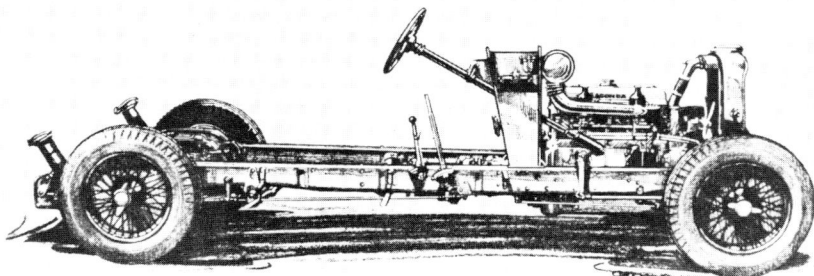

from the other without lifting the bonnet. However, the Saloons were noticeably different, the early example (SB1) having the upright appearance of the M45R, while the later model (SB3) was more rounded and rakish.

The LG45 was a more sober car than the M45, even though it had a similar performance despite an extra weight penalty. But the taut, perhaps vintage, feel loved by so many had gone forever, and this quiet refined style of motoring catered for the taste of a completely different type of driver.

The attractive Frank Feeley-designed Drop
Head Coupé was designated simply DHC.

The elegance of the Tourer is captured in this
drawing by Connolly, but his imagination
seems to have run awry with this impression
of the Saloon. The Tourer was designated TB,
and the Saloon SB3. Inset, leather cases were
£7 extra.

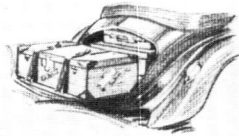

Tools and Jackall controls in nearside matching wheelcase. No SB2 body was manufactured.

LG Motors entered two LG45 Tourers for the 1936 Monte Carlo Rally, both fitted with M45 wings, these obviously being more suited to rally conditions and the expected heavy snow. The cars are seen at Staines, with Alan Good (left) and Major A. T. (Goldie) Gardner, prior to leaving for the start at Tallin in Estonia. In the event, the second car, DPE 120, was driven by T. G. Moore of *Motor Sport*, who did extremely well, finishing 41st overall. Alan Good, however, crashed near Riga and, though he was uninjured, the car was too badly damaged to continue. Private entries this year were R. E. Dobell (M45) who finished a very creditable 29th and T. C. Mann who was 60th overall. (Photo: Chas K. Bowers)

T. G. Moore (in flying helmet) on his arrival at Monte Carlo on 29
January 1936. (Photo: Alex Moore)

The sheer magnificence of the LG45 Tourer is clearly shown in these photographs. For the first time on a Lagonda a bumper was fitted as standard equipment, to the front only, though a rear one was sometimes supplied to special order. The bumper was of the harmonic stabilising type, and was fitted to improve handling rather than to protect the car from knocks. During his testing of the 3½ Litre Derby Bentley, W.O. had found that a bumper of this type transformed the car's road behaviour, which in fact was causing some concern at high speed on poor road surfaces. The vehicle illustrated was first registered in June 1936, but the photographs are recent. As can be seen, the car is still in pristine condition. (Photos: David Crow)

Though the two LG45 Saloons appear identical at a glance, close examination reveals the car on the right of the picture to be one of a few that were made with a rear-mounted spare wheel. This was half set in the boot lid, and fitted with an aluminium cover. The Jackall system controls on this version were situated as on the M45 Rapide. NTB 550 was one of the cars originally supplied engineless to Gardner Ltd for diesel engine testing, but for a period after the war a Jaguar XK 150 engine was fitted, when it became known as a 'Laguar'. The majority of saloons are as shown top left and below. Resplendent in dark red, there can be few finer examples than the car shown from the side view. The boot lid, open here, served as an extra luggage platform on all LG models. (Photos: Lagonda Club and Geoffrey Seaton)

(Above)   The first of a long line of both Lagonda and Aston Martin cars to feature Frank Feeley's superb styling was the LG45 Drop Head Coupé. The excellent example shown was first registered in April 1937, and has been in the hands of its current owner since the early 1950s. Though extensively used, it must rank as one of the finest of this model existing today.

The car's beautifully turned out Sanction 3 engine. (Photos: Richard Hare)

(Above)   The LG45 DHC is equally attractive with the hood up as down. The Ace wheel discs, in my opinion, enhance the appearance of the car. (Photo: Lagonda Club)

An elegant razor edge Saloon by Freestone and Webb. (Photo: Lagonda Club)

(Above)   A long wheelbase (11ft 6in) chassis was introduced in 1937, and the G10 gearbox, with synchromesh second, third and top, was now standard equipment, centre or right-hand change being optional. The final drive ratio for most of these heavy saloons was 3.818:1. The Lagonda-bodied car shown above was catalogued as the de Ville. Fitted suitcases were supplied with the car. The boot lid, when open, formed a platform for additional luggage. The price was £1,195, with wind-down division £30 extra. (Photo: Lagonda Club)

An attractive Cabriolet on the long wheelbase chassis by Salmons and Sons. This car is now in the USA. (Photo: Lagonda Club)

(Above)   The LG45 racing team cars on the forecourt of the Fox and Nicholl Service Station at Tolworth, 1936. The four-seaters are extreme left and right, the opening for the rear seats covered with a tonneau, clearly visible on the car shown side view. As for the two- seaters, the car on the left is without doubt a different colour, thought to have been blue, and was possibly the mount of French driver Marcel Lehoux in the French Grand Prix, 28 June 1936. (Photo: Lagonda Club)

LG45 TEAM CARS

The new Lagonda management were keen to keep a close association with motor sport, so backed the building of four competition chassis for 1936. These were built under the guidance of Arthur Fox, who had long experience both in racing and with Lagonda. Two of the cars were entered for Le Mans in June and, to comply with race requirements, were fitted with four-seater bodies. The other cars were two-seaters and were primarily built for the French Grand Prix to be held at Montlhery on 28 June, just two weeks after Le Mans.

The cars were based on the standard production 10ft 9in wheelbase LG45 chassis, and it is thought few modifications were made other than ratio changes to gearbox and back axle to suit race conditions. First gear of the G9 gearbox was changed from 3.14 to 2.618:1, and the axle ratio became 3.14 as opposed to the 3.66:1 used in the production car. Later, other axle ratios were used from time to time, together with a variation in wheel and tyre sizes.

The LG45 engine had now reached the development stage of Sanction 3, and this engine was used in the team cars. Tuning was carried out by Fox and Nicholl, a Fox-designed exhaust replacing the normal system. Engine test results no longer exist, but it is believed brake horse-power figures were in the region of 150 at 3600 r.p.m.

Again the cars' stark bodies were to the design of Arthur Fox and, though there was some updating, closely resembled the 1934 Tourist Trophy cars. The four cars were almost identical, the four-seaters being just slightly longer in the tail, due to the repositioning of the petrol tank when the two extra seats were squeezed in, even though they were only token affairs. Three of the cars

It is my belief that HLL 534 was the car originally used by the Leoz brothers in the French Grand Prix. This photograph was taken in the late 1950s and shows the car as it was when purchased by Lord Dunleath, who still owns it. The car, now restored, is back to pre-war race specification (see Ards TT Commemoration, page 234). (Photo: Lord Dunleath)

were finished in the usual Fox and Nicholl red; the original colour of one two-seater is uncertain, though it is usually accepted as being blue.

The four-seater cars were registered in May 1936 and became EPB 101 and EPB 102. However, both these cars completely vanished late in 1936, or perhaps during 1937, and no records for them are known to exist. Hence chassis numbers are uncertain but were possibly 12108 and 12109, as these numbers are not recorded against existing cars. The numbers are also in the correct sequence; both two-seaters are in the hands of Lagonda Club members and are 12110 and 12111. Unlike the four-seater cars, the two-seaters were not immediately registered, but 12111 became EPE 97 in August 1936, 12110 becoming HLL 534 almost ten years later, in March 1946.

THE 1936 RACING SEASON

Due to strikes in France, the 1936 Le Mans 24-hour race was cancelled, the Biennial Cup entries being carried over to 1937. However, the French Grand Prix at Montlhery on 28 June went ahead as planned. The race was split into three classes: 750–2000cc, 2000–4000cc and over 4000cc, and was run over 80 laps of the circuit, a total of 1,000km. Of the 37 starters, there were only five cars in the over 4000cc class; three straight eight Hudsons, and the two-seater Lagondas of Lehoux/Rocatti and the Leoz brothers. Due to bad driving by both parties, this turned

Possibly the Marcel Lehoux mount for the French Grand Prix, but certainly the Hon. Brian Lewis' car for the 1936 Ulster TT, the Brooklands 500-mile race, and many other exciting adventures, EPE 97 as it is today. (Photo: David Dunn)

out to be a disappointing race for the Lagonda team. Lehoux ran out of brakes twice and had to retire at 750km as no more linings were available. The Leoz brothers, also driving beyond the capacity of their brakes, did, however, fight off the Hudson challenge. Finishing without brakes they won the class at 64.39 m.p.h. The race was won by the Wimille/Sommer Bugatti at 77.85 m.p.h., with the Delahayes second, third, fourth and fifth, the Riley of Trevoux/MacLure taking Class One at 68.87 m.p.h. The Leoz brothers' Lagonda was 18th overall.

Just a week later, Lehoux took his Lagonda to Rheims for the Marne Grand Prix. From a field of 22 starters, he finished 12th overall, at an average speed of 79 m.p.h., the outright winner again being Wimille in his very fast Bugatti. This turned out to be Marcel Lehoux's last drive in the Lagonda as, sadly, he was killed when driving an ERA at Deauville on 19 July 1936.

Arthur Fox entered just one car for the Belgian Grand Prix, a 24-hour race to be held on 11 and 12 July 1936. This was one of the four-seater cars originally intended for Le Mans. The nominated drivers were Richard Seaman and Freddie Clifford, two very experienced men, though both were new to Lagonda motoring. The race was divided into six classes: 1100cc, 1500cc, 2000cc, 4000cc, over 4000cc and supercharged cars of any capacity. There were 34 starters and, though it was dry at the fall of the flag, the weather soon deteriorated, and continued to do so for the entire weekend. Despite the rain, however, the Lagonda was lapping at an average speed of around 78 m.p.h. After six hours, the Sommer/Severi Alfa Romeo was well in the lead, their competitors either blowing up or having spectacular crashes, of which there were many. The Lagonda was now in third position, but its performance was somewhat marred by its heavy tyre consumption, forcing many long, unscheduled pit stops, with only the drivers being allowed to work on the car. The Alfa Romeo continued to build up its lead and, as the 24th hour ran out, the car had covered some 3,002km at an average speed of 76.12 m.p.h. A Delahaye won the 4 Litre class at 75.03 m.p.h., and the Lagonda won its class at 72.33 m.p.h., fourth overall.

THE 1936 RAC TOURIST TROPHY

Arthur Fox entered three of the LG45 cars for the 1936 TT. These were driven by the Hon. Brian Lewis (racing number 1), Pat Fairfield (racing number 2) and Earl Howe (racing number 3). This year the race covered only 30 laps of the Ards circuit, but a change of rules permitted the ladies to drive for the first time in the history of the race. Mrs Elsie Wisdom took up the challenge with a Fiat, and Mrs D. Phipps with an Aston Martin. Others were reserve drivers, some in fact taking a turn at the wheel.

The day, 5 September, was grey and wet, the rain continuing well into the afternoon. Undaunted, the crowds turned up in larger numbers than ever before, no doubt determined to witness the now annual duel between Brian Lewis and Eddie Hall, the latter this year driving a 4¼ Litre Derby Bentley. They were not disappointed. Battle commenced from the fall of the flag in the large car class. On the 12th lap, Seaman (Aston Martin) retired with engine trouble and Dixon (Riley) was building up his lead, closely followed by Hall and Lewis.

The 17th lap saw the race marred by one of the sport's greatest tragedies – local driver Jack Chambers (Riley) skidded into a lamppost, killing eight spectators and injuring many more. Though the race continued, this disaster finished further racing at Ards for all time. The Lewis and Hall duel went on until the Lagonda skidded into the sandbags at Newtownards, badly damaging a wheel and losing much time limping to the pits for it to be changed. Of the 31 starters, 15 finished. Freddie Dixon's Riley, this year co-driven by C. J. P. Dodson, was the overall winner on handicap, with Eddie Hall's Bentley second overall (first in its class), and the Frazer Nash BMW of A. F. P. Fane third (first in its class). In his first race at the wheel of a Lagonda, Pat Fairfield did well to finish fourth (second in his class), Earl Howe was fifth (third in his class) and the Hon. Brian Lewis well down the field due to his mishap, 14th overall (fifth in his class).

The cars of Pat Fairfield and Brian Lewis,
Fairfield's in prominence, at the Dundonald
pits, await battle to commence. (Photo:
Martin Whitehead)

Earl Howe (number 3) makes a fast start in the large-car class, closely
followed by Lewis (number 1) and Fairfield (number 2). Also quick
off the mark were the Embiricos' Bugatti (number 16) and the

Mongin Delehaye (number 14). The two cars were only to collide
later on, each choosing its own ditch in which to retire. (Photo: Cyril
Posthumus)

A fine action shot of Earl Howe at speed on the Ards circuit during the 1936 TT. He finished fifth overall (third in his class). The car is one of the four-seaters originally built for the 1936 Le Mans 24-hour race, which was cancelled that year due to strike-torn France. (Photo: A. W. Fox Collection)

The fate of these four-seater LG45 team cars is uncertain, but the general consensus of opinion is that they were returned to standard production specification, fitted with touring or saloon coachwork back at Staines, then sold through the normal channels, presumably as second-hand vehicles.

Eddie Hall's Bentley leading the Brian Lewis Lagonda during their final duel on the Ards circuit.

Lewis and Howe 'floating' round Quarry Corner during the early stages of the 1936 TT. The wet road, however, proved a saviour for the tyres until the track dried out in the late afternoon. (Photos: Cyril Posthumus)

THE BRDC 500-MILE RACE
Brooklands 19 September 1936

With only minor modification, EPE 97 took on the might of purpose-built track cars for the BRDC 500-mile race, and held its head high. Jointly driven by Earl Howe and the Hon. Brian Lewis, the car lapped consistently at around 120 m.p.h. Its average speed for the race, including pit stops, was in excess of 113 m.p.h., and it finished a creditable third overall.

For this race, all road equipment was removed, along with the radiator slats to improve cooling. The front brakes were also removed, considerably reducing the unsprung weight, a common practice on outer circuit cars. At the back, the rear axle was fitted with a 3:1 special straight-cut crown wheel and pinion, the 21in wire wheels carrying 7.00 × 21in track tyres. In order to clean up the car, the passenger seat was cowled over and the front dumb-irons were neatly faired in. Surely, the car never looked more beautiful than on this day.

'Ebby' Ebblewhite drops the flag to start the large car class. As the 500 was a handicap race, most of the entrants were well on their way round the track when this photograph was taken. First off the line is number 22, the Pacey Hassan Special, jointly driven by Pacey and Baker-Carr. Half a wheel behind, number 21, the Lagonda driven by Howe and Lewis and, still on the line, number 20, Jack Duller's single-seater Duesenberg, driven by himself and Gwenda Stewart. Just visible behind them, and on the extreme right of the picture, is scratch car, the giant 8 Litre Barnato Hassan Special to be driven by Bertram and Marker. They later had a good run lapping around 129 m.p.h. until a connecting rod broke and put a stop to it, much to the disappointment of the crowd and no doubt themselves. Standing behind the Lagonda, the tall mechanic is Donald Wilcockson (Fox and Nicholl's chief mechanic) with, on his right, Earl Howe who drove the later stages of the race, and, on Wilcockson's left, Arthur Fox. The Lagonda, in fact, entered in Arthur Fox's name as in previous races, though it is believed the car was always the property of L. G. Motors. (Photo: Quadrant/ Autocar)

This pit stop took just 1 minute 58 seconds. The photograph was taken just after the car had stopped. Donald Wilcockson pours the first 5-gallon churn of petrol into the 40-gallon tank, and the offside wheels are off. Arthur Fox holds a replacement rear at the pit counter, in readiness for his mechanic, Lionel Taylor. (Photo: Quadrant/*Autocar*)

Holding the Lagonda high on the banking to ease the load on its tyres, Brian Lewis flies past the Cotton/Black supercharged MG Magnette with Billy Cotton at the wheel, on the run up to the Railway Straight. The MG also finished the gruelling race, covering 176 creditable laps. (Photo: The Brooklands Society)

THE LE MANS 24-HOUR RACE
19–20 June 1937

EPE 97 was the only Lagonda entry for the 24-hour race at Le Mans in 1937. By this year the clouds of war were on the horizon, and an armament drive was under way. Fox and Nicholl had taken on sub-contract work for the Hawker Aircraft Co., and, to cope with this commitment, their Tolworth site was being extended. Due to these events, race preparation on the car was carried out at the firm of Pudney, Turner and Vincent, where these photographs were taken, just five days before the race. It is believed Fox's mechanics carried out this work, but it is likely the Lagonda works also had a hand in things. EPE 97 was allotted race number 3, and the nominated drivers were Charles Brackenbury and John Hindmarsh.

The race itself was marred during the opening laps by an appalling accident at the notorious White House corner, when Bugatti driver René Kippeut was killed in a collision with Pat Fairfield's Frazer Nash BMW, Fairfield dying from his injuries the following day. Fortunately the Lagonda was not involved, but the car soon developed engine trouble and, after a succession of pit stops, had retired by 10 p.m. The race was won by the Wimille/Benoist works Bugatti, with Aston Martin winning the Rudge Whitworth Cup. Sadly, John Hindmarsh also died a few days later at Weybridge when test flying the prototype Hawker Hurricane; the cause of the accident has never been disclosed. (Photos: Chas K. Bowers)

THE RAC TOURIST TROPHY RACE
Donington Park, September 1937

Owing to the tragic events at Ulster in 1936, all racing there had been stopped. The new venue for this classic race became Donington Park, a far shorter circuit than Ards, and one less suited to the heavy metal; the Lagonda was in fact the largest car entered this year. As is often the case, the change of scene brought a change of rules and doors now became a mandatory item. Hurriedly, Fox had what can only be described as token affairs fitted, useless for the purpose intended, but somehow they satisfied the scrutineers. As small as they were however, the exhaust had to be altered in order that the nearside one would open.

Twenty-one cars left the line for this 312-mile race, the Lagonda EPE 97 along with the Delahayes and Darracqs starting scratch. With some disappointment to entrants and spectators alike, Eddie Hall's 4¼ Litre 'Derby' Bentley was a non-starter, so breaking his record of competing in every TT since 1928. Driven this year by Charles Brackenbury and Charlie Martin, just one refuel stop was planned for the Lagonda, at the change-over point for the drivers. Though unsuited to the Donington circuit, the car ran faultlessly throughout until, with only three laps to go, a stub axle broke; Martin, who was at the wheel, managed to keep the car under some sort of control during its gyrations and fortunately walked away unharmed. The race winner was Comotti in a Darracq who averaged 68.7 m.p.h. on this twisting circuit.

Charles Brackenbury in EPE 97 at the Fox and Nicholl service station prior to the drive to Donington Park in 1937. This rare photograph clearly illustrates the minute door and modified exhaust system fitted for this race. A similar door was fitted on the other side of the car. (Photo: Tim Lee/Elliott)

THE BROOKLANDS SPORTS CAR HOUR RECORD

During a run at Brooklands in May 1937, observed by the RAC, Sammy Davis had become the holder of the unofficial one-hour sports car record, having covered 102.22 miles, at the wheel of a Type 328 Frazer Nash BMW; no passenger was carried. Alan Hess, who at that time was editor of *Speed Magazine*, also had his sights on this record and managed to persuade L. G. Motors' Managing Director Dick Watney into loaning him EPE 97 for a similar attempt. A gentleman's agreement was made that out of pocket expenses would be met by the company. With this in mind, Hess took the car to Fox and Nicholl for tuning, and on 7 October drove it to Brooklands for this run, to be observed by the RAC. The attempt was made during the afternoon of this miserably cold and wet day.

With the car in full road trim, passengered by Jeff Leitner, Alan Hess covered some 104.4 miles in the hour, easily breaking Davis' record. The car was then driven to Staines where Hess presented Watney with the good news, together with the Fox and Nicholl bill for tuning, in the order of £25. But, despite the success and the gentleman's agreement, Watney refused to pay it, an incident Hess felt bitter about until the day he died. This was the last occasion EPE 97 was run by either Arthur Fox or L. G. Motors; however, the car continued to pursue its racing career, but under new ownership. For reasons unknown, the long Fox and Nicholl/Lagonda association had also by now come to an end. Perhaps hard words were passed between Fox and Watney over the car's dismal showing at Le Mans, but this we will never know.

After the war, EPE 97 was owned and raced by Joe Goodhew who, in an attempt to extract more speed, progressively modified the car by lowering, lightening, and eventually shortening the chassis. Fortunately, this was achieved by overlapping the sideframe members after they were cut. During the 1960s the car was fairly extensively raced in Lagonda Club and VSCC events by Lt. Col. Billy Michael, and later owned by David Dunn, who had success at Phoenix Park with the car in this form. However, during his recent restoration of the car, David put matters right, and EPE 97 is now once again resplendent in its pre-war form, a commendable and worthwhile undertaking. The car has since been sold.

Alan Hess, Jeff Leitner and EPE 97 at Brooklands after their successful record run in October 1937. (Photo: Alan Hess)

David Dunn on his way to winning the 1978 Gold Flake Trophy at Phoenix Park, one of the car's last appearances in its lightweight form. (Photo: David Dunn)

(Below)   Alan Hess re-acquainted with EPE 97 at a Brooklands Society Reunion in 1980, David standing proudly behind his famous and beautifully restored car. (Photo: Arnold Davey)

THE ARDS COMMEMORATION RUN
8 August 1986

An exciting week of motor sport in Ulster came to its climax with a commemoration run to mark the 50th anniversary of the last race on the world-famous Ards road circuit, and to pay tribute to those who died there on that tragic day, 5 September 1936.

This three-lap, non-competitive event, organised by the Ulster Vintage Car Club, embraced the full 13½ miles of the Dundonald–Newtownards–Comber–Dundonald triangle, and attracted a massive 85 entries, many from overseas, predominantly driving genuine TT machinery. Amongst the historic line-up were the LG45 Lagonda team cars of Lord Dunleath and David Dunn, Lord Dunleath remarking:

'It was one of the most gratifying moments of my life to be able to line up beside David Dunn at the pits near Quarry Corner on the evening of 8 August, and see two of the team cars back in original condition, in exactly the same place they were prior to the 1936 TT'.

This highly successful and authentic re-enactment of this historic race was only made possible by the help and leniency of the RUC, together with the co-operation of the public authorities, and, indeed, the public themselves. One can only hope it will be repeated.

The President of the Ulster Vintage Car Club, Lord Dunleath, enjoying his 1936 LG45 Lagonda team car during the Ards TT commemoration run. Lord Dunleath remarked after the run that his riding mechanic said they had pulled 105 m.p.h. on one of the sections, but as he was so busy shouting abuse at the people who got in the way, he had no time to look at the rev counter. Clearly an occasion that will provide happy memories for years to come. (Photo: Esler Crawford Photography)

THE LG45 RAPIDE

Promenade Percy's ultimate sports car: flash, flamboyant, extrovert, it has been dubbed them all, but the Rapide was a wolf in sheep's clothing, very fast, a masculine machine, yet silent and impeccably mannered. It was hailed by the Company as the fastest production car in the world, even though a couple of continental models may have had an edge on it. However, these were without doubt of temperamental nature, something untrue of any Lagonda.

The Rapide was based to some extent on the successful racing models and, like these cars, the backbone was the conventional LG45 chassis, again reduced in weight. All unnecessary equipment was removed, with the exception of the Tecalemit automatic chassis lubrication system. The twin bulkheads developed for the standard models were discarded, and the old cast aluminium bulkhead was reintroduced, though to keep body dimensions to a minimum, it was slightly reduced in width. The synchromesh third and top speed G9 gearbox was retained, but the G10 with synchromesh second, third and top speed gears was soon offered as an alternative, with right-hand change only for the Rapide. In both cases, the top and final drive ratio was 3.31:1, with one exception, this being 3.14:1 (chassis number 12277R) to the

special requirement of the original owner. Centre lock wire wheels with 6.00 × 18in tyres were standard equipment.

Almost all the Rapides were powered by the Sanction 3 engine, just a couple being fitted with the Sanction 4. The letter R followed the LG45 engine number in both cases.

High compression pistons raised the ratio from the standard 6.68:1 to 7:1, with 7.5:1 available for those with racing in mind. The Lagonda catalogue stated that every Rapide engine was specially selected, and quoted the brake horsepower as 150, though this is generally considered to be optimistic, 140 b.h.p. being a more likely figure. As on previous 4½-litre models, twin SU H5 carburettors were fitted, but the air cleaner was deleted to improve breathing. For the same reason, the exhaust was based on the design developed by Arthur Fox, but the exposed area of the external pipes was now covered with chromium-plated flexible tubing for ornamentation, and it was no doubt this embellishment that gave rise to the car's playboy image in the early days, an image soon dispelled however when the road test reports were published.

The Rapide made its début towards the end of August 1936 and, with the reluctance of the British to accept

235

change, was perhaps too advanced in styling for Mr Average. For all that, Feeley had retained the hand-crafted look of quality associated with the marque, but with an added 'something' that created personality and excitement – an excitement it continues to exude some fifty years on, to the young in heart at least. The performance was equally sensational, from rest to 60 m.p.h. in little over 12 seconds, and a maximum speed approaching 107 m.p.h. was beyond the dreams of the enthusiast of the day, and even now is satisfactory for most. I was recently entrusted with one of these fine cars for a run of some 50 miles or so, rekindling an immense desire to

own a Rapide from boyhood days, the machine fully living up to all the expectations conjured up over more long years than I care to remember. To many, the Rapide is the ultimate Lagonda, and few will deny that it ranks amongst the élite of all PVT sporting cars today. Certainly a Rapide would be one of life's greatest pleasures and most valued possessions.

Of the 25 LG45 Rapides built, the first was chassis number 12141R, the last 12277R; all but one can be accounted for, and most of these cars are still in use. The car was priced at £1,050.

Advanced for its day, but in no way flashy, the Rapide radiator was in fact identical to the standard LG45 models. (Photo: Alec Downie)

The impressive sight seen by a passenger looking overboard. (Photo: Herb Schofield)

Nearside of the engine showing the exhaust manifolds, manufactured to a design developed by Arthur Fox. Chromium-plated flexible tubing concealed the exposed area of the rigid pipes and, in order to prevent heat discoloration, distance pieces maintained an air gap between the two. The twin Scintilla Vertex magnetos can also be seen below the forward manifold, the forward one firing the inlet side plugs, the rear the exhaust side plugs.

Due to good accessibility, maintenance and cleaning of the Sanction 3 engine became a pleasure rather than a chore; this beautifully turned out example has had many enjoyable hours spent on it. (Photo: Herb Schofield)

(Above)   The view seen by most when the Rapide is given its head. The boot housed the spare wheel, and perhaps an overnight bag at a squeeze. Seen at Silverstone in 1973, this car was first registered in 1937. (Photo: Phil Ridout)

Though extremely narrow, the Rapide was a full four-seater of considerable comfort for average-sized occupants, but the lack of luggage accommodation created a problem when touring with four up. The hood could be erected by one person and in no way detracted from the car's appearance when raised. Side screens were secured by quick-release catches on the inner side of the doors, so avoiding the unsightly peg-type fixings standard at the time. The excellent example shown was first registered in February 1938 and is seen almost at the end of a complete restoration. (Photo: Alec Downie)

Both photographs of this very fine machine are recent, but the car could have looked little, if any, different when it was first registered during 1938. Chassis 12277R was the last of the 25 LG45 Rapides built, differing in some respects from the remainder of the production by sporting chromium-plated brake drums and front axle while, at the back, the axle ratio was changed from 3.31 to 3.14:1. The modifications were incorporated to comply with the customer's order. Frank Feeley's artistry is seen to full advantage here: the wings taking the form of a Gothic arch at their centres became a Feeley trademark and the design was subsequently a feature of the marque into the post-war David Brown era. Feeley also paid great attention to detail design and the mountings for the windscreen are typical – clever concealment by the body mouldings cleaned up what is often an untidy area on a sports car. The screen, of course, could still be folded flat if desired; provision was also made for wind deflectors to be fitted at its side posts, these complementing the car's weather equipment. (Photos: Herb Schofield)

(Above)   This very fine Rapide is seen at the Davies Motor Sales and Service Department at Staines in the late 1950s. The premises, extensively enlarged, are now owned by a multiple motor group. (Photo: Mrs V. E. Davies)

Bruce Spollon enjoys himself with a perfectly standard car at a VSCC Donington Park Meeting, May 1979. (Photo: Tony Wood)

Bob Freeman-Wright, Lagonda Club Chairman for many years, at speed with his LG45 Rapide 'The Scarlet Woman' during practice at Silverstone, August 1949. (Photo: Richard Hare)

The Scarlet Woman, face duly lifted, presents herself at a Lagonda Club Southern Rally in the 1950s. She has aged little since. However, one wonders if such drastic surgery really improves her behaviour, or is it perhaps just in the mind! (Photo: Geoffrey Seaton)

Chapter Twelve

BORN BY THE HAND OF A GENIUS

THE LAGONDA V12

We have now to cast our minds back to August 1935, the time of the demise of Lagonda Ltd and the formation of L. G. Motors, the new company headed by A. P. Good, W. O. Bentley and R. G. Watney. When these gentlemen arrived at Staines, Good called together the small remaining staff and, after formal introductions, to the astonishment of all announced, 'We are going to build the best car in the world, and there are just two years to do it in'. The reason for this tight schedule, however, was not disclosed. The proposed car was to have a completely new chassis, this to be offered with the choice of either 11ft or 11ft 6in wheelbase, and powered by an equally new 4½-litre 12-cylinder engine developing such power that even with heavy closed coachwork, the magic 'ton' could be easily exceeded in complete silence.

Bentley's hand-picked design and development team wasted no time in getting to work on this ambitious project but, if the company were to remain viable, something had to be produced in the short term. Frank Chasemore, a survivor from the old company, was given the task of rounding up the staff who had been paid off and sorting out material requirements to get M45A production once again under way. This, as we have seen, was soon superseded by the LG45, nowadays often referred to as Mr Bentley's 'interim' car. Of course, the LG45 also required a considerable amount of design and development work, but despite this and to the surprise of many, a prototype V12 appeared on the Lagonda stand at the Olympia Motor Show in October 1936.

From a clean sheet of paper, the prototype of this complex motor car had been produced in a mere 15 months, even though, to meet the deadline, some of the engine components had been knocked up in the carpenter's shop. However, few were to know, so skilfully were they manufactured and, though the car was displayed with transparent bonnet sides, these were kept locked. As on the LG45, Girling brakes were fitted, and the body closely resembled the SB3 fitted to that car, though with a more rakish rear end. For all this, the V12 was the sensation of the show. Provisional prices were quoted at £1,050 for the 11ft chassis, the Saloon £1,450; 11ft 6in chassis, £1,075, Hooper Limousine £1,670. Prospective customers were informed that deliveries would not commence before June 1937, but when both June and July came and went without a single delivery, August saw the Company publish the following statement:

'The making of the new 12-cylinder Lagonda has been a deliberately retarded process – for a vintage wine may not be hurried to maturity or a new motor-car launched precipitately upon the market. Today, after two years' active experiment, the 12-cylinder Lagonda has attained full stature. Figures, which cause even its designers (Mr W. O. Bentley – and others) to pause and marvel, are available to show that this new motor is destined to eclipse anything of its type so far produced. We built, indeed, better than we knew. Of the half-dozen patrician motor cars still remaining on the world market, none ever inherited so rich a patrimony of design as the 12-cylinder Lagonda. The new car is no mere recapitulation of a good – but tired – design in terms of 1937. It is a new-born car, unrelated to any yet on the road – here or on the Continent. New ideals of performance were set up and these have been exceeded in the sheer versatility of the new car. Such is the 12-cylinder Lagonda – a car destined to rank, from now on, among the greater names in motoring history.'

It was early October of that year, in fact, before the company made any further announcement, and then the full 1938 model range was published. The announcement was not without its surprises: a short chassis (10ft 4in) was to complement the standard 11ft and the long 11ft 6in chassis and, in addition to the V12, a new 6-cylinder 4½ Litre model was to be introduced. This was designated LG6 and was unveiled at the Olympia Motor Show later in the month, together with the relaunch of the V12. During the months which had lapsed since the showing of the prototype V12, many changes had been made, but perhaps the most noteworthy regarding the chassis was discarding the Girling brakes in favour of the Lockheed hydraulic braking system. The body came in for some considerable restyling, the production Saloon bearing little resemblance to the prototype car. Frank Feeley's influence was again shown to full advantage on these new models.

The first running of the prototype V12 engine. Witnessing the event is Lagonda Technical Director and Designer W. O. Bentley with, on his left, the Head of the Development Department, Stan Ivermee. Completing the picture are Stuart Tresillian and Charles Sewell of the design team. Other important members of this team were Frank Ayto and Leslie Stark. Ex-Bentley mechanic from Cricklewood days, Percy Kemish, held the responsible position of Experimental and Racing Shops Foreman. The engine shown above is fitted with a specially made Stromberg twin choke carburettor, and thermostatic mixture control. This large carburettor fed simultaneously into the manifolds of each cylinder block. However, carburation was to be the cause of many sleepless nights for the development team, several alternatives being tried in the period before production got under way. Eventually twin downdraught SU carburettors became standard equipment, one fitted with a thermostatically controlled starting device. (Photo: The Late W. O. Bentley Collection)

Objectives

In a brief synopsis published when the V12 was first introduced, W. O. Bentley gave the following objectives in designing the 12-cylinder Lagonda:

'1. To give a top gear range from zero to approximately 110 m.p.h.
2. To render gear changing practically superfluous, yet to provide through the gears acceleration superior to any non-racing car.
3. The entire mechanism to function so smoothly and silently that passengers are unaware of anything but mere motion.
4. To provide, for the first time, springing which gives absolute suppleness with perfect stability by utilising an entirely new system of independent front suspension by torsion bars, in conjunction with hand-controlled shock absorbers and a wide low-slung frame.
5. To provide a steering layout which is the first perfect compromise between direct action, fingertip lightness, with complete selectivity at the highest speeds.
6. To possess the essential characteristics of early models designed by me, namely, absolute reliability and durability, even when driven consistently at maximum speeds.
7. An engine which *without adaptation* is sufficiently versatile, smooth, quiet and powerful as to be *equally suitable* for a town car or the Rapide sports model.
8. To provide hydraulic brakes which are inherently compensated and can be used with absolute confidence in any emergency at no matter what speed the car is travelling.'

To achieve these objectives, the following methods were adopted:

'1. To obtain good acceleration on top gear calls for a low axle ratio. In the past, to get high maximum speeds, it was necessary to have a high axle ratio. But in the 12-cylinder Lagonda this problem has been overcome by designing an engine which has an unusually wide range of engine revolutions running up to 5,500 r.p.m. without effort and well within all factors of safety. Acceleration and speed have thus been simultaneously achieved with

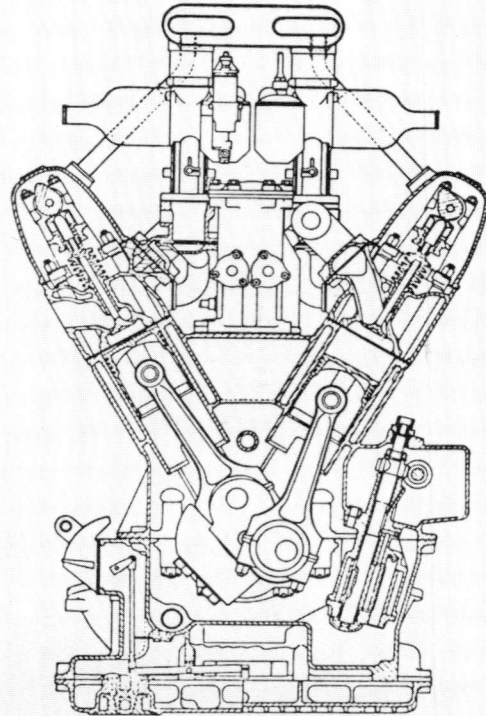

Cross-section of a production 12-cylinder engine. The carburettors are SU. A single Burgess air cleaner/silencer was common to both. Also visible are the gear type oil pumps with their skew gear drive from the auxiliaries shaft, and the unusual anti-surge baffle system in the wide, shallow sump. (Illustration: Arnold Davey)

this short-stroke 12-cylinder engine. It is necessary here to emphasise certain specific points:

(a) The piston speed at 5,500 r.p.m. is no higher than normal.
(b) The crankshaft is quite exceptionally rigid.
(c) Due to the lightness of reciprocating parts, inertia forces even at 5,500 r.p.m. are lower than in many engines at 4,000 r.p.m. and the bearings are more lightly loaded than is the common practice.
(d) The compactness of the design and the high grade materials used give this 12-cylinder engine a

really remarkable power to weight ratio: likewise, the unit is so short that the maximum body space is available.

The valve gear is so designed that it can easily handle these high revs without calling for springs above normal strength. There is no side thrust on the valves owing to the absence of rockers and the fitting of a light tappet interposed between the overhead cam and the valve stem. In this short stroke engine the valves are exceptionally large because the bore is so great in relation to the capacity of the cylinder. The engine delivers 180 brake horsepower at 5,500 r.p.m., at which point the power curve is still rising. The cylinder and crankcase are in one piece, made of cast iron, which design is much facilitated by the short stroke because the depth and weight of the castings are correspondingly reduced.

2.   The factors enumerated above explain how it has been possible to retain a low axle ratio while the numerous power impulses from the 12-cylinder engine ensure the utmost smoothness at lower speeds. If it is desired to use the close ratio four-speed gearbox provided, startling acceleration is available over a wide range of road speeds on the lower ratios.

3.   This (minimum vibration) feature is attained through:

(a)   Low gear ratio.
(b)   Stiff cast iron crankcase.
(c)   Stiff short stroke balanced crankshaft.
(d)   Double the number of smaller power impulses per rev (12 cylinders).

4.   The front springing of a car without independent suspension is always made less flexible than it need be owing to steering difficulties arising when real flexibility is introduced. This point is covered in the Lagonda independent suspension design, the geometry of the steering being consistently correct. Weight distribution and wide-spaced back springs, with a large range of shock absorber control, greatly help the stability and cornering. An anti-rolling torsion bar is also fitted.

5.   A type of independent front springing for which the geometry is correct for all wheel positions. This feature is unobtainable with orthodox suspension systems and is also absent in a number of independent suspensions already in production, owing to the inclusion of either rubber bushes or lack of rigidity in frame or arms. If the steering geometry is correct there is no tendency to steering wheel shocks – therefore there is no necessity to introduce frictional damping, which enables one to use a higher ratio steering without impairing its lightness. The rigidity of the frame at the front end of the Lagonda chassis is also an important factor in the steering control of the car. This is largely due to the fact that the torsion bar is five feet long and is anchored at its rear end to the cruciform centre section of the frame, thus relieving the forward part of the frame from practically all racking.

6.   It may be argued that the weight of the new Lagonda models exceeds that of certain other high performance motor cars. We have obtained our power to weight ratio by providing surplus power; for, in my view, one of the essential justifications for the expensive and exclusive car is that it should be capable of giving noticeably more performance than cheaper vehicles, and that with an expectancy of life without loss of edge and with all stamina unimpaired.

7.   The versatility of the 12-cylinder Lagonda engine is its predominant feature. We have got such surplus power, and almost unlimited revolutions characterise this engine, that only very infrequently can it be extended. Logically, therefore, during 90 per cent of its life, the engine is operating at little more than two-thirds of its capacity. It can, indeed, be regarded as a de-tuned unit – an immediate impression gained by all who drive it.

8.   Road stability as interpreted by Lagonda is still inadequate in the majority of cars, irrespective of price. The highest speeds are permissible on the Lagonda, because:

(a)   The steering is direct and selective.
(b)   The suspension ensures stability in emergencies.
(c)   The brakes are not only powerful, but make the driver master of any untoward situation. Lockheed

brakes with 16-inch drums and dual master cylinders, as fitted to Lagonda, are of the same type as are found on the fastest racing cars in the world.'

W. O. Bentley

Cost was completely eliminated as a primary factor in the design of the 4½ Litre 12-cylinder Lagonda, and without such restriction the ability of this genius W. O. Bentley was shown to the fore. Hailed by the motoring press as a masterpiece of engineering, and as one of the world's most advanced and desirable cars, the V12 was a direct challenge to Rolls Royce. Once again, history was being repeated, as the magnificent 6½ and 8 Litre Bentley cars of the 1920s and early 1930s were in direct competition with that company's products too.

A synopsis by W. O. of the objectives for the design of the V12 and the methods adopted to achieve these objectives was published when the car was introduced in 1936. These are reproduced on page 244. Apart from making interesting reading, they emphasise many of the important design features of this complex vehicle. The following, then, is simply intended to add a little detail to some of these design features, together with the general specification of the production models.

To ensure complete rigidity, the chassis side frames were deep box sections, these side frames being cruciform braced. This large X bracing assembly was mounted as far forward as possible to minimise twisting moments at the forward end of the frame. The front suspension was independent, with unequal length wishbones locating the swivel pin and hub assemblies, and torsion bars as the springing medium, secured in adjustable housings at the cruciform X bracing. At the rear, conventional semi-elliptic springs were used, but the shackle pins were special, designed to eliminate excessive side loads at the spring hangers. Damping was by special Armstrong piston-type shock-absorbers, the rears controllable for rate by a control on the steering column. An anti-roll bar was fitted between the levers of the rear pair. A centre change G10 gearbox had synchromesh on second, third and top speed gears, the box being separately mounted from the engine, driven by an intermediate shaft that passed through the centre of the cruciform. The rear 'V' of the X bracing provided the

gearbox location, the arrangement resulting in the advantage of a short propeller shaft. A Salisbury hypoid rear axle was chosen with the following ratios: 4.27, 4.45 and 4.72:1, these applying respectively to the available chassis lengths of 10ft 4in, 11ft and 11ft 6in. The track for all three models was 5ft. A Lockheed hydraulic braking system, with twin master cylinders, was used, but the handbrake remained on the offside; a unique feature was that adjustment of its mechanism also compensated for lost motion on the foot-brake pedal. Steering was low geared compared to previous Lagonda models at 3¾ turns from lock to lock, but it was said to be light and precise at all speeds. Automatic chassis lubrication and Jackall jacks were standard equipment. Normal tyre sizes were 6.00 × 18in for the 10ft 4in wheelbase car, and 6.50 × 18in for the 11ft and 11ft 6in models, on centre lock wire wheels.

In order to obtain smooth, silent power throughout the speed range, W.O. designed a comparatively short stroke 12-cylinder engine, this in V configuration, with a bore and stroke of 75 × 84.5mm, 4479cc (41.85hp). The two banks of six cylinders were set at an angle of 60°, and the blocks staggered to allow the connecting rods to run side by side on the crankpins. Both cylinder blocks and the upper half of the crankcase were an integral casting of nickel iron, with detachable cylinder heads of the same material; the lower half of the crankcase and the sump unit were of aluminium. The fully counterweighted crankshaft ran in four conventional steel-backed white metal bearings, and carried a Lanchester-type damper at its nose, housed within the timing chest.

To prevent the large hollow journals of the crankshaft becoming sludge traps, the usual arrangement of end caps was discarded and, instead, the internal bores of the journals were plugged with aluminium, drilled in a complex system of oilways for bearing lubrication. The bearing surfaces were nitride hardened, and duralumin connecting rods ran directly on the crankpins, no white metal being interposed, a design that proved completely trouble free. So trouble free, in fact, that almost fifty years on, Lagonda Club members talk of engines still running with no visible evidence of a bottom end overhaul. Anodised alloy, Specialloid pistons with fully floating gudgeon pins were fitted, the gudgeon pins secured by circlips. Though two gear-type oil pumps were contained in a common housing, these were in effect self-contained systems, each with its own relief valve, bypass pipe and filter, the latter again in a common housing. The mains and big end bearings were supplied at 70 p.s.i., while the camshafts, timing gears and ancillary equipment were fed at about 15 p.s.i. The oil pick-up was from the centre of a wide, shallow three-gallon capacity tray-like sump, fitted with gravity operated baffles to prevent pump cavitation when on hills or during hard braking. The oil content was indicated by a float operated rod.

Each bank of cylinders had a single overhead camshaft running in seven bearings in an alloy gallery, the gallery itself housing the adjustable tappets and tappet guides. The valves were in line and fitted with double springs, but were not interchangeable, the inlets being slightly smaller than the exhausts. Each cylinder bank had its own Delco-Remy coil ignition set, and the distributors, driven off the rear of the camshafts, were fitted with vacuum advance, and fired one 14mm sparking plug per cylinder. The firing order was 1–2–9–10–5–6–11–12–3–4–7–8. (Offside cylinders odd numbers, nearside even numbers.)

The SU downdraught carburettors, one fitted with a thermostatically controlled starting device, were mounted on separate manifolds, part of which was cast into the head. The cylinder heads were of crossflow design, and to create a hot spot for the incoming charge, two exhaust ports were connected by external plumbing to the inlet manifolds. A single Burgess silencer filtered the air for both carburettors, and drew part of its supply from the cam covers. The exhaust manifolds had just one outlet each, and the pipes remained separate throughout their run, with large silencers fitted forward of the rear axle. The clutch was a conventional Borg and Beck, and transmitted the drive through the previously mentioned intermediate shaft and fabric couplings to the gearbox.

The radiator was both taller and wider than that fitted to the LG45, and its filler cap shallower; it was also mounted two inches lower, and slightly raked in angle. For most 11ft wheelbase cars, and all of the 11ft 6in models, an extra tall radiator was fitted, in keeping with the more sedate body styles fitted to these chassis.

Though the Lagonda catalogue quoted the power output at 180 b.h.p. at 5,500 r.p.m., test bed figures in the hands of the Registrar of the Lagonda Club suggest these figures were optimistic. The above specification relates to the first Sanction V12 (S1), of which there were approximately 86 chassis.

Sanction 2

Produced from about May 1939, the specification was as Sanction 1, but the firing order was changed to 1–12–9–4–5–8–11–2–3–10–7–6. The oil filler position was also changed to the offside camshaft cover and both oil pressure relief valves were set at 70p.s.i. The secondary system was fitted with a pressure reducing valve downstream of its filter. The mixture hot spot was improved by exhaust gases impinging on a copper plate in the pipe to the induction manifold. There was a G11 gearbox (with wider spaced intermediate gears).

Sanction 3

Not produced.

Sanction 4

As Sanction 2, but with the rear pressed steel chassis cross member replaced by a tubular member. Brakes were improved to minimise fade.

Many of the early cars had at least some S2 modifications incorporated by the factory after delivery. The total production of models other than S1 was 42 chassis, plus two or perhaps three cars built during 1946–47 from parts in stock.

W. O. Bentley's greatest achievement. This partly dismantled 4½-litre V12 Lagonda engine gives an insight into the superb engineering, but reveals little of its complexity. However, clearly visible is the gear train, culminating in a duplex chain drive for the overhead camshafts. Also visible is a similar chain from the nearside timing drive for the auxiliaries shaft, shown here with the water pump impeller and generator fitted, and the pump body placed in front of the engine. From the centre of this shaft, skew gears drove the two oil pumps. The Lanchester type damper is not shown, but was fitted on the exposed section of crankshaft, and butted against the spacer forward of the master timing gear. The assembly was concealed once the timing chest cover was fitted. The cylinder heads were removable without disturbing the valve timing. (Photo: The Late W. O. Bentley Collection)

FPK 550 (later re-registered NPJ 680), the prototype V12 Standard Short Saloon, made history at Brooklands on 10 October 1938. Driven by Earl Howe, it became the first production Saloon to cover 100 miles in one hour (the actual distance was 101.5 miles). The big car lapped consistently at 105.52 m.p.h. until, on the 22nd lap, a tyre deflated. Making use of the car's built-in jacking system, the wheel was changed in 2 minutes 42 seconds, and the car then went on to finish with a remarkable lap at 108.27 m.p.h. With the exception of racing tyres, the car was to standard production specification, and the officially observed run was carried out on normal pump fuel.

NPJ 680 seen at Potters Bar on 28 August 1980. Sadly, shortly after this photograph was taken, the body of this important car was removed and replaced with a competition body in the style of the Le Mans machines (see V12 racing cars); to the purist, an unparalleled act of vandalism. Note the spatted rear wings and absence of wheel cases on this early car. (Photo: Arnold Davey)

The late Ken Lipscombe with a production engine on test. Ken left Lagonda to take charge of chassis erection for Rapier Cars Ltd at Kew, but returned to the fold when that company went into liquidation. Note the old two-litre petrol tank high on the wall, still giving yeoman service.

The Lagonda Motors advertisement in the *Motor* announcing the 12-cylinder model range. No tourers, however, were manufactured, the model being superseded by the Rapide (see V12 Rapide).

The new Twelve Cylinder Lagonda de Ville

★ The new Twelve Cylinder Lagonda

10' 4" chassis	...	...	...	...	...	£1,200
Tourer	...	...	...	...	...	£1,485
Saloon	...	...	...	...	...	£1,550
Drophead Coupe	...	...	...	...	...	£1,575
11' chassis	...	...	...	...	...	£1,225
de Ville	...	...	...	...	...	£1,625
Sedanca de Ville (Coachwork by Thrupp & Maberly)	...	...	...	£1,870
11' 6" chassis	...	...	...	...	...	£1,250
Seven passenger Limousine (Coachwork by Thrupp & Maberly) ...						£1,850

The new Twelve Cylinder Lagonda Saloon

LAGONDA MOTORS LTD · STAINES · MIDDLESEX
Telephone: Staines 1122 (5 lines)

A V12 Sanction 2 engine *in situ*. The camshaft-driven distributors, each with their own coil, twin SU carburettors (Burgess filter removed) and, at the front, deep in the V, the aluminium top of the double oil filter housing are all visible, as are the exhaust manifold shrouds, which ducted the hot air through vents in the bonnet side panels. The engine shown is that of a car still in service, and credit must be given to the owner for its immaculate turn-out.

A seven-passenger limousine by Thrupp and Maberly on the long chassis. (Photos: Ivan Forshaw and Lagonda Club)

An early Drop Head Coupé. In the model above, the swage line commenced at the radiator cap and continued in one sweep to the rear wings – effective, very costly, and an endless problem for the 'tin basher'. The idea was quietly dropped in favour of a conventional moulding, as seen below. Both cars are beautiful, though perhaps the styling of the later model is more in keeping with the 'best car in the world' image (designation V12 DHC). The maximum speed of the Coupé was in the order of 104 m.p.h., with acceleration from rest to 50 in under 10 seconds. (Photos: Mrs V. E. Davies and Ivan Forshaw)

The beautifully styled Standard Short Saloon (V12 SS) is shown top, and, above, a similar body on the medium chassis. Both these cars are fitted with the short radiator, and the coachwork in both cases is Lagonda. These cars were capable of about 104 m.p.h. in complete silence.

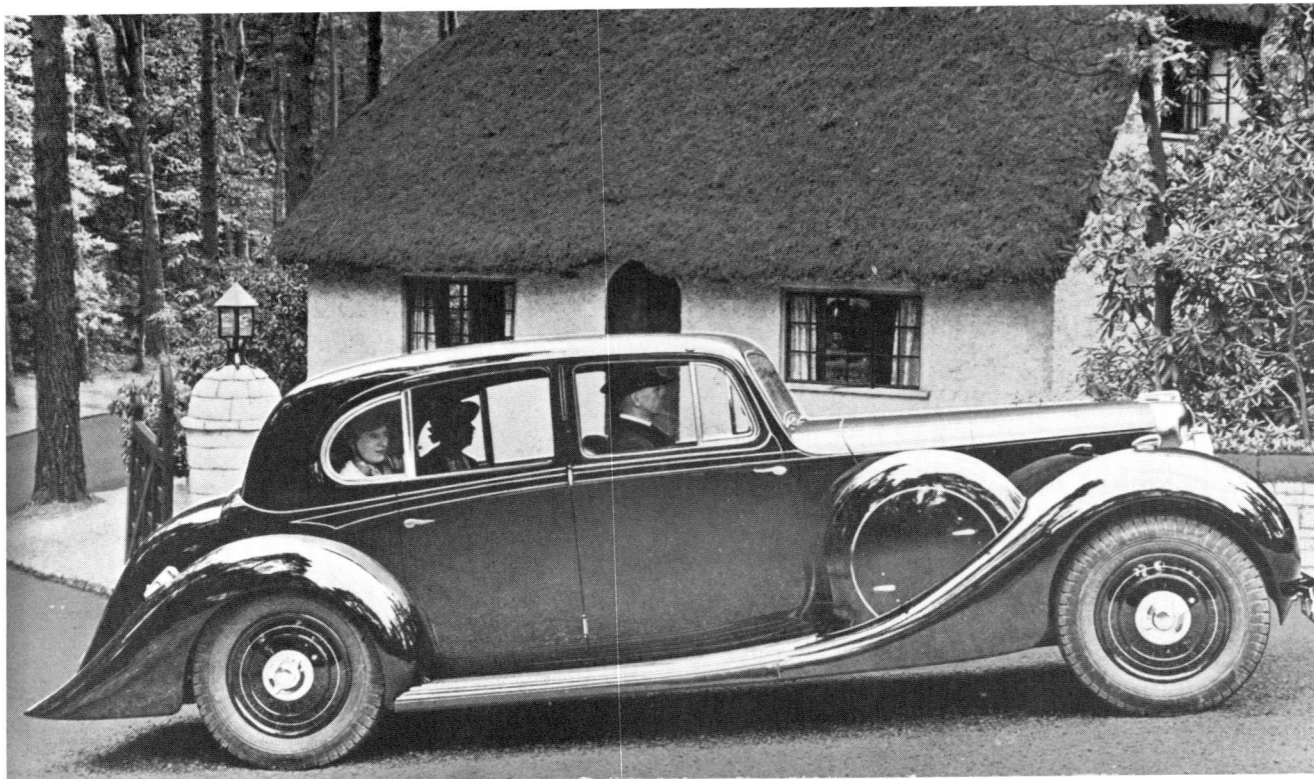

(Above)   The 11ft wheelbase de Ville. In order to blend with the higher coachwork, a taller radiator was used on most of the 11ft wheelbase cars and all 11ft 6in wheelbase cars. The coachwork was Lagonda and designated V12 de Ville. (Catalogue Illustration: Ivan Forshaw)

A similar car, this time without sidemounts, the spare wheel being housed within the boot. A Sedanca de Ville by Thrupp and Maberly was also available on the 11ft chassis. (Photo: Mrs V. E. Davies)

(Above)   This 1939 DH Coupé was built to the order of the Maharajah of Jawhar and was reconditioned by the Lagonda service department in 1951. The spare wheel is housed in the boot, and the hydraulic jack controls and pump were accessible through a panel in the forward floor. (Photo: Lagonda Club)

A more familiar sight to most enthusiasts is the standard short chassis V12 Coupé, with side-mounted spare contained in a case on the offside and a dummy wheelcase nearside to house the Jackall controls and tool kit. This magnificent example was first registered in 1938, but is seen here at a Lagonda Club meeting in 1985. (Photo: Phil Ridout)

An entire book could be devoted to special coachwork on the Lagonda chassis, and many fine examples from the specialist companies have been shown earlier in this book. The V12, with three available chassis lengths, softer suspension, and large reserve of power, offered even more scope for the bespoke carriage trade. Virtually all the respected companies of the day produced coachwork to grace this advanced chassis.

A magnificent two-seater Roadster by Vanden Plas. (Photo: Hartop Collection)

A Razor-Edge Saloon on the 11ft W/B chassis by H. J. Mulliner. (Photo: Dan Margulies)

This elegant carriage on the long chassis was a Lagonda design but built by Thrupp and Maberly for W. J. Lyons of teashop fame. (Photo: Chas K. Bowers)

Two well-balanced designs by Barker: a touring limousine on the medium chassis (above) and a Sedanca de Ville on the long (left). (Photos: The Hartop Collection)

As modern as the hour, it is hard to believe that this superb saloon was built almost 40 years ago. The coachwork is H. J. Mulliner, the chassis one of the V12s assembled just after the war from parts that remained in stock. The whereabouts of this desirable car is unknown. (Photo: *The Motor*)

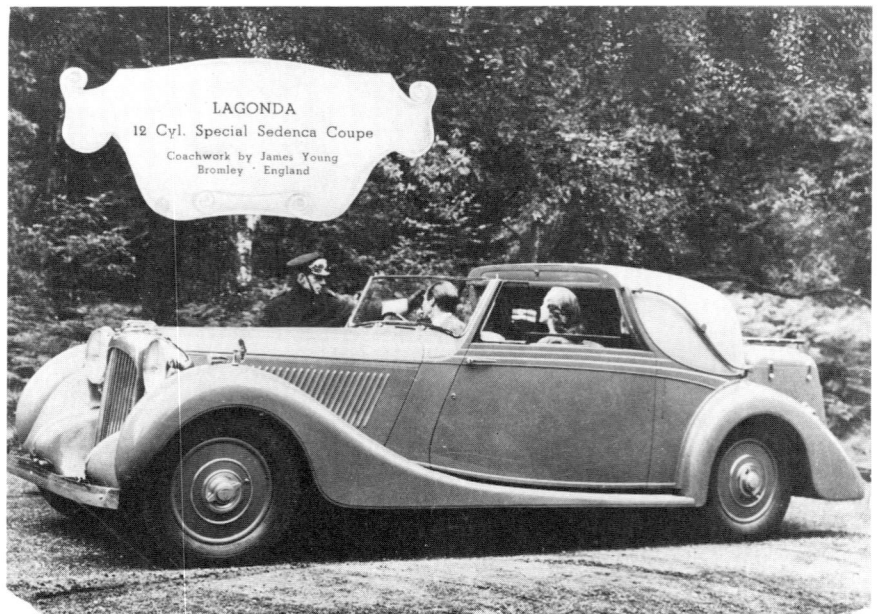

LAGONDA
12 Cyl. Special Sedenca Coupe
Coachwork by James Young
Bromley · England

The ultimate in 1930s motoring, this magnificent V12 by James Young is on the 11ft W/B chassis. Two cars of this style were produced and both are now in the USA. (Photo: Arnold Davey)

The Lagonda became the 'in' car during the 1930s and anyone who was anybody owned one, from the aristocracy to the showbiz personalities of the day.

Ralph Richardson (later Sir Ralph Richardson) registered this V12 DH Coupé (above) on 28 April 1939. It later became the property of His Highness the Maharajah of Jawhar, who enjoyed it for over eleven years. The car is currently owned by a Lagonda Club member who purchased her in November 1967, and recently completed a long but authentic programme of restoration. (Photo: Henry B. Morris)

Originally the property of Lagonda Motors Company Chairman Alan Good, this car (left) was first registered in December 1940. This was possibly the last V12 to be completed during the war years. These later models were fitted with two leading-shoe brakes at the front. The car is shown at a post-war meeting, but is now being restored. (Photo: Laurence Hanham)

W. T. Watson (left) poses with this V12 H. J. Mulliner Razor-Edge Saloon, along with the Hon. Peter Mitchell-Thomson (later Lord Selsdon), Lord and Lady Waleran, spaniel Waleran, and their Lagonda-bodied V12 Drop Head Coupé, on completion of the 1939 Scottish Rally. Both cars won the coachwork award in their respective classes, plus the premium prize for open and closed cars in the over £1,000 section. For performance, Lord Waleran was seventh in Class 5, and Watson nineteenth in Class 6. (Photo: National Motor Museum)

This new, silent, high performance 12-cylinder car from Staines was beginning to make inroads into Rolls Royce sales figures, and the threat to the Derby-based company was becoming a reality. The reason was not hard to see: the V12 was as well equipped as the Rolls Royce Bentley, far less cumbersome than their flagship, the 12-cylinder Phantom III, and faster than both. In an attempt to combat this threat, the 4¼ Litre Bentley was offered with the option of overdrive, but perhaps more important was the testing of a specially tuned version of this car, its engine developing 142 b.h.p., an increase of 17 b.h.p. on the production model. The coachwork was a special, lightweight, very streamlined close coupled saloon, with flush fitting windows moulded to follow the contours of the body. This was, of course, the famous Embiricos Bentley, wittily referred to as the Rolls Royce Lagonda chaser by Arnold Davey, co-author of *The Marque Lagonda*.

This lightweight Bentley was extensively tested on the German autobahns, and frequently returned speeds in excess of 110 m.p.h., which was genuinely faster than the V12 Lagonda, at least in standard form. Even so, Alan Good was spurred on to building an answer to this car but, in the mean time, both companies entered into an extensive advertising campaign, with Lagonda usually listing the titled or stage celebrities who had been supplied with these cars. In order to maintain a high standard of quality, Dick Watney developed the habit of picking a car at random and taking it home for the weekend, where he would go over it with a fine tooth-comb. Armed with a list of defects, he would return to his office on the Monday and immediately call in the department heads to demand explanations for any faults. Watney was a hard man, so it was not long before every Lagonda was virtually perfect when it left the factory.

THE V12 RAPIDE

The V12 Rapide was introduced in October 1938 and seemingly came into being through lack of demand for the catalogued Tourer; in fact, no record exists of an open touring body being fitted to this sophisticated chassis. However, there was a market for a car of more sporting appearance, providing that such a car retained the luxury and refinement of the existing models, and perhaps offered even more in the way of performance.

Earlier models bearing the Rapide label had been breathed on in some form or other, in order to improve their performance compared to that of their standard counterpart. This was not so with the V12: the short 10ft 4in chassis and engine remained unchanged from that of the DH Coupé or Short Saloon, though an increase in acceleration and maximum speed did result from reduction in body weight.

The superb body styling of this Rapide made the car a trend-setter from the word go but, though advanced, it retained typical Lagonda elegance from every angle. Likewise, the finish and quality of its furnishings were second to none and provided this new era of the sporting motorist with the best of saloon car comfort when the hood was erected. Flapping sidescreens were not in keeping with this silent sports car, so the side windows were glass and could be wound open or closed but, true to sporting traditions, a fold-flat screen was fitted. The car was a full three-seater, the single rear seat being sideways mounted in order to provide ample leg room. The price of this model was £1,600, and Ace wheel discs were an optional extra. Though the following photographs of the V12 Rapide give some idea of the car's magnificence, no photograph can really do this Lagonda justice. Model designation V12R.

Originally registered AT 1 in 1939, this superb V12 Rapide was finished in scarlet and grey, with grey leather trim and, to special order, stainless steel dashboard and ebonised door cappings with pewter inlays. During the war, the car was sold back to the factory by the first owner's widow, who retained the original number, it having been in the family since 1903. In July 1946, the car was reregistered LPF 158 and was then used for a time by Dick Watney. It was later sold, it is believed, to Lord Selsdon who had a four-carburettor Sanction 2 engine fitted, and the coachwork repainted black. The present owner purchased LPF 158 in 1962 and at that time regularly drove it at speeds well in excess of 100 m.p.h. but now, in deference to its age, reluctantly, but wisely, keeps the speed down to around the legal limit. Note the change in side lamp treatment on the later car from that of the earlier models. (Photo: M. A. Walker)

September 13, 1938.

The Motor

The
LAGONDA
A New Body on

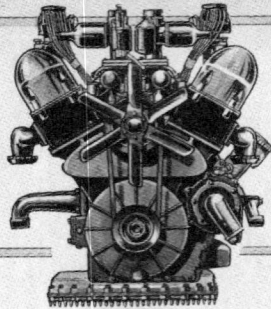

12 cyl.
RAPIDE
the Short Chassis

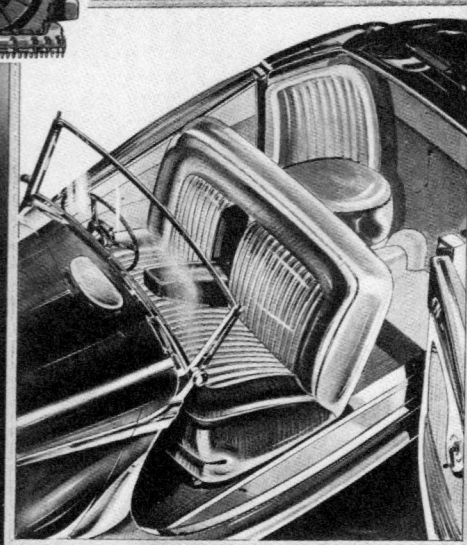

These 1938 cars show the perfection of
styling of the Rapide from every angle. Few
cars today can emulate its beauty or quality.
(Photos: Herb Schofield)

The Rapide retained its beauty even with the hood up. Though this photograph is fairly recent, the car is correct in every detail, even to its radio aerial. (Photo: Herb Schofield)

THE LG6 LAGONDA

Introduced just in time for the 1937 Motor Show, the LG6 was a direct descendant of the V12 and, in appearance, the two cars were almost identical, so much so that even those familiar with the marque may have trouble identifying one car from the other unless viewed from fairly close quarters.

A short and a medium length chassis was offered, these in both cases 3½in longer than the corresponding V12 models, giving a wheelbase of 10ft 7½in and 11ft 3½in respectively; with this exception, the chassis frames of the two cars were virtually identical. The main difference was, of course, the engine, and this was again the well-proven 4½ Litre Meadows 6ESC, to Sanction 4 specification (see LG45). Surprisingly, this engine was slightly longer than the V12, and alone necessitated the increase in chassis length. The only other difference of any importance was the back axle and here a return was made to a spiral bevel unit of Lagonda manufacture, as opposed to the American Salisbury hypoid assembly used on the V12. The axle ratios were 3.58:1 for the 10ft 7½in W/B car, and 3.818:1 for the 11ft 3½in W/B model. As on the V12, the gearbox was a centre change G10, which was replaced by the G11 at about the time of its

introduction into the V12 (see V12 Sanction 2). This model was designated LG6 Sanction 2. No cars were produced as Sanction 3. Sanction 4 had its rear pressed-steel cross member replaced by a tubular member. Anti-fade brakes were fitted.

With the exception of minor detail, the Lagonda-built coachwork for the LG6 and V12 models was virtually identical, the most pronounced distinguishing features being the horns, which were exposed on the LG6 and cowled on the V12 and, from the rear, the protrusion of a single exhaust pipe on the LG6, the 12-cylinder car of course having two. Regarding special coachwork, with the exception of those built for the long wheelbase V12, all other length bodies were available on the LG6 chassis.

The LG6 was quite a brisk performer, with a genuine maximum of around 95 m.p.h., and good acceleration for a 30hp car of such size and weight. From rest, through the gears, to 50 m.p.h. in 11 seconds was about the norm for the Saloon and the DH Coupé.

At the same time as Earl Howe broke the 100 miles in an hour unofficial record at Brooklands with the prototype V12 Short Saloon, Stan Ivermee drove an LG6 standard Short Saloon, covering some 95.87 miles in the

The Motor   October 13, 1937.

The new Six Cylinder Lagonda Drop-head Coupé

New
LAGONDA
programme

★ TWO ENTIRELY NEW
MOTOR CARS BY
W. O. BENTLEY

New low-built ultra-rigid frame.

New Lagonda-design independent front-wheel suspension.

New shock-free precision steering.

New light-action Lockheed Safety Brakes.

All quiet centre-change gear-box, all synchromesh except from 2nd-1st.

New Lagonda coachwork of advanced design, a perfected combination of sheer beauty and comfort.

★ The new Six Cylinder Lagonda

10' 7½" chassis	...	...	...	...	...	£875
"Rapide"	...	...	...	...	...	£1,150
Saloon	...	...	...	...	...	£1,195
Drophead Coupe	...	...	...	...	...	£1,220
11' 3½" chassis	...	...	...	...	...	£895
de Ville	...	...	...	...	...	£1,275
Sedanca de Ville (Coachwork by Thrupp & Maberly)				...	...	£1,540

LAGONDA

hour, and putting in a flying last lap of 98.43 m.p.h. Like the V12, with the exception of the racing tyres, the car was in standard trim and run on normal pump fuel.

An extremely handsome LG6 Drop Head Coupé. This car was first registered in April 1939, but the absence of body mouldings suggests the car to be of 1938 manufacture. The photograph is recent. (Photo: R. J. Jenner)

Though there were no V12 Tourers, five or six LG6 Tourers were manufactured, and two of these are known to exist. This car was first registered in 1940 and is now in the USA. Body designation LG6T. (Photo: Hartop Collection)

A very fine Drop Head Coupé – this car has more familiar body
mouldings. Body designation LG6DHC. (Photo: Herb Schofield)

The standard Short Saloon, in my opinion looking 'undressed' without
wheel discs, but these were always optional. Body designation LG6SS.
(Photo: Herb Schofield)

(Above) This photograph brings back many memories of wartime motoring and the long distances covered, usually at night, sometimes in dense fog, all in the course of duty. My mount, however, was never as luxurious as this superb LG6. For those not old enough to remember such times, the white paint on the bumpers and running boards was mandatory, and all lamps not cowled had to be rendered inoperative, with the exception of side and tail lamps which had to be dimmed. (Photo: L. S. Armandias)

The LG6. Faired-in rear wings were fashionable in the late 1930s and for the 1940 model they were made available for those who preferred them, on the standard V12 as well as on this model. (Photo: Lagonda Club)

THE LAGONDA LG6 RAPIDE

Surprisingly few LG6 Rapides seem to have been built. Seemingly the extra performance of the 12-cylinder model was felt by most to warrant the additional expense, though this was quite considerable. The difference in price amounted to £325 and, in those far off days, that was enough to buy three Ford Eights, or perhaps a small house in the country.

For the LG6 Rapide, the chassis remained unchanged from that of the standard short chassis model apart from two important exceptions: the compression ratio of its Sanction 4 engine was increased from 6.68 to 7.5:1, and the rear axle ratio became 3.31:1, which was in fact the same ratio as the earlier LG45 Rapide.

With the exception of minor detail changes, the coachwork was as the V12 Rapide. For comparison, the 1939 catalogue illustration is that of a V12R, and the photograph an LG6R. Note the price increase on those quoted in a previous advertisement. (Photos: Ivan Forshaw and Stanley Mann)

Chapter Thirteen

THE END OF AN ERA

THE LE MANS V12

W. O. Bentley's cars had dominated the scene at Le Mans and elsewhere during the late 1920s, and it was therefore reasonable for Alan Good to believe that a racing version of the V12 could once again return the laurels to Britain. Given satisfactory time for development, this would undoubtedly have been so, but Good was a man who believed all could be done at the drop of a hat and, with less than six months to go before the 24-hour race, he dropped his new brainchild on W.O.'s desk. W.O. was incensed at the idea, resenting making a racer of what he had conceived as a sophisticated road machine, to say nothing of the lack of available time, only agreeing to go ahead on the understanding that no attempt would be made to win and that the outing in 1939 would be nothing more than a proving run for a serious attempt in 1940. Two cars were to be built, one of them privately entered and driven by Lords Waleran and Selsdon, who, in fact, may well have planted the seed in Good's mind in the first place.

The 10ft 4in wheelbase V12 chassis frame was chosen, but its weight was considerably reduced by holes cut in the sides of the box section main side frames. These holes were interconnected with tubes to prevent canting, and the tube ends were then sealed with thin aluminium covers. Similarly, almost every component was reduced in weight, either by extensive machining of the castings or, in the case of the suspension wishbones and brake drums, by lightening holes, the latter again fitted with aluminium dust covers. The brakes themselves were Lockheed hydraulic with twin leading shoes; cooling was assisted by intakes in the backplates. An extensive reduction in weight at the rear meant new road springs, and these were softer than those used on the production car, but they were again damped by controllable Armstrong

hydraulic dampers. At the front, an additional pair of friction shock absorbers assisted the non-controllable Armstrong hydraulic type. Cooling air was ducted to the dampers from intakes formed in the horn fairings, and at the rear by scoops. The gearbox was fitted with a higher than standard first gear and the remote control was discarded, the gear lever now protruding from the top of the box and cranked to bring it close to the steering wheel. Top and final drive ratio was 4.09:1. A 38-gallon tank was mounted close behind the cockpit and, in order to increase the weight over the rear wheels, the batteries and spare wheel were fitted as far back as possible. Centre lock wire wheels carried 6.50 × 19in tyres at the front, and 7.00 × 19in at the rear.

Extensive development of the engine was limited to some extent by the grade of fuel specified for Le Mans, and the most compatible compression ratio was found to be 8.8:1, though given the right brew, it is understood that W.O. would have opted for a higher figure. The cylinder heads however were very different from those on the production engine, and were also fitted with modified valves and special valve springs of American manufacture. Alterations were made to the valve timing, and four SU carburettors replaced the twin set-up used in the production engine. The gas flow was further improved by beautifully fabricated six into one exhaust manifolds. Other modifications included a spacer between the crankcase and the sump, to increase its capacity; an auxiliary tank, its tap accessible to the driver, to replenish the sump while the car was in motion; and the radiator reduced in height, but fitted with a larger header tank. In this form the press quoted the brake horsepower as 220 but, in reality, it was 206 at 5,500 r.p.m., and the car was theoretically capable of 140 m.p.h. at 6,000 r.p.m. if conditions were such that this r.p.m. figure could be reached.

In keeping, the body was ultra light and consisted of five major parts, all hand-beaten from aluminium. It was mounted directly to the chassis and secured by quick-release fasteners, while the one-piece bonnet was secured by leather straps, and the pretty, quick detach-able wings weighed a mere 5¾lb each. Both cars were finished in British racing green, the works car identified by white paint around the horn fairings.

The cars were chassis numbers 14089 (works car) and 14090, registered HPL 448 and HPL 449 respectively; the former car was re-registered as GRK 77 in 1948.

This photograph was taken on 7 June 1939, when Alan Good threw a cocktail party at Staines to show off the cars and generally publicise the Le Mans team. Many ex-Bentley Boys and, of course, W.O. were among the guests. The team consisted of Arthur Dobson and Charles Brackenbury, who were to drive the works car, and Lords Waleran and Selsdon, owners and drivers of the sister car. Also present were the back-up team of mechanics and technical staff, including Stan Ivermee, Percy Kemish, Jack Sopp and Lionel Taylor who, along with W.O., had done such a magnificent job by producing the cars on time at such short notice. For this occasion the cars were fitted with slatted radiators, but they were never run in this form, the slats being replaced by wire mesh prior to departure for Le Mans. (Photo: Laurence Hannam)

The two Le Mans cars had been built virtually behind locked doors, but, as a morale booster, a few days after the cocktail party the works car was put outside for general viewing by the factory staff, who were allowed out in batches to inspect it. However, the man studying his watch suggests it is time the lads were back on the job. Note that the wire mesh stoneguard has already replaced the vertical radiator slats fitted for Alan Good's publicity party. (Photo: Bob Lewis)

Prior to the race, there was literally no time for testing or proper tuning. In fact, the Waleran/Selsdon car was filled with petrol and driven straight to the ferry, running in to be completed *en route* to Le Mans and during practice. However, the works car did have a couple of circuits of the Brooklands track and a few runs around the block and it is shown here on trade plates returning to the factory after one of these short road tests. Its driver on this occasion is unknown. (Photo: Geoffrey Goddard)

THE LE MANS 24-HOUR RACE
17–18 June 1939

W. O. Bentley made it clear from the outset that no attempt would be made for a Lagonda win at Le Mans this year, though there would be every effort to ensure both cars finishing, and it was considered imperative they should, as a bad showing would seriously affect sales of the production models. W.O., of course, was very experienced at Le Mans, and had worked out a speed that should not unduly stress these new cars, yet was faster than the 82.35 m.p.h. average of the previous year's winning Delahaye. The drivers of both cars were therefore under strict instructions to keep as near as possible to this pre-arranged speed, with no speeding up unless instructed to do so from the pits. The opposition was formidable, especially from the French who were fielding Delahayes, Delages, a 3.3-litre supercharged Bugatti, and Talbot Darracqs. From Italy came Alfa Romeo, and from Germany both Adlers and BMW. The main interests from Britain were, of course, the two 12-cylinder Lagondas but, in pursuit of the Rudge Whitworth Cup, MG, Singer, Morgan, Riley, Aston Martin and HRG were all present, plus an interesting little car, made not more than a stone's throw from the Lagonda works, the 1495cc Atalanta.

From an initial entry of 49 cars, only 40 were lined up for the start. Amongst these were the V12 Lagondas, the works entry driven by Arthur Dobson and Charles Brackenbury, and the private car by Lords Waleran and Selsdon. They carried the racing numbers 5 and 6 respectively. At the fall of the flag, Dobson was first away, hotly pursued by a gaggle of cars whose drivers were determined to get amongst the traditional Le Mans blind of the opening laps and, behind them, the private Lagonda with Lord Selsdon at the wheel, who had made a bad start. First car round was Chinetti's Talbot Darracq, with Dobson six seconds behind. Driving strictly to W.O.'s schedule, he soon settled into a consistent lap time of around 5 minutes 40 seconds in 12th place. Meanwhile Selsdon was averaging 6 minutes 14 seconds, and was in 18th position. He made a 20-second pit stop on the eighth lap, thereafter speeding up slightly, and was inside six minutes by his 11th lap. However, he was lapped by Dobson on the 18th, and in order to increase the distance

between the two cars, Dobson was given the speed-up signal. The 19th lap became the fastest Lagonda lap of the race, the distance being covered in 5 minutes 35 seconds (89.82 m.p.h.). Lagonda controllers, it seems, still had memories of the accident in 1928 when two of their cars collided through running in close proximity.

Refuelling was only permitted after 24 laps, and Stan Ivermee called the cars in on their 25th laps (after 209.58 miles). However, from the second refuel and driver changeover, the distance was increased to 27 laps, fuel consumption working out at 6 m.p.g., slightly better than the estimated figure. By this time, the longstanding Le Mans lap record had been broken by a Delahaye, with Mazaud at the wheel, who was locked in a battle with Gerard's Delage; the new record stood at 5 minutes 12.1 seconds (96.74 m.p.h.). Lord Waleran proved to be faster than his team mate, after taking over at the change on the 25th lap. He was soon down to 5 minutes 40 seconds, in keeping with the times being returned by the very experienced partnership of Dobson and Brackenbury. By the second change and refuel, darkness was falling, and Selsdon was soon in with a lighting problem, followed by Dobson who was worried about the charging rate. Both were soon on their way again, running two laps apart.

All the cars had slowed a little with the onset of darkness, and both Lagondas were now lapping consistently at 6 minutes (83.84 m.p.h.). Both cars ran like clockwork through the night, the drivers changing at their pre-set intervals, but the Mazaud Delahaye was out by 2 a.m., having caught fire at speed when Mongin was at the wheel, and Gerard's Delage took the lead. At 7 a.m., the Dobson/Brackenbury Lagonda was fourth, with Waleran/Selsdon sixth, but by 8 a.m. fortunes changed when a crash put Hug's Delage and Chinetti's Talbot Darracq out of the race, leaving the Lagondas in third and fourth places. With daylight, all the cars had, of course, speeded up, but were holding their respective positions. Brackenbury handed over to Dobson at about 9 a.m., complaining of difficulty in changing gear, and seven minutes were lost attending to a sticking clutch; a further 17 minutes were lost for the same reason when Dobson handed the car back to Brackenbury on lap 184, with the private car now on the same lap. About this time, the Wimille/Veyron Bugatti was beginning to put pressure on the leading Delage. By midday Gerard brought the car into the pits with ignition problems but, as little could be done, they pressed on hoping for the best. When Brackenbury handed the Lagonda over to Dobson at 1 p.m., three minutes were lost due to a broken offside exhaust bracket. However, to get the car back on schedule after a lost running time now totalling 27 minutes, Dobson was given the speed-up signal, and

pushed his average up to 88 m.p.h., with the private car still consistent at 85 m.p.h. By 3 p.m. the Bugatti was three laps ahead of the Delage, and for the final hour the positions remained unchanged, the race running out with the Wimille/Veron Bugatti winning at 86.85 m.p.h. (2,084 miles), a record for the race. The Gerard/Monneret Delage was second, the Dobson/Brackenbury Lagonda third, and the Waleran/Selsdon Lagonda fourth, first and second in their class respectively.

The Dobson/Brackenbury V12 (HPL 448) gathers an admiring crowd during its pre-race preparation at Le Mans. The official syphoning the tank is no doubt about to check to see if it is the regulation brew.

(Above) The start of the Le Mans 24-hour race, 4 p.m. Saturday 17 June 1939. Though Selsdon seems to have been the best sprinter, Dobson (number 5) was first away. (Photos: The Late Harold Nockolds Collection)

Lord Selsdon at speed with the V12 Lagonda HPL 449 during the 1939 Le Mans 24-hour race. (Photo: Geoffrey Goddard)

The Lagonda team return to the pits on completion of a gruelling but gratifying 24 hours. The 1939 Le Mans was unexpectedly fast, and W. O. Bentley's schedule would have won any previous race. Third and fourth places were no mean feat, however, and one the company was justifiably proud of. Driving number 5 is Arthur Dobson, while Charles Brackenbury rides on the tail, and Percy Kemish hangs on the nearside. Lord Selsdon is at the wheel of number 6 with, just visible behind him,

Lord Waleran. A happy Alan Good, in dark sweater, rides on the tail. The photograph, enlarged from a snap, was given to me by Bob Lewis, who was a member of the staff at the time. Bob unearthed this historic picture from his wallet where, judging from its crumpled state, it had remained from pre-war days, the ageing process somehow increasing its charm.

The French were jubilant at the outcome of the race, and had every right to be. Not only was this their third Le Mans win in a row, they had also broken the flying lap record for the circuit and covered the greatest number of miles in the history of the race – a magnificent effort. However, equally pleased were the British; both Lagondas had performed impeccably and proved themselves well capable of winning when fully developed. As it stood, third and fourth place overall (first and second in their class) was a very creditable showing, and one that

would have been good enough to win just twelve months earlier.

Naturally there was speculation as to whether the cars could have won had W.O. set a higher average, and evidence exists to suggest that this bothered Bentley too. The cars were clearly capable of maintaining a higher average and were seemingly still running well at the end of the race. True, the works car had lost 27 minutes running time due to minor problems, but the private car had run faultlessly throughout the 24 hours. As it turned out, the Dobson/Brackenbury car had covered 2,006 miles at an average speed of 83.61 m.p.h., with Waleran and Selsdon covering exactly 2,000 miles at 83.35 m.p.h., almost dead on Bentley's target.

During the 1950s, a Lagonda Club member writing in the Club's magazine suggested the Le Mans cars were in poor shape after the race. W. O. Bentley was quick to dispute this. In a letter to the magazine's editor he made it clear, in no uncertain manner, that both cars ran the 24 hours without a tyre change or brake adjustment, the only fault being a fractured exhaust bracket on one car. He went on to point out that both cars were successfully raced at Brooklands just a few weeks later without being touched. W.O. made no reference to the clutch problems

but, as these are known to have occurred, one can only assume they were overlooked due to the passage of time. However, Percy Kemish has gone on record as saying that both engines were dismantled after the race with disappointing results, claiming that all but three of the combined total of 96 special valve springs had broken, that the valve seats and heads had cracked in the areas where the exhaust valves were adjacent, and evidence existed of oil starvation. You will have to form your own opinion as to the most likely story, but certainly the cars were running well enough to maintain their target lap speeds and, in fact, for one to be substantially speeded up during the closing laps of the race.

THE BARC BANK HOLIDAY MEETING
Brooklands 7 August 1939

The last three races on this historic day were outer circuit handicap events, to be run over three laps. The Le Mans cars were entered for the first two of these races, on this occasion stripped of wings and fitted with Brooklands regulation silencers. Brackenbury drove the works car and Selsdon the private one. Selsdon again made a bad

start, but soon got into his stride to finish second to Brackenbury, who won at an average speed of 118.45 m.p.h. Baker was third in a Graham-Page. The Lagonda lap speeds are interesting, Brackenbury's 111.92, 120.01 and 127.70, and Selsdon's 104.85, 128.03 and 127.70 m.p.h. laps hardly suggesting engineering maladies.

'Ebby' Ebblewhite had undoubtedly underestimated the capabilities of the Lagondas, so for the second of these three-lap races they were rehandicapped by 21 seconds, and with this severe penalty had no hope of winning, but both cars again ran well. This event was won by Maclure in his very fast Riley at 122.71 m.p.h.

The last race of the day was won by Baker in his Graham-Page, and the fall of the chequered flag marked the end of 32 years of motor racing on this important and popular track. The day also ended a chapter in the life of the late A. V. Ebblewhite; 'Ebby', as he was affectionately known, became chief timekeeper and starter at the track in 1908, a position he held until Brooklands closed for racing on this sad but memorable day.

Percy Kemish steers the works V12 to the start line for the first of the three-lap outer circuit races which it won at 118.45 m.p.h. Brackenbury, in pullover, walks behind, whilst Stan Ivermee assists on the nearside, followed by an unknown mechanic. (Photo: National Motor Museum)

TENTH RACE

DISTANCE ABOUT 9 MILES. (FORK START.)

(Cars will run three complete laps and finish in the Railway Straight.)

5.5 p.m. THE FIRST AUGUST OUTER CIRCUIT HANDICAP. (The entrant of the winner to receive £25 ; the entrant of the second £10 ; and the entrant of the third £5. Two to start, or no race ; four to start, or no second prize ; seven to start, or no third prize.) For motor cars in racing or touring trim propelled by means of internal-combustion engines only.

Entrance 3 Guineas. Closed 26th July, 1939.

No.	Entrant.	Car.	No. of Cyl.	Bore.	Stroke.	Cubic Capacity.	Driver.	Colour. Car : Wheels.		Start. m. s.	No.	
1	Mr. J. B. Emmott ...	Multi-Union II S	8	68·5	100	2,946	C. S. Staniland	Silver :	Silver	0 0	1	N/S
2	Mr. G. P. Harvey-Noble	Bentley-Jackson	6	100	140	6,597	Entrant ...	Silver :	Black	0 19	2	26
3	Mr. I. F. Connell ...	Darracq ...	6	90	104·5	3,996	Entrant	Blue :	Silver	0 26	3	
4	Mr. Hugh C. Hunter ...	Alfa-Romeo S	8	68	100	2,904	Entrant ...	Red :	Red	0 30	4	
5	Lord Selsdon ...	Lagonda ...	12	75	84·5	4,480	Entrant ...	Green :	Black	0 37	5	← 2
6	Mr. F. E. Elgood ...	Bentley ...	4	101	140	4,487	R. Seys ...	Green :	Green	0 37	6	
7	Mr. G. B. C. Sumner ...	M.G. ... S	6	57	71	1,087	Entrant ...	Red :	Silver	0 37	7	
8	Mr. A. P. Good ...	Lagonda ...	12	75	84·5	4,480	C. Brackenbury	Green :	Black	0 37	8	← 1
9	Capt. A. G. Miller ...	Lagonda ...	6	88·5	120·6	4,467	P. Nuttall ...	Blue :	Black	0 43	9	
10	Mr. P. Courtney ...	Amilcar S	6	56	74	1,093	Entrant ...	Black :	Red	0 53	10	
11	Mr. F. R. Gerard ...	Riley	4	69	100	1,496	R. M. Turner ...	Blue :	Ivory	1 8	11	
12	Mr. G. L. Baker ...	Graham-Paige	8	88·6	114	5,387	Entrant ...	Blue :	Blue	1 25	12	
14	Mr. R. F. Oats ...	Alvis	4	68	103	1,496	Entrant ...	Red :	Black	1 48	14	

BLACK

BLUE

S denotes supercharged engine.

Competitors in any previous handicap at this Meeting may be re-handicapped at the discretion of the Handicappers.

RESULT.

Winner............ 8 .... Second .... 5 .... Third.... 12 .... Speed of Winner....118·45....m.p.h. Won by.... 6·8 seconds

PASSING AT FORK.

When passing the Fork in Outer Circuit Races, competitors marked " Black " or " Blue " on the Race Card must keep the line of that colour painted on the Track on their right.

BETTING.

In order to avoid any mistakes or misunderstandings as to the competitors in a Brooklands Race on whom, or against whom, odds are laid, all betting should be on the number of the car, as stated in the Race Card. There will be no objection to the names of the drivers being put on the Bookmakers' slates, but these names will in no way govern the betting.

The Public are warned not to bet with Bookmakers who do not display their Official Brooklands Permit.

All Bookmakers will pay " First Past Post," irrespective of objection.

Lap Speed Table for Races on OUTER CIRCUIT appears on page 35.

„   „   „   „   „   MOUNTAIN CIRCUIT   „   „   34.

„   „   „   „   „   ROAD CIRCUIT   „   „   34.

Lap Speed Table for Races on OUTER CIRCUIT appears on page 35.

27

NOTICE

Any Races which the Stewards may decide to postpone may be run on
SATURDAY, 12th AUGUST, 1939.

A 1939 August Bank Holiday race card (reproduced by kind permission of the Brooklands Museum).

THE V12 LAGONDA SPECIAL LIGHTWEIGHT SALOON

Lagonda Motors' reply to the Rolls Royce Embiricos Bentley was, of course, the V12 Special Lightweight Saloon. Due to the priority of the Le Mans cars, completion of the prototype model was well behind schedule.

However, a few laps of the Brooklands track were managed before everything came to a halt there in August 1939, the car returning average speeds in excess of 120 m.p.h., a good 10 m.p.h. faster than its Derby-built rival.

Basically the chassis was the 10ft 4in wheelbase V12 Rapide, but fitted with a four-carburettor engine tuned to Le Mans racing specification and, like the Le Mans cars, a 4.09:1 ratio rear axle. The all-aluminium Airflow coachwork was designed and built by Lancefield, and closely resembled the Portout-built body of the Embiricos Bentley, featuring perspex side and rear windows contoured to conform with the body shape. The styling was years ahead of its time. In fact, the R type Bentley Continental of the 1950s had more than a passing resemblance, especially when viewed from the rear. Had the car gone into production, the estimated price was said to be little short of £2,000, a vast amount of money pre-war. Hitler, however, put an end to such luxuries and, with the company now concentrating on the war effort, the car stood around gathering dust until bought by Lord Fraser in the summer of 1940, when it was registered JPG 492. It later passed through many hands, eventually being purchased by Brian Morgan in 1966, who spent some eight years restoring it. Both the Lagonda and the Bentley survive to this day. (Photos: The Hartop Collection)

Chapter Fourteen

THE AUSTERE YEARS

WORLD WAR II 1939–1945

When the rearmament programme was getting under way during 1936, Alan Good and a former chief operations engineer from Imperial Airways, one F. Wyndham Hewitt, formed a company to subcontract to the Bristol Aeroplane Co. Wyndham Hewitt Ltd, as the company became known, arranged to buy out the Lagonda machine shop, together with its stocks and plant, in order to manufacture controllable cooling Gill rings for the Bristol range of radial engines. It was also agreed they would take over all machining operations for Lagonda Motors, a massive undertaking, as at this time the W. O. Bentley-designed G10 gearbox was in production and his complicated 12-cylinder engine soon would be. Alan Good was again Company Chairman, and F. Wyndham Hewitt took the position of Managing Director. Herbert H. Wheeler was Secretary to both companies, with Watney and Bentley as Directors of both firms.

Car production came to a halt at Staines on 26 September 1939, though vehicles nearing completion were eventually finished and delivered, most of these cars bearing 1940 registrations. Alan Good took delivery of a V12 Drop Head Coupé as late as December of that year, a car now owned by a Lagonda Club member.

As the war progressed, the relative importance of Lagonda Motors and Wyndham Hewitt became reversed and, on 23 April 1943, the entire shareholding of Lagonda Motors, with the exception of Watney's one share, were sold to Wyndham Hewitt Ltd. However, 12 months later, an Extraordinary General Meeting changed the name of Lagonda Motors back to L. G. Motors (Staines) Ltd, and at the same time Wyndham Hewitt Ltd became Lagonda Ltd, a reintroduction of the pre-1935 name. During 1944, L. G. Motors was voluntarily wound up, a paper exercise that was not finalised until 12 months later.

Returning to September 1939, within a remarkably short space of time the vast resources of the Staines factory were in full swing producing the essentials of war. The workforce, reinforced by almost an army of unskilled labour, operated machines that ran 24 hours a day, seven days a week. As in the 1914–18 war, a large section of the works was devoted to the production of shells and almost 4,500,000 were produced, a further 6,000,000 shell parts being made for assembly elsewhere. In addition to the Bristol Gill ring, many other important aircraft parts were made, and almost every operational type eventually became fitted with components of one sort or another manufactured by Lagonda. An entire machine shop was set up for the manufacture of Messier undercarriage shock absorber legs, and no less than 12,480 of these units were produced for the Halifax heavy bomber. Old hands skilled in making car petrol tanks were soon employed on aircraft self-sealing petrol and oil tanks, and in the production of coolant header tanks for the Rolls Royce Merlin power plant, the heart of the Spitfire, Seafire, Mosquito and many other aircraft.

Percy Kemish had a hand in experiments with a marine version of the V12 car engine, and outboard transmission gears with contra-rotating propellers were developed and manufactured for the Royal Navy. A number of Meadows gearboxes were produced for the Tetrarch tank, along with many other Crusader and Centaur tank components. Ordnance equipment included gun body assemblies for the 20mm Polsten heavy machine guns, plus anti-tank and Howitzer gun carriages. Lagonda Ltd were also responsible for the development and manufacture of Flamethrowers, and over 6,200 of varying types were produced. Stan Ivermee was awarded the MBE for his work in this field.

The magnificent contribution made by Lagonda, its associated companies and staff, with their high volume production of weapons, aircraft components, and support equipment, played a significant part in achieving a satisfactory conclusion to the war.

August 8th—October 31st, 1940

" The battle was fought, and won by sheer quality of men and material . . . by the technical achievements of a small body of craftsmen, working patiently, devoting all their talents, energy of mind and skill to the task."

. . . in appropriate measure and degree the same spirit

inspired those who, in so few years, have placed Lagonda

in the very forefront of the world's finest cars.

LAGONDA

LAGONDA MOTORS LIMITED   LAGONDA   STAINES, MIDDX. ENGLAND

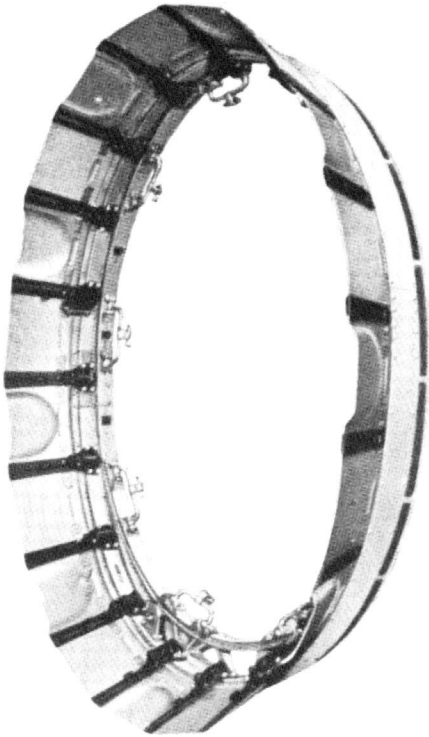

The Bristol Gill Ring. The Gill ring was developed to control the flow of cooling air over the cylinders of radial aero-engines, and was fitted to all Bristol engines after the design was finalised in 1936. From that date Lagonda Ltd produced in their Staines and Slough factories 90 per cent of the Gill rings fitted to Bristol-engined aircraft, some 97,792 units.

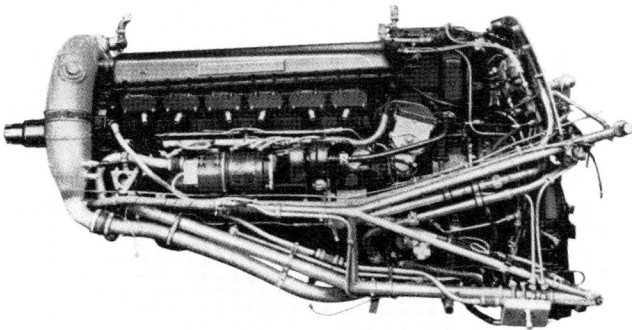

A Rolls Royce Merlin power plant fitted with a Lagonda-manufactured coolant header tank, 6,700 of which were produced in the Staines factory.

COMPRESSOR
SET

A two-stage compression unit for aircraft servicing, powered by the Petter 2A 8hp, horizontally opposed petrol engine. Thousands of these engines were produced by Lagonda and its associated companies. In addition to powering compressor sets, they were also used for 4kW generator and lighting sets, water pumping and filtration. Three-ton air conditioning plants for use in the Far East were also made in large numbers.

The 6pdr anti-tank gun carriage. Hubs and sighting gear sets were also made for the 95mm howitzer carriages, plus 8,062 gun body assemblies for the 20mm Polsten heavy machine gun.

The Cub oil engine. In 1942 Lagonda took over Oil Engines (Coventry) Ltd and within two years increased the output by 900 per cent. These engines were in heavy demand, and amongst the many uses were combined generator and compressor sets, lifeboat propulsion units, and portable fire pumps.

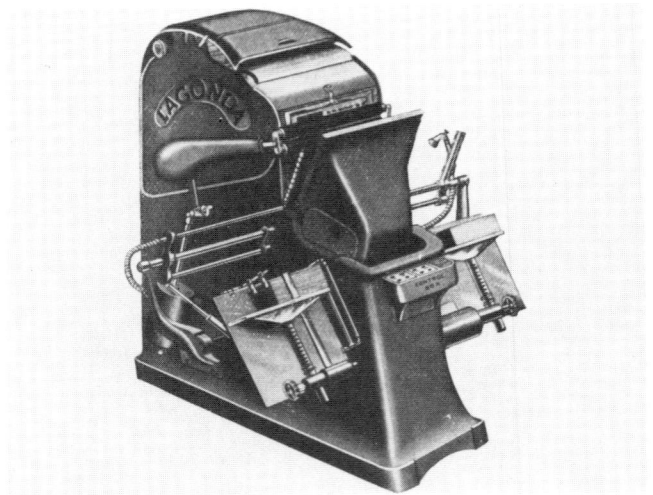

The Lagonda Auto-Platen. Perhaps one of the company's more unusual productions, this automatic printing machine was of all-British design, and far in advance of any pre-war machine. Lateral automatic feed and delivery permitted a battery of machines to be linked up for colour work; 5,500 prints per hour were possible with great ease of operation. (Illustrations from Lagonda Achievements: Ivan Forshaw)

THE LB6

By early 1944 consideration was being given to a new model Lagonda for what would undoubtedly be, after the cessation of war, an austerity Britain. For most, large exotic machinery would be a thing of the past, so the post-war car would need to be smaller, more economical, and comparatively cheaper than its predecessors, yet still endowed with good performance and, by the standards of the day, of a quality that would uphold the name Lagonda.

At the outset, the project was little more than a part-time job for W. O. Bentley, much of the preliminary design work being carried out during evenings and weekends, often on Frank Ayto's billiard table. However, one W. G. Watson was engaged full time on this work, and later in the year he was joined by Donald Bastow, who had left Rolls Royce to take a responsible position in the Lagonda design team.

Engines of four, six and eight cylinders were considered, these designated LB4, LB6 and LB8 (LB standing for Lagonda Bentley). The LB4 had a bore and stroke of 78 × 85mm (1625cc), but calculations soon proved it

unsatisfactory for the car envisaged, and it was shelved in favour of the 78 × 90mm (2580cc) LB6. The LB8 was never to get beyond the drawing board.

The first LB6 engine was running on the test bed by the end of the war in Europe. It was of advanced design, and patents were taken out on many of its important features. The design of the crankcase itself was of special interest, as it dropped well below the centre line of the main bearings. It was iron, and integrally cast with the cylinder block, the latter being fitted with wet liners. A four-bearing crankshaft ran in a conventional front main bearing, whilst the other three were special, being housed in semi-circular Duralumin 'cheeses'. These located the bearings in the crankcase webs and were fitted after the crankshaft itself had been entered from the rear of the case, the design subsequently proved, however, in racing versions of the engine. The cylinder head featured hemi-spherical combustion chambers, and twin overhead cam-shafts operated the valves via inverted bucket tappets directly under the cams. The camshafts were chain driven, and a further chain drove an auxiliary shaft for the

Left to right, Stan Ivermee, Percy Kemish W. O. Bentley, Charles Sewell and Donald Bastow gathered round a 2.6-litre LB6 engine. This engine differs in many respects from the first prototype shown in *The Cars in My Life* by W. O. Bentley, including a complete change in cylinder head design. The head shown has valves set at an angle, suggesting that it has hemispherical combustion chambers, as did the engine that eventually went into production; the valves on the first prototype were vertical. The position of the generator was later moved to the top of the engine for accessibility. (Photo from Lagonda Achievements: Ivan Forshaw)

distributor. An Autoklean oil filtration system was used. Pool petrol was the only available fuel, and the low octane value restricted the compression ratio to 6.4:1. Even so, the engine during test recorded 106 b.h.p. at 5,000 r.p.m. With further development it was, of course, this engine that powered the DB2 Aston Martins that were so successful in the Mille Miglia, and at Le Mans, Spa, and elsewhere.

Prior to the war, W.O. had experimented in the design and manufacture of automatic gearboxes, but abandoned the exercise when the French Cotal electric gearbox became available, and this box in modified form was chosen for the LB6. The Cotal box had as many reverse ratios as forward and, consequently, a car fitted with this box could be driven as fast in reverse as it could forward, though it would take a brave man to do it. However, this was not acceptable to the British, so a smaller version with no reverse was manufactured for the Lagonda, the reverse gear then being incorporated within the back axle and operated by an independent selection.

The chassis of the LB6 was a conventional cruciform frame, but with tubular side members for added rigidity. Independent suspension was employed all round; the front by unequal length wishbones and coil springs, while at the rear, torsion bars were used as the springing medium. The swing axles were splined, and were fitted with universal joints at both ends, these drive shafts then being located by double tubular arms. To reduce unsprung weight, the brakes were mounted close up to the differential assembly, which itself was fitted directly to the frame.

As Lagonda were still committed to essential contracts, and the body shop was fully engaged on aircraft components, the coachwork for the prototype cars was sub-contracted to Vanden Plas. However, Frank Feeley had a hand in their design and his influence is evident, as can be

seen in the photograph of the first prototype, taken at Staines in 1945. This car was finished in a dull grey and the painted, as opposed to plated, radiator shell was typical of the times, chromium being almost impossible to obtain other than for essential work. The cars were subjected to exhaustive road testing, each with a target of 50,000 miles in the shortest possible time. As you would expect, problems arose but, on the whole, the tests seem to have been reasonably satisfactory, as Dick Watney announced the car to the press in September 1945, with *Autocar* lending some pages to its description and creating great excitement amongst the new car starved public. The price was not quoted, however, nor was it to be for the next two years or so.

Originally it was intended that the LB6 would be known as the 2½ Litre Lagonda Bentley, but as soon as the name was released, Rolls Royce demanded that Bentley's name should be removed from the car, claiming it infringed their trademark. Apparently, when Rolls Royce bought out the Bentley Motor Co. in 1931, W.O. had signed a contract that allowed Rolls Royce to register the Bentley name as a trademark, a contract that was to stand for ten years. However, Rolls Royce claimed they held the name permanently. In an attempt to iron matters out, W.O. met Lord Hives of Rolls Royce and, surprisingly, agreed to sell his name for all time. Naturally, the Lagonda Chairman Alan Good was furious with this agreement, and within a few weeks the whole affair was in the courts: Rolls Royce proved their case and the legal charges cost Lagonda £10,000 they could ill afford. the company had no alternative, of course, but to change the name and, from then on, the LB6 was described in all advertising as the new 2½ Litre Lagonda, designed under the supervision of W. O. Bentley. His name, of course, was also removed from the radiator.

The first prototype LB6 at Staines in 1945, the complete rear wing detached for wheel removal. (Photo: Louis Klemantaski)

The early post-war years were extremely difficult for the manufacturers of consumer goods and, due to the large demand for steel, this was particularly so for the motor trade. Supplies of raw materials were tightly controlled, and priority was rightly given to the needs of the high volume, mass produced and shoddy end of the motor business, where a ready and waiting export market existed, even though virtually all of these cars were only updates of pre-war models.

Lagonda of course had its exciting brand new car under development and, as a result of advance publicity, there was a fairly full order book. But the 2.6, though relatively cheaper than most of its predecessors, was again a car for the connoisseur and ostensibly the home market. This being so, the allocation of steel and other essential mater-

ials to Lagonda Ltd was such that it was impossible to put the car into production, at least in the immediate future. The overheads of the large Staines factory were considerable and, like many lesser companies, Lagonda was on the open market by 1947. Fortunately a buyer was in the wings, David Brown (now Sir David) of David Brown & Sons (Huddersfield) Ltd, who bought the name Lagonda, the three prototype 2.6 Litre cars, and all drawings, stocks and spares, but not the factory itself. Thus came to an end the marque's long association with the Thames-side town of Staines where, from such humble beginnings at the turn of the century, had evolved over the years one of the most respected companies in British motor engineering.

THE V12 LE MANS CARS: POST-WAR

When war was inevitable, both the Le Mans cars were put into storage at a small garage in Staines. Whether this was considered a safer haven, or simply the space they occupied at the factory was needed, is uncertain. Certainly the large Staines site would be a prime target for the German bombers, but as things turned out, the Lagonda factory came through the war unscathed. Fate played its hand, however; in 1942 the small garage that housed the cars was demolished by a bomb, killing the occupants of the flat above and, of course, severely damaging the cars. One suffered more than the other but, with the exception of bodywork, both were restorable.

After the war Charles Brackenbury, who had somehow acquired the cars, offered them for sale as desirable restoration projects, which, of course, they were. The works car, chassis number 14089 (HPL 448), was bought by R. M. Cowell, who re-registered it GRK 77. Bob Cowell was a partner in a coachbuilding firm at Egham and so had the facilities to refurbish the chassis and provide it with quite an attractive body. In this form, he drove it on at least two occasions at Jersey, but the car lacked its pre-war sparkle and his best placing seems to have been ninth overall. Disillusioned, Cowell sold the car and, after changing hands a couple of times, it was eventually bought by Lord O'Neill, who gave it a sheltered life

for some years, during which time the body was replaced by one that closely resembled the original. The current owner is John Rees, who has rebodied the car yet again but, like the chassis, to a degree of perfection that must be a lesson to every enthusiast with originality in mind. The car has now also been reunited with its pre-war number, HPL 448.

The car of Lords Waleran and Selsdon, chassis number 14090 (HPL 449), became the property of Robert Arbuthnot who fitted a stark and ugly body on completion of the necessary mechanical work. Arbuthnot had his sights set on Indianapolis, but his average laps of 104 m.p.h. in practice proved too slow to qualify. A second attempt was planned, but the car was crashed *en route* to the track and, though repairable, Arbuthnot sold it in America as it stood. In the ownership of R. H. Sabourin, the car turned up at Watkins Glen in 1950. However, it was sold again in the November of that year, and then led a hard competitive life in the hands of various owners until it threw a connecting rod. Then followed a sequence of events that has become the fate of far too many historic vehicles once in the wrong hands. The engine was eventually bought as a box of bits by the Lagonda Club American representative Bob Crane, who used the cylinder heads, camshafts and four carburettor set-up on his V12 DH

Bob Cowell with the rebodied ex-works V12 during the Jersey Road Race of 1948. (Photo: Hartop Collection)

Coupé, apparently with electrifying results. During 1976, the chassis frame was located and purchased by Lagonda enthusiast James E. Dale of Toronto, who persuaded Bob Crane to part with the engine parts not in use, in order that they might be reunited with their rightful chassis, but the project was eventually abandoned. There is a happy ending to this story, however. The chassis and much of the original engine are now back in Britain, and its new owner is currently carrying out an authentic restoration.

These excellent photographs show the factory-sponsored Le Mans V12 Lagonda as it is today, though the authenticity of the restoration is such that the pictures could well have been taken just prior to the car's departure for the race in 1939. (Photos: Phil Ridout)

The new Lagonda factory was to be at Hanworth Air Park near Feltham, at the original Aston Martin Works. David Brown, having recently acquired Aston Martin, then merged the two firms to form a new subsidiary to his long-established company, in the name of Aston Martin Lagonda Ltd. Fortunately, David Brown and Sons were themselves a respected firm in quality engineering and, in keeping, the old traditions and standards of both Aston Martin and Lagonda were strictly maintained. The company moved to Newport Pagnell in 1953 where both Aston Martin and Lagonda cars are made to this day, though yet again 'under new management', as the saying goes.

When Lagonda was bought by David Brown, Alan Good, Dick Watney and W. O. Bentley went their own ways. Good had lost interest in cars, and by the end of the war had virtually cornered the small diesel engine market. He died at the early age of 46. Dick Watney returned to his old firm, Rootes, and was killed in a car accident when on business in Australia. Bentley, together with Donald Bastow and a few key men from Staines, set up a design office at Weybridge. It is believed it was a short-lived affair, though an experimental 3-litre engine was designed and built for Armstrong-Siddeley, but it was never used due to a change of plans regarding prospective models. W. O. Bentley died on 13 August 1971, aged 83.

Sir David Brown

THE DB 2.6 LAGONDA, MARK I AND MARK II

The prime purpose of this book has been to illustrate the products of the Lagonda Company, together with some of its competitive achievements and misfortunes, during the years the company was at the Causeway Works at Staines. The move to Hanworth effectively severed this long Staines/Lagonda association and, without doubt, cut short a significant era of motoring history, never to be repeated. The 2.6 was of course conceived at Staines, so it is fitting that this model should be followed through to its conclusion, even though in its production form it was made elsewhere.

Further to the LB6 prototypes, three development

cars were built, the chassis and engines of which were made at the David Brown branch at Parsley, near Leeds; the completed chassis was then transported to Bournemouth where Tice & Co. manufactured and fitted the coachwork. The bodies for the production cars were, however, made and fitted at Hanworth, and it was from here that final tuning and road testing were carried out.

The DB 2.6 was simply the production version of W. O. Bentley's last brainchild, the LB6; obviously there were modifications, but mostly in the styling. Mechanical changes were generally of a minor nature, perhaps with

This early production DB 2.6 Litre car dates back to 1949, though it was not registered until 1951. There are a few subtle differences from the mainstream production models, all relating to coachwork; they included a slight change to the shape of the windscreen and rear window, the length of rain gulleys, instrument panel, and so on. The car shown, despite a long hard life, continues to give enjoyable motoring. (Photo: J. Caine)

the exception of discarding the Cotal gearbox for one of David Brown's own manufacture. This excellent manual four-speed gearbox, with synchromesh on all but first gear, was only slightly marred by the then fashionable steering column change.

The first public showing of the DB 2.6 was at the Earls Court Motor Show in October 1949. Available as a Saloon only, the car was priced at £1,998, plus £1,111 tax, but the price steadily rose during 1951 to £2,250, again plus tax. During 1951 a Drop Head Coupé was introduced, a little more expensive at £2,325, plus tax. For

1952, the Mark I was replaced with a Mark II version. Though there were few mechanical changes, the body was increased in width by 4in and the front of the car was generally tidied up, being fitted with a new type of Lucas headlamp. Improvements were also made to the heating and ventilating system, and hydraulic jacks became standard equipment.

In all, 550 DB 2.6 Litre cars were produced, the model being replaced with a DB 3 Litre Lagonda in 1953. In later years this was followed by a 4 Litre model, but that is another story.

This is a later Mark I Saloon than that pictured on the previous page. These very under-rated cars were extremely advanced for their day, with rack and pinion steering and hypoid rear axle. In a design that dated back to 1944, these were features that few of its competitors could boast a decade later. As for the performance, a genuine 91 m.p.h. was claimed by the manufacturers. (Photo: Ivan Forshaw)

(*Above*)   The Frank Feeley touch is very evident in this front view of the Mark I Drop Head Coupé. His favourite Gothic arch wing and lamp fairing treatment is seen to full advantage, and the car from this angle, in many respects, resembles the V12. Had the latter been developed and produced after the war, it may well have been very similar in appearance, but on a larger scale. (Photo: Hartop Collection)

Though the design of the rear of the car was the responsibility of another stylist, it is in complete harmony, resulting in an attractive, well proportioned machine. (Photo: Ivan Forshaw)

The 2.6 Mark II Saloon was an elegant machine. Note the change in front end styling, and the new type Lucas headlamps. A Drop Head Coupé was also available on this chassis. (Photo: Louis Klemantaski)

Chapter Fifteen

THE POST-WAR CAR CLUBS

THE 2 LITRE LAGONDA REGISTER

As we have seen, the Lagonda Car Club formed in 1933 by C. G. Vokes was wound up just prior to the outbreak of war. After the war, two clubs came into being; firstly, the 2 Litre Lagonda Register and, secondly, the Lagonda Car Club. The aims and interests of these clubs were really quite different, the 2 Litre Register concentrating on the exchange of technical information and the formation of a spares pool, mostly for the 2 Litre models; the Car Club focusing on competitive and social events, all models of the marque being acceptable. Today's very successful Lagonda Club is an amalgamation of these clubs, and embraces the policies of both with its full competitive and social calendar, and excellent spares and technical service for all models of the marque Lagonda in current use.

At this point a brief insight into the history of these post-war founder clubs may be in keeping. The 2 Litre Lagonda Register was the brainchild of the late P. A. (Peter) Densham and, to quote his words:

'In October 1946 I found myself with a 2 Litre Lagonda and a gratuity. Many others had to choose between the two. Unfortunately, by the time some very necessary repairs had been carried out at post-war prices, I also was among those who had a Lagonda and no gratuity!

In view of the high cost of repairs and the scarcity of spare parts, I decided that Lagonda owners should unite. I advertised the car for sale in *Motor Sport*, and immediately found myself in touch with that select body known as 'Lagonda enthusiasts'. They wrote from many counties, a few wanting to buy my car, but generally, after a short introductory paragraph, they threw themselves into a rapturous description of their own Lagonda.

I bought a notebook and ruled columns down each page, paid 2/6 to a printer to print forms setting out the idea I had in mind, and calling for certain particulars of the car. I sent a dozen of these forms to the addresses which my advertisement had produced. Six forms came back with their half-crown subscriptions, and I opened the register by writing the names and car particulars on a foolscap sheet. Each day I found at least one Lagonda letter in the post, and from these I composed the first *Notes*. Things went well. I found a great similarity in all letters received, a genuine love of the Lagonda car, an honest, though sometimes misguided desire to help, and great need for a spares pool and advice bureau.

Very many letters were received. I used my bank as a forwarding address and remember the manager's horror when someone sent a gearbox – dripping the worst type of oil – to me at the bank: "You will please remove this large piece of engineering at your first opportunity, as we have no room in these premises for such things."

In April 1947 we advertised a rally at Farnborough, and no words can describe the thrill and surprise with which we surveyed the 60 Lagondas that were present. We held a meeting after the rally and a President and various officers were elected, and the Register became recognised. We no longer searched for members, they came willingly.'

The main officers elected were Densham, Forshaw, Norris, Halford and Watson. However, at the time of the amalgamation of the Register and Car Club in 1951, the 2 Litre Lagonda Register officers were:

President: Air Marshall Sir Alec Coryton, KBE, CB, MVO, DFC
Vice-Presidents: R. G. Goslet, MC and P. A. Densham

Peter Densham in 1947.

Joint Hon. Secretaries: A. C. Rees and J. M. Bosworth
Technical/Spares Register: Captain I. Forshaw

Committee: Audsley, Coates, King, Allen, Gabb, Hibbert, Martin and Vessey

THE LAGONDA CAR CLUB

The Lagonda Car Club had a more conventional start in life. Simply, a number of enthusiastic Lagonda owners had been discussing the prospects of forming a Lagonda Car Club, and a very successful meeting was held on Sunday 29 June 1947, at the home of Mr and Mrs J. E. Davies at Shepperton-on-Thames, where it was unanimously agreed to form a Lagonda Car Club immediately. The aims of the club were to be:

1. To perpetuate the Lagonda tradition.
2. To keep all owners in touch with one another with a view to maintaining their views and interest.
3. To promote social events, for example competitions, trials and rallies.

To further these aims it was agreed that:

1. Membership of the Lagonda Car Club should be open to owners of all models.
2. The entrance fee should be 10/-, and the annual subscription £1–1–0.
3. An organisation might be set up whereby instruction books and technical help could be exchanged between members.
4. A club badge should be designed and made available to members.

It was also decided to hold a rally in Bournemouth on the weekend 27–28 September 1947, and a dinner/dance in London in December.

The 2 Litre Lagonda Register was discussed. The opinion of the meeting was that there was no need for conflict of interest to arise, as the Lagonda Car Club would cater for all Lagonda models. Amongst those

elected to act on a provisional committee were: Squadron Leader C. E. L. Powel (Chairman), Mrs V. E. Davies (Hon. Secretary), Paston-Green, Major Pillitz, Deller, Child and Nicholas.

Though Mr J. E. Davies was the prime mover in the forming of the Lagonda Car Club, due to his business interests with the marque he opted out of taking an official role in the club.

THE LAGONDA CLUB

The Lagonda Club was formed in October 1951, by the amalgamation of the Lagonda Car Club and 2 Litre Lagonda Register. The aims of the club may be summarised briefly: to maintain the traditions of the marque Lagonda and to engage in or promote any motoring activity by which the members of the club may benefit. To provide:

1. Competitive and social events for all models.
2. The exchange of technical knowledge and experience.
3. Spare parts scheme.
4. The issue of a quarterly magazine and regular newsletter.

Current officers of the Lagonda Club are: President: J. W. T. Crocker; Vice-Presidents: A. Davey, A. W. May; Secretary: Mrs V. E. May; Chairman: J. G. Ody; Events Secretary: J. A. Batt; Membership Secretary: B. R. Hyett; Area Secretaries: J. Stoneman, H. Taylor, H. Schofield, A. Downie; Treasurer: A. T. Elliott; Spares and Technical Services: Captain I. Forshaw, A. Brown, P. Whenman. Australian Rep: B. A. Jacobson; USA Rep: B. Happe.

Enquiries should be sent to the Secretary, Mrs V. E. May, 68 Savill Road, Lindfield, Haywards Heath, Sussex RH16 2NN.

The following set of photographs offer prospective Lagonda enthusiasts an insight into club activities. They may also bring a few nostalgic memories to some of our members. The emphasis is on Lagonda enthusiasts doing their own thing in whatever form it takes, be it racing, rallying or simply enjoying the company of fellow club members.

Farnborough, April 1947. The first meeting of the 2 Litre Lagonda Register. Despite the miserable weather, some sixty cars were present, many arriving from far afield. Left to right: founder members Air Marshal Sir Alec Coryton, Mrs S. Fane de Salis and Captain Ivan Forshaw. Mrs de Salis' 1931 blown 2 Litre has been in the family from new, and is currently owned by her grandson. The 2 Litre shown is an H/C car, and was first registered on 21 March 1929. It was the mount of the late Edward Sawers but since the mid-1950s has been owned and extensively used by Phil Ridout. (Photo: The Late Peter Densham Collection)

One of the most enjoyable social events on the Lagonda Club's calendar is the Annual General Meeting and *Concours d'Elégance*. This 1960s scene is typical of one of these occasions. Peering under a bonnet are, left, Ben Walker, and the late Don Roberts, who expertly carried out this difficult task of judging for many years.

All these photographs were taken at Silverstone during the 1950s and 1960s.

(Above)   Slender budget racing, 2 Litres in the paddock on a typical summer's day. (Photo: Richard Hare)

Jeff Ody at Woodcote with a very desirable 1929 L/C car. (Photo: Tony Wood)

(Above)   Driven by Sharon and Stone, this 2 Litre finished ninth in the 1930 Brooklands Double Twelve. It is shown 31 years later with the late G. T. (Tweedie) Walker at the wheel negotiating Copse Corner, followed by Billy Michael in the LG45 team car, EPE 97, when in its Goodhew form. The 2 Litre is now owned by Tweedie's son Bruce, editor of the club's magazine, The Lagonda. (Photo: Harold Barker)

Without doubt, the great authority on all matters Lagonda is lifelong enthusiast Ivan Forshaw, shown left at an AGM in the late 1960s. Still smiling, despite the fact that in his capacity of Technical Adviser he was at that time averaging over 1,500 letters a year in response to club members' queries and problems. I have lovingly preserved every letter received from him, and these span more than 36 years, not only for the valuable information they contain, but also for the art of his writing – encouraging, humorous, and always technically correct to the smallest detail. (Photos: Lagonda Club)

Perhaps some of the most memorable AGMs were those held at Ascot and Runnymede during the 1960s. The *Councours de'Etat* Merit Award winners at the Royal Ascot Hotel (now sadly demolished) are, left to right, 1954 DB 3 Litre DH Coupé, 1934 M45R Tourer, and 1930 2 Litre L/C Tourer.

Amongst many desirable cars at Runnymede were this 1936 LG45R and the 1934 M45TT car, Le Mans winner in 1935, BPK 202.

Again at Runnymede, a superb 1934 M45 Tourer. In the centre of this picture, hands behind his back, the late Bert Hammond admires an 11.9 Model K. (Photo: Richard Hare)

During the 1960s and 1970s the Lagonda Club tracked down several of the old hands at Staines, and they soon became familiar faces at the AGMs. Often they were driven to the venue in club members' cars, and this annual event became an enjoyable outing for many of them. Inevitably, with the passage of time, few are left to share the pleasures they created so many years ago, but they are not forgotten.

Left to right are Ted Bibby, the late Frank Feeley, Ron Kerridge (not ex-staff), the late Fred Shattock and the late Percy Kemish. (Photo: Arnold Davey)

Bert Hammond still admiring Mrs Freda Roberts' 11.9 Model K, and no doubt chatting to her about his exploits on and off the track with Lagonda cars during the pioneering days. Freda had a successful trip of some 1,300 miles with this car in the FIVA Sicily Rally of 1981. Quite an achievement for this elderly lady – the car of course. (Photo: Richard Hare)

Club membership is not entirely made up of pre-war car enthusiasts. Indeed, many members run the later cars, sometimes as one in a collection of Lagonda models, such as the 1955 DB 3 Litre Tickford DH Coupé. This car was originally built for HRH The Duke of Edinburgh. (Photo: Louis Klemantaski)

Dignity and impudence. This fast and imposing DB4 Saloon was first registered in 1964, but the 4 Litre models were first introduced in 1961. The car is seen at a Lagonda Club meeting in 1985, its next-door neighbour a Rapier Special. (Photo: Geoffrey Seaton)

For those with around £80,000 to spend, what could be finer than the new Aston Martin Lagonda. This factory demonstrator is seen at Great Fosters, Egham, for the 50th anniversary of the Lagonda Rapier in 1984. (Photo: Phil Ridout)

Continental rallying is enjoyable and popular with many Lagonda Club members. Though some can be a test of man and machine, the majority are fairly light-hearted affairs, but fun all the same. This is an old hand at the game, Richard Hare, with his LG45 at the start of a rally in the South of France. In 1985 no fewer than 50 Lagondas journeyed to celebrate the 50th anniversary of the Lagonda Le Mans victory in 1935.

Maintenance and restorations form an important part of the club activities during the drear winter months and many enjoyable hours can be spent within the confines of your own garage. However, only the brave would undertake a restoration of the magnitude shown here.

Where there's a will there's a way. The H/C 2 Litre Speed Tourer, MP 3654, as it was purchased by Alec Downie, the car having been destroyed by vandals who set fire to the building in which it was housed.

The lower picture shows the car as it is today after many hundreds of hours work by its owner, such is the enthusiasm for these cars. This car, despite covering a reasonable annual mileage, has won many *Concours de'Elégance* awards, and is a frequent visitor to Lagonda Club and VSCC meetings up and down the country. (Photo: Alec Downie)

(Above)   The Brooklands Society Reunion is always an enjoyable day, and one usually well attended by Lagonda enthusiasts. This photograph, taken in June 1976, shows Mrs Robby Hewitt awaiting the fall of the flag in her 1934 M45 Tourist Trophy car, BPK 203, her passenger for this event the late Kaye Don. To her right on the banking is A. F. Rivers-Fletcher in his very quick Alvis.

Closed cars are a rarity these days, and Jeff Ody's superb 1931 Type Z3S 3 Litre Saloon gathered many admirers at the 1986 Lagonda Spring Social, held at the new museum complex at Brooklands. Invited clubs on this day were Aston Martin, Singer, Alvis and Austin, and a very memorable occasion it proved to be. (Photos: Phil Ridout)

The Lagonda-Based Racing Specials

A fine action shot of Nigel Hall with his 1936 LG45 Special at Cadwell Park in August 1979. (Photo: Tony Wood)

Ian MacDonald, 1937 LG45 Special, on his winning lap of the Brooklands Memorial Trophy Race at Llandow, September 1973. (Photo: Tony Wood)

The V12 chassis is an obvious choice for the special, or replica enthusiast, and here we see Alistair Barker going well at Silverstone with his 1938 Le Mans Replica. (Photo: Tony Wood)

This 1935 Lagonda Rapier is a replica of the famous Eccles car but, unlike the original machine, the two-stage blowers are mounted on the flywheel bell housing and are belt driven. Boost pressure is about 15 p.s.i. at maximum r.p.m. Built, owned and raced by Paul Morgan, the car is shown at a VSCC Silverstone meeting in the 1970s. (Photo: Tony Wood)

David Fletcher-Jones at speed with the 1934 Lagonda Rapier Racing Special on his way to winning the Spero Trophy Race for the third time in a row, VSCC Llandow 1975. (Photo: Tony Wood)

President of the Lagonda Club, James Crocker with his 1935 Lagonda Rapier two-seater Special. Amongst the successes with this car are the Ashcroft Trophy, Lagonda Club Michael and Fox Trophies, *Motor Sport* Brooklands Memorial Trophy Race (second), and many more. Equally happy on the road as on the track, it is seen arriving at Great Fosters for the Rapier Promotion Anniversary, July 1984. (Photo: Geoffrey Seaton)

The Daniel Richmond Special, a car with a long and successful racing career. It is hard to believe it started life as a sober Rapier Abbott Fixed Head Coupé. (Photo: Dan Margulies)

(Above)   A very fine replica of the LG45 four-seater driven by Earl Howe in the 1936 TT (see page 225). Though the chassis of this car is basically to standard specification, the body is an authentic reproduction of the Fox and Nicholl-prepared four-seaters. The car is extensively raced in club events. (Photo: Colin Bugler)

A group of Lagonda enthusiasts enjoying themselves at a BDC Silverstone race meeting during the summer of 1959. In the centre foreground of the party is the late Mike Wilby who, for 18 years, devoted most of his spare time to Lagonda Club activities and, during these years, held practically every executive position on the committee until his untimely death in 1971. (Photo: Jeremy Mason)

(Above)   A fine line-up of cars belonging to members of the American section of the club. BPK 201, in the centre of the picture, has now returned to Great Britain. (Photo: Lagonda Club)

A happy Wood–Batt team. Tony Wood and John Batt with their Rapier Wood–Batt Special at Prescott, August 1971.

The Harry Gostling Prize, awarded annually to the writer of the best Lagonda Club magazine article.

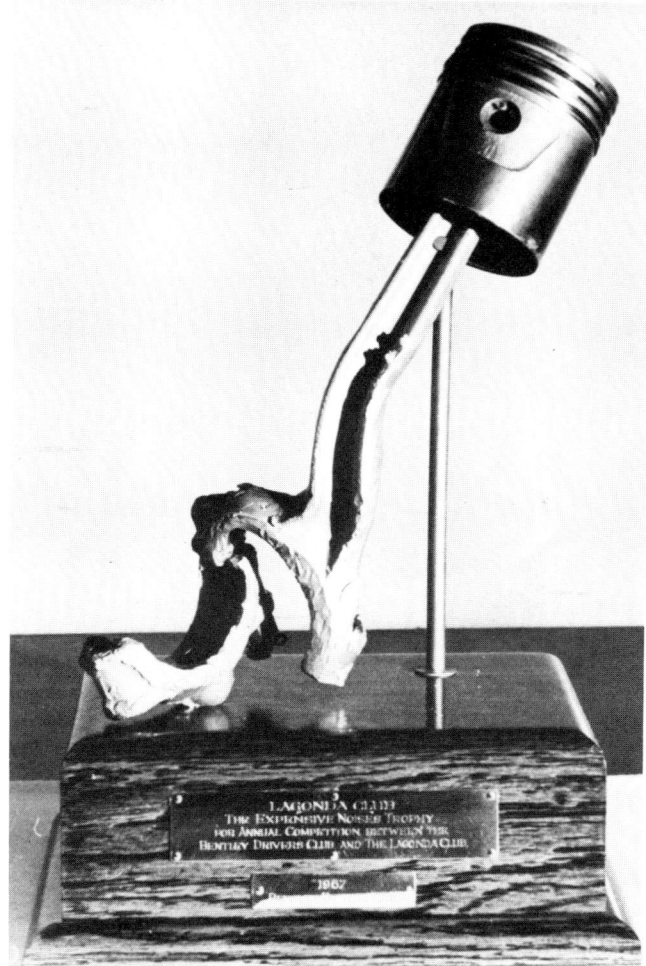

The Expensive Noises Trophy, an annual award for competition between the Bentley Drivers Club and Lagonda Club. No prizes, though, for guessing the Lagonda components that make up these trophies.

Trophies . . .

. . . and sweet dreams.

INDEX